Love♡Hina

「ラブひな」

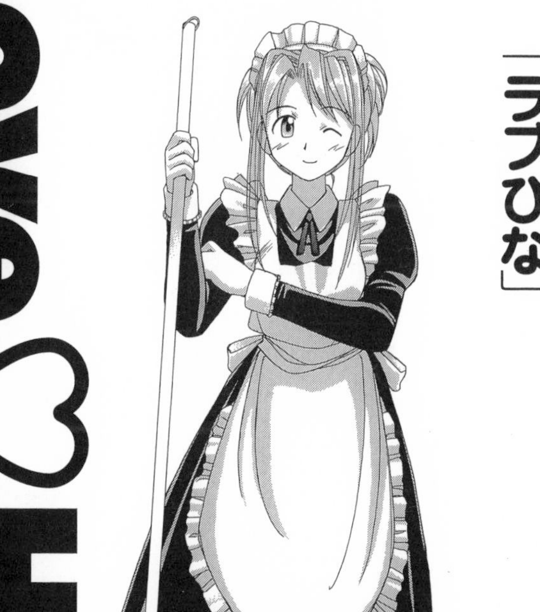

Vol.1

Ken Akamatsu

赤松　健

CONTENTS

Originally published in Japanese in 1999 by Kodansha Ltd. as LOVE ♡ HINA 1.

Published by Kodansha International Ltd.,
17-14 Otowa 1-chome, Bunkyo-ku, Tokyo 112-8652.
Copyright © 1999 by Ken Akamatsu.
English translation copyright © 2000 by Kodansha International Ltd.
All rights reserved. Printed in Japan.

ISBN 4-7700-2715-X
First Edition, 2000
00 01 02 03 04 05　10 9 8 7 6 5 4 3 2 1

LOVE♡HINA

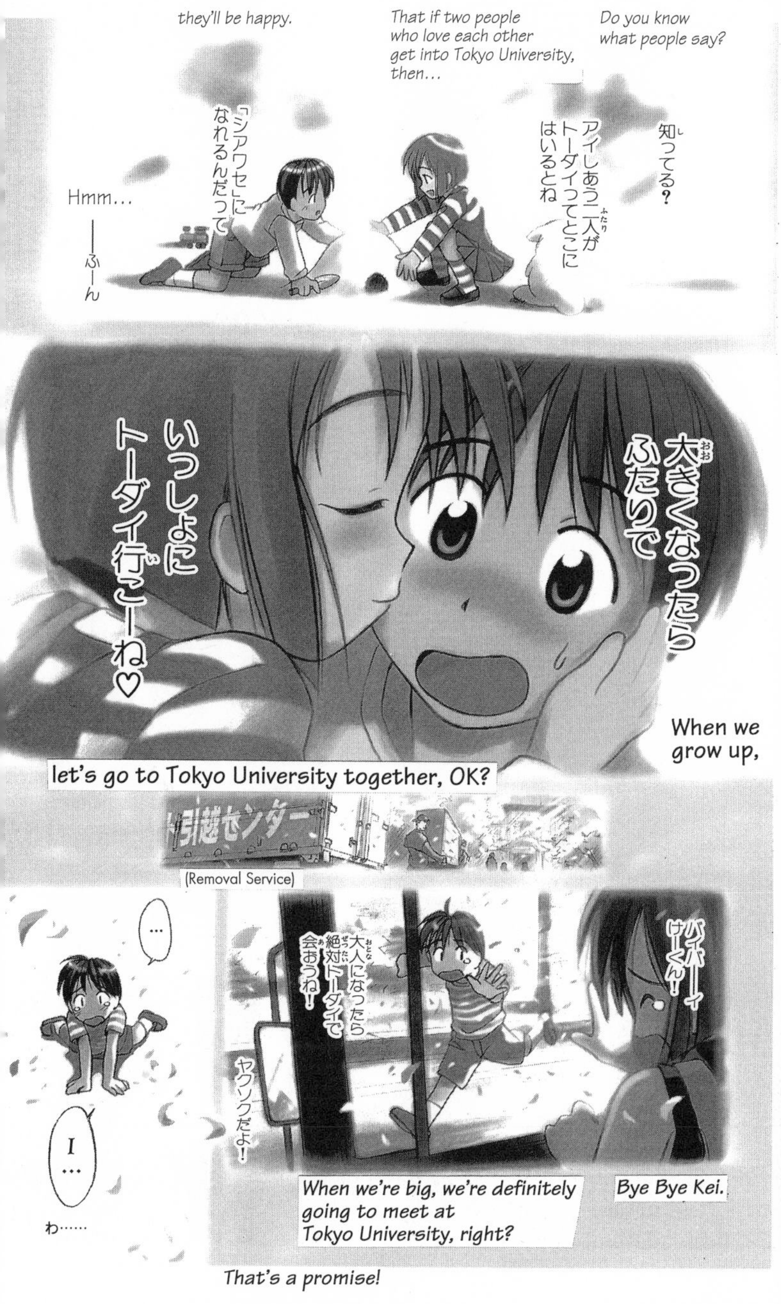
知ってる？
Do you know what people say?
アイしあう二人がトーダイってとこにはいるとね
That if two people who love each other get into Tokyo University, then…
「シアワセ」になれるんだって
they'll be happy.
——ふーん
Hmm…
大きくなったらふたりで
いっしょにトーダイ行こーね♡
When we grow up,
let's go to Tokyo University together, OK?
引越センター
(Removal Service)
バイバーイけーくん！
Bye Bye Kei.
大人になったら絶対トーダイで会おうね！
When we're big, we're definitely going to meet at Tokyo University, right?
ヤクソクだよ！
That's a promise!
…
I…
わ……

Me, I'm Keitaro Urashima,
age 19, no girlfriend.

And anyway, that's why I find myself
in my second year as a drifter,
still trying to get into university.

わかった!!

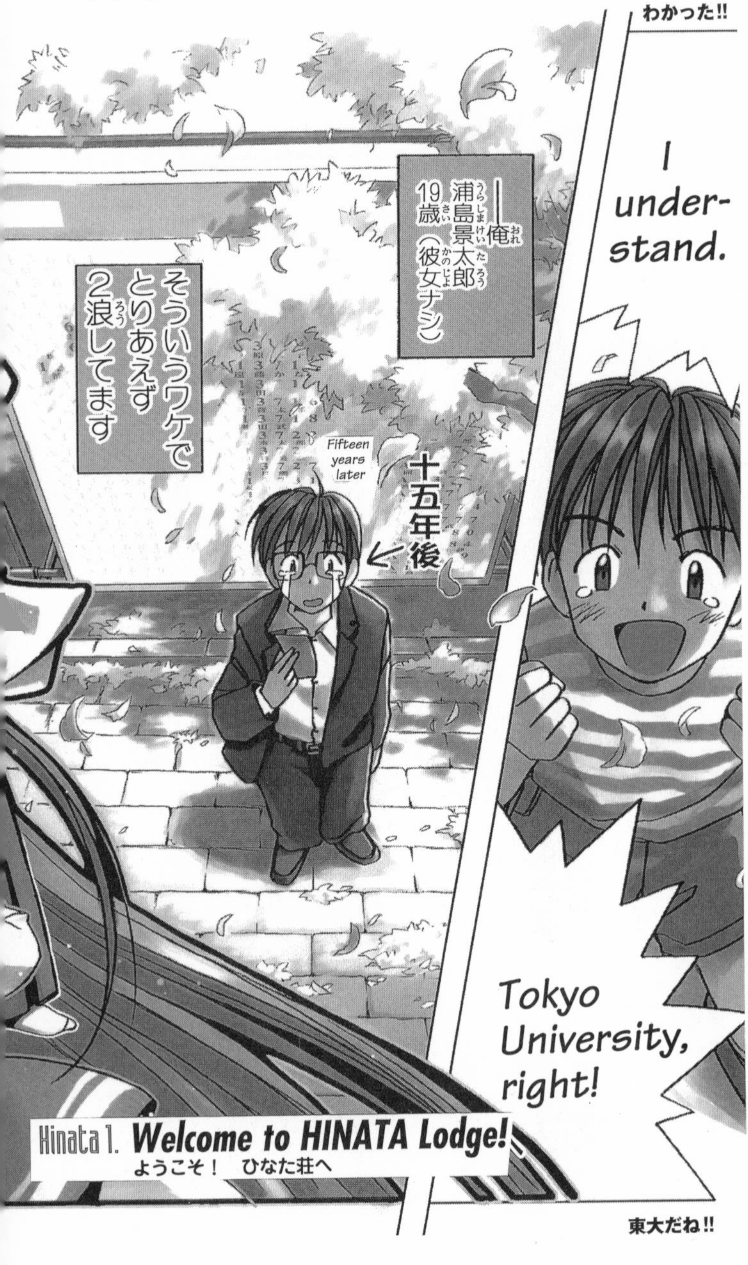

I understand.
Tokyo University, right!
—俺　浦島景太郎19歳（彼女ナシ）
そういうワケでとりあえず2浪してます
Fifteen years later
十五年後
Hinata 1. Welcome to HINATA Lodge!
ようこそ！　ひなた荘へ

東大だね!!

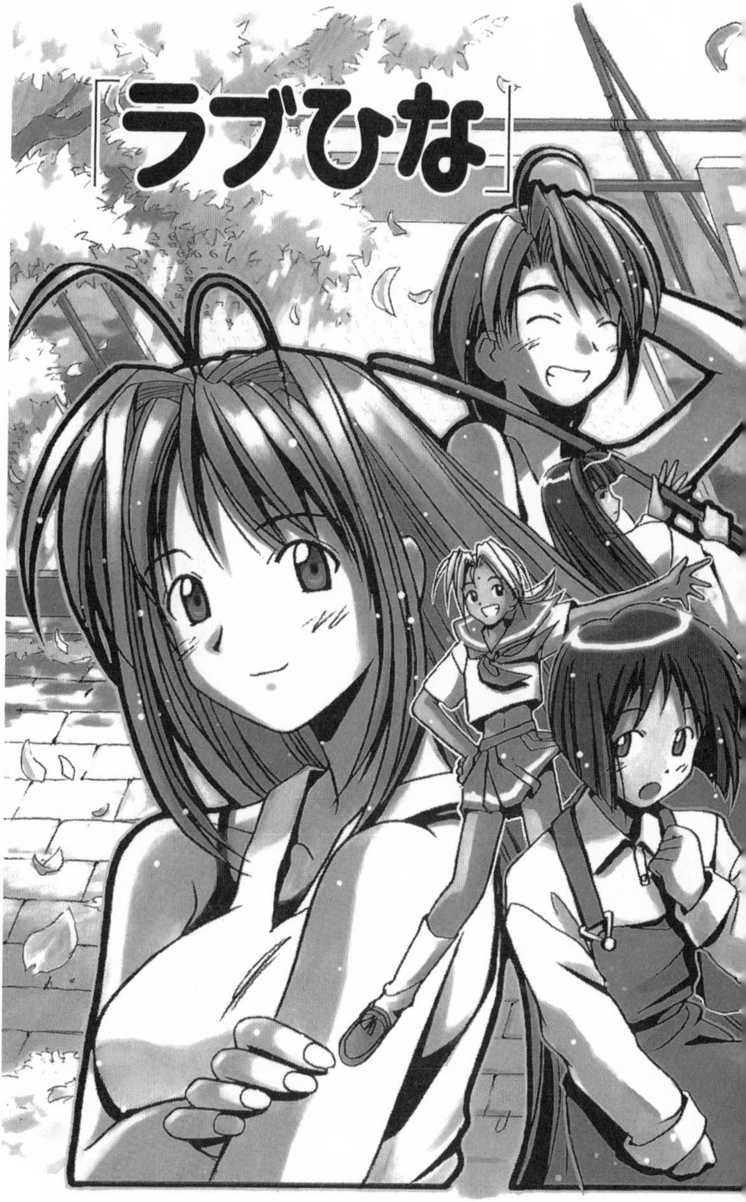
「ラブひな」

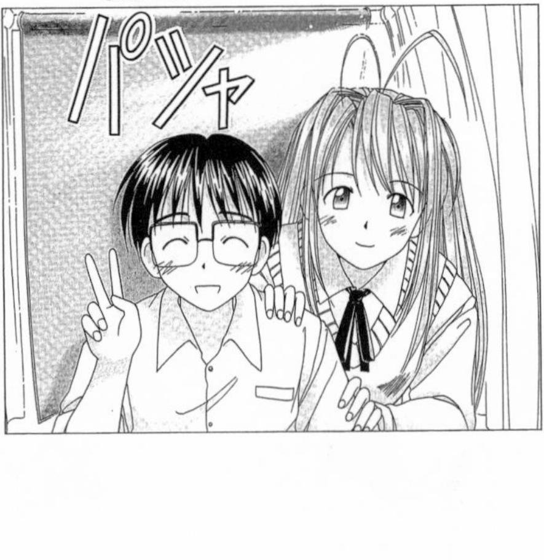
Click-whirr
パッシャ

東大のみを受けつづけ
落ちつづけて３年目 ―――

とうとう家を追い出された俺は
その温泉街へやってきた

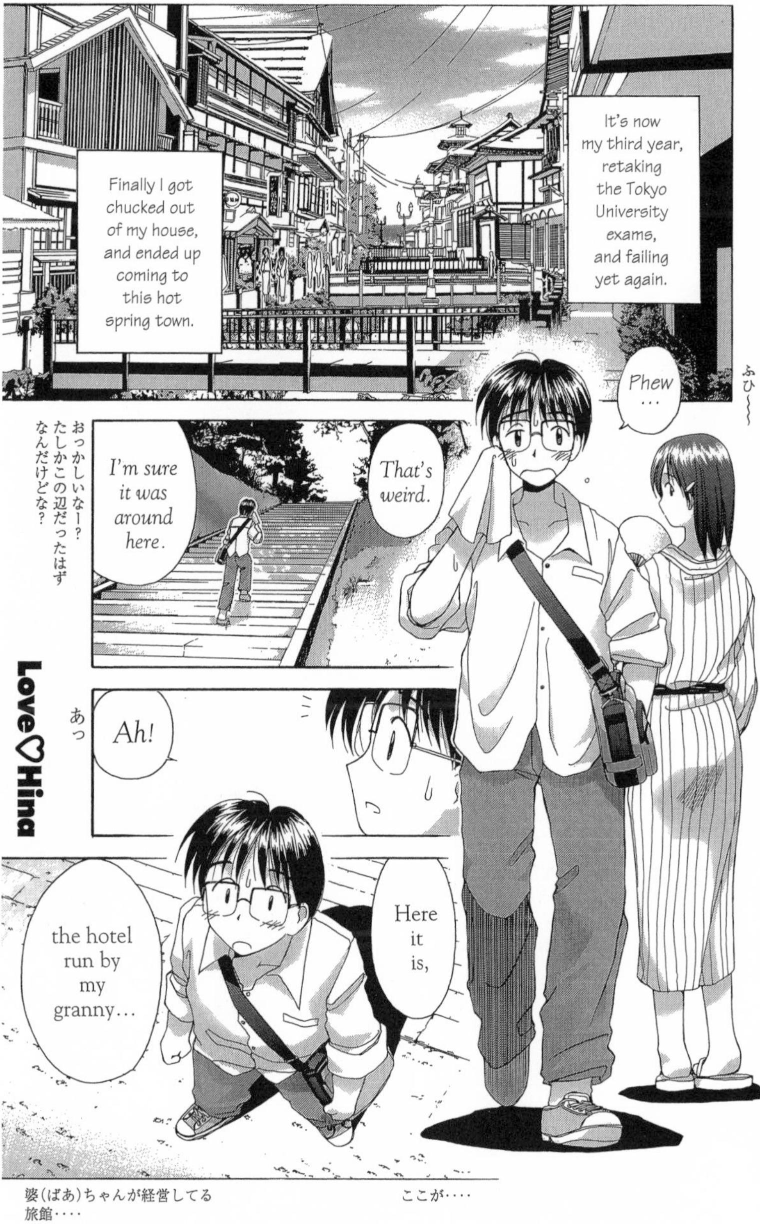
It's now my third year, retaking the Tokyo University exams, and failing yet again.
Finally I got chucked out of my house, and ended up coming to this hot spring town.
Phew …
ふひ〜〜
That's weird.
I'm sure it was around here.
Ah!
Here it is,
the hotel run by my granny…

おっかしいなー？
たしかこの辺だったはず
なんだけどな？

あっ

ここが‥‥

婆(ばあ)ちゃんが経営してる
旅館‥‥

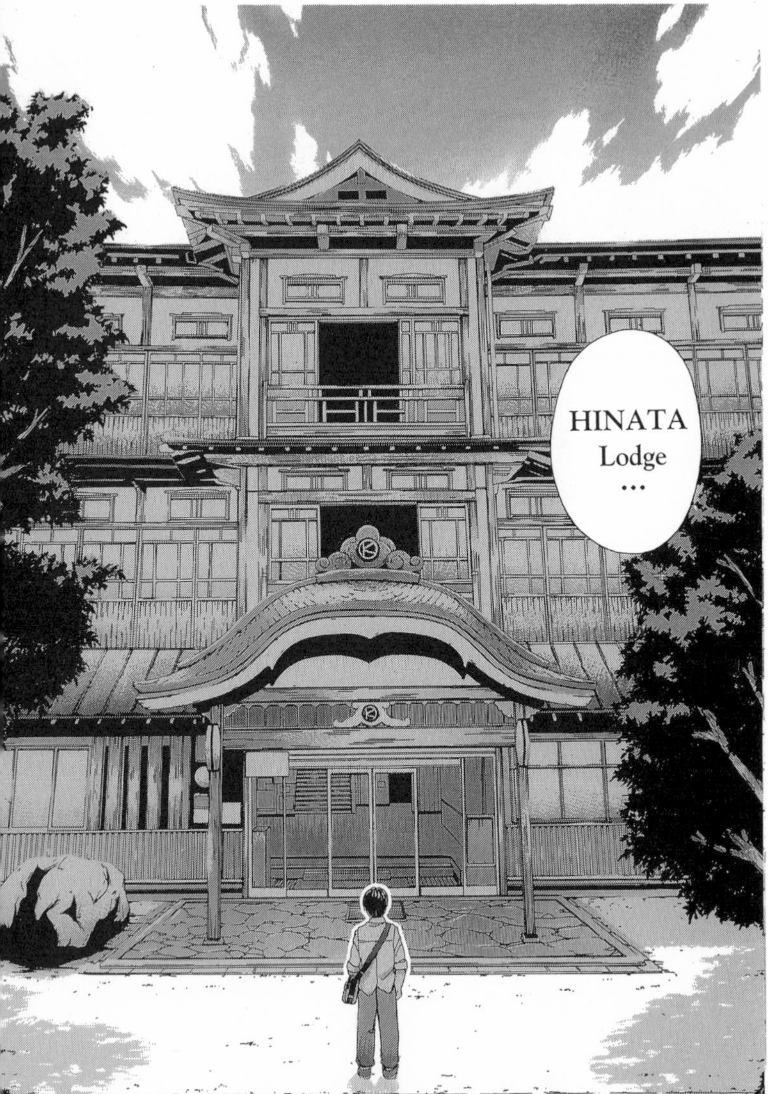
HINATA Lodge ...

ひなた旅館か‥‥

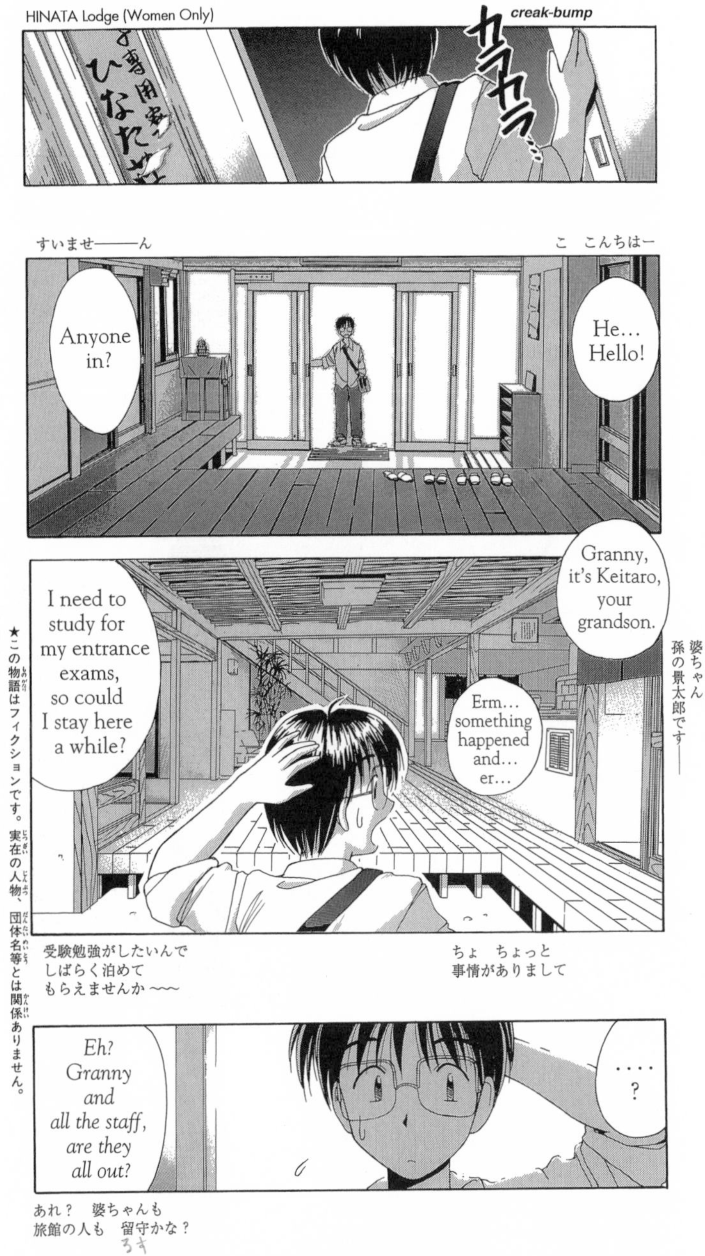
HINATA Lodge (Women Only)
creak-bump
カラカラ…
ひなた荘
こ　こんちはー
He… Hello!
すいませーーーん
Anyone in?
婆ちゃん　孫の景太郎ですーー
Granny, it's Keitaro, your grandson.
ちょ　ちょっと事情がありまして
Erm… something happened and… er…
受験勉強がしたいんでしばらく泊めてもらえませんか〜〜
I need to study for my entrance exams, so could I stay here a while?
…
?
あれ？　婆ちゃんも旅館の人も　留守かな？
Eh? Granny and all the staff, are they all out?
★この物語はフィクションです。実在の人物、団体名等とは関係ありません。

This story is a work of fiction. No real people or organizations are referred to.

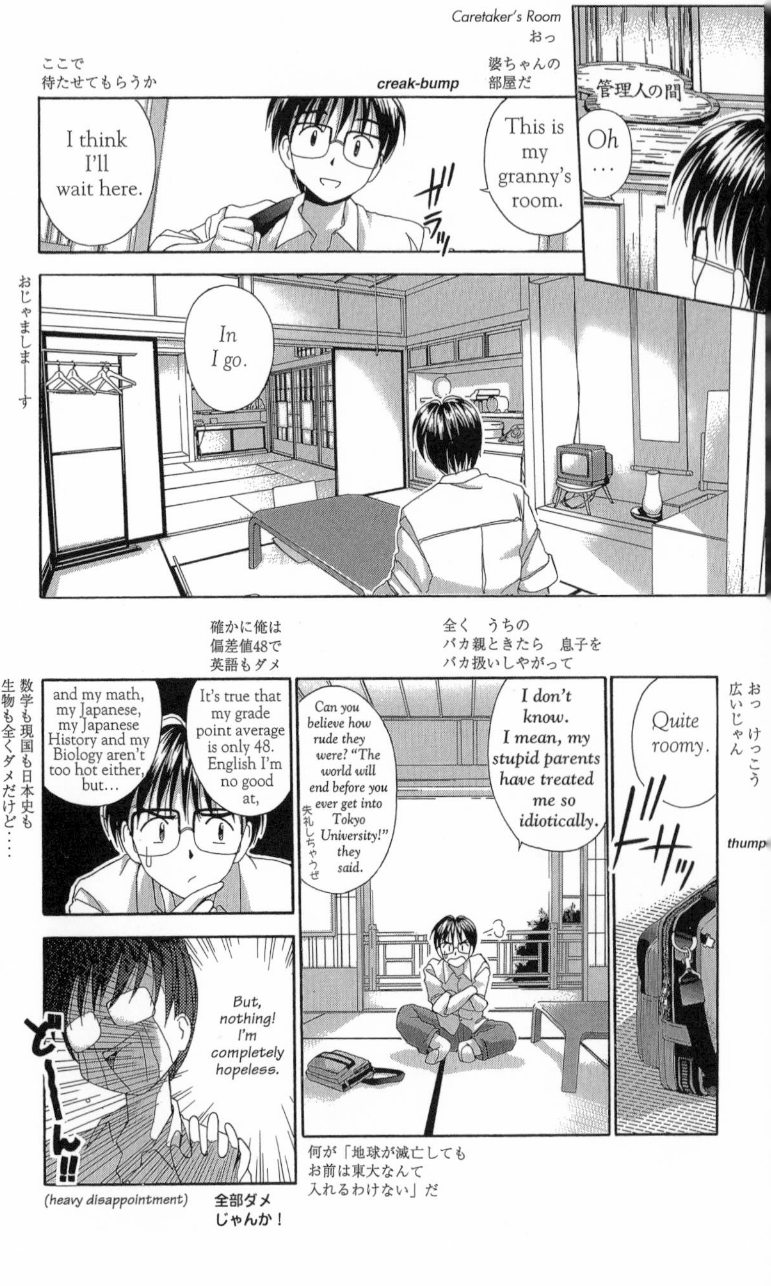
Caretaker's Room
おっ
管理人の間
Oh …
婆ちゃんの部屋だ
This is my granny's room.
ガラッ
creak-bump
ここで待たせてもらうか
I think I'll wait here.
おじゃましま――す
In I go.
おっ けっこう広いじゃん
Quite roomy.
ドサッ
thump
全く うちのバカ親ときたら 息子をバカ扱いしやがって
I don't know. I mean, my stupid parents have treated me so idiotically.
何が「地球が滅亡してもお前は東大なんて入れるわけない」だ
Can you believe how rude they were? "The world will end before you ever get into Tokyo University!" they said.
失礼しちゃうぜ
確かに俺は偏差値48で英語もダメ
It's true that my grade point average is only 48. English I'm no good at,
数学も現国も日本史も生物も全くダメだけど……
and my math, my Japanese, my Japanese History and my Biology aren't too hot either, but…
But, nothing! I'm completely hopeless.
どーん!!
(heavy disappointment)
全部ダメじゃんか！

ほんっと　モテる
要素が全然ない
男だよな

sigh (lies down)

考えてみれば
勉強だけじゃなく　スポーツもダメ
顔もパッとしないし
とりえもないし

はあ‥‥

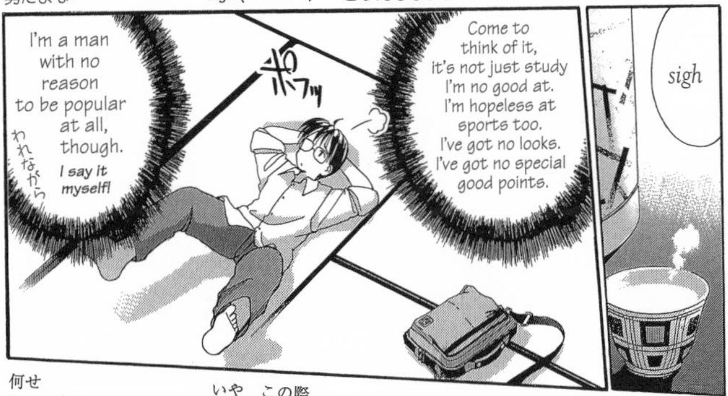
I'm a man with no reason to be popular at all, though.
われながら
I say it myself!
ボフッ
Come to think of it, it's not just study I'm no good at. I'm hopeless at sports too. I've got no looks. I've got no special good points.
sigh

何せ
この20年の
俺の人生‥‥

いや　この際
お話しできるだけでも
いい

あ〜〜あ　一度でいいから
女の子とデートしたいな〜〜

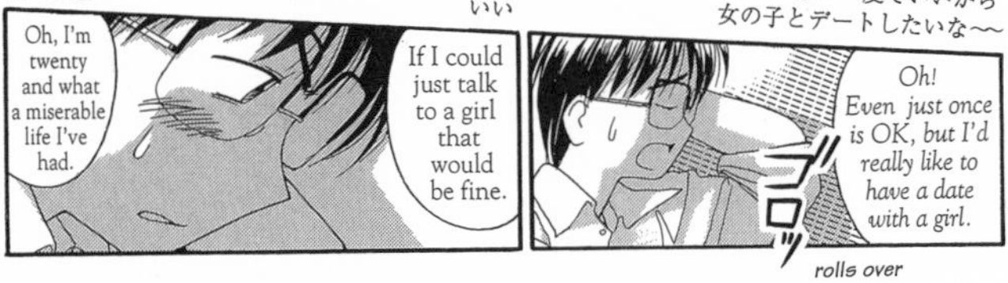
Oh, I'm twenty and what a miserable life I've had.
If I could just talk to a girl that would be fine.
Oh! Even just once is OK, but I'd really like to have a date with a girl.
ゴロッ

rolls over

フォークダンスの
相手は　いつも男

体育祭でも
出番がなくて

小中高と　女子には
避けられ　バカにされ

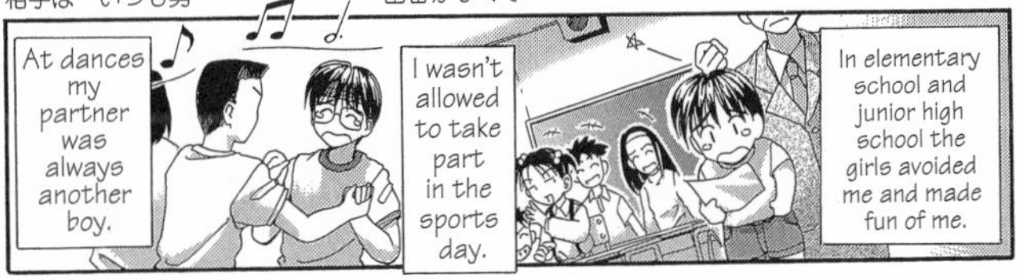
At dances my partner was always another boy.
I wasn't allowed to take part in the sports day.
In elementary school and junior high school the girls avoided me and made fun of me.

全部ひとりで
うつってる!!

おまけに趣味の
プリクラ集めは

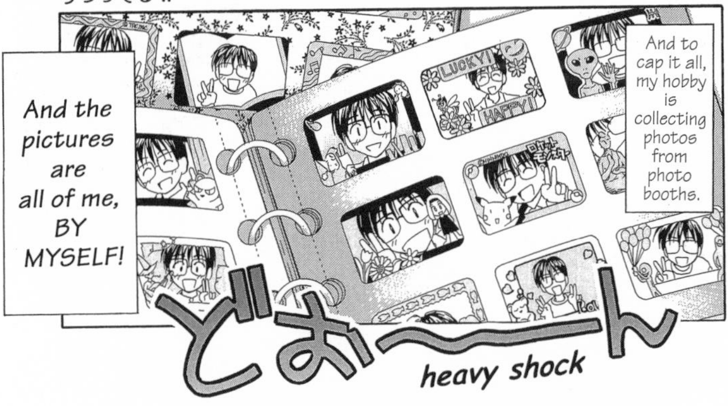
And the pictures are all of me, BY MYSELF!
LUCKY!
HAPPY!
And to cap it all, my hobby is collecting photos from photo booths.
どぉ〜〜ん
heavy shock

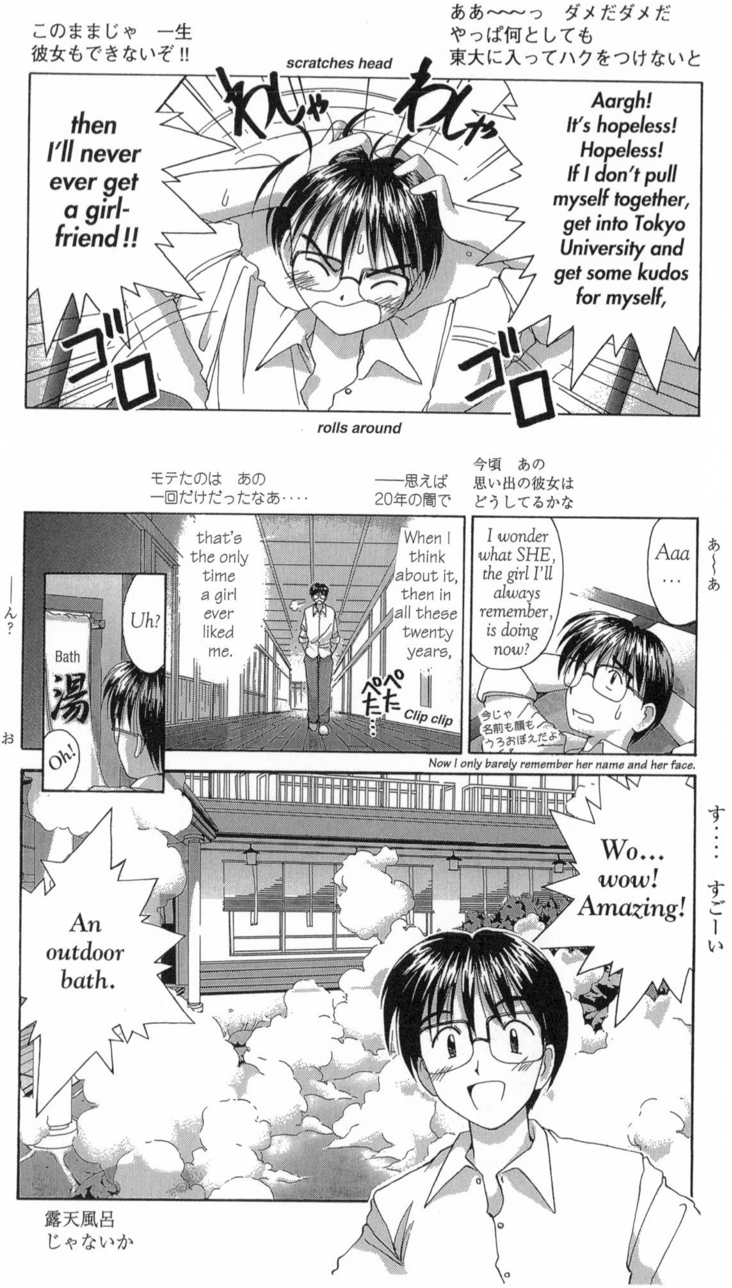
ああ〜〜〜っ　ダメだダメだ
やっぱ何としても
東大に入ってハクをつけないと
Aargh! It's hopeless! Hopeless! If I don't pull myself together, get into Tokyo University and get some kudos for myself,
わしゃ　わしゃ
scratches head
このままじゃ　一生
彼女もできないぞ!!
then I'll never ever get a girl-friend!!
ゴロ　ゴロ
rolls around
今頃　あの
思い出の彼女は
どうしてるかな
I wonder what SHE, the girl I'll always remember, is doing now?
あ〜あ
Aaa …
今じゃ名前も顔もうろおぼえだよ
Now I only barely remember her name and her face.
――思えば
20年の間で
When I think about it, then in all these twenty years,
モテたのは　あの
一回だけだったなあ‥‥
that's the only time a girl ever liked me.
ぺたぺた‥‥
Clip clip
――ん?
Uh?
Bath
湯
お
Oh!
すごーい
す‥‥
Wo… wow! Amazing!
露天風呂
じゃないか
An outdoor bath.

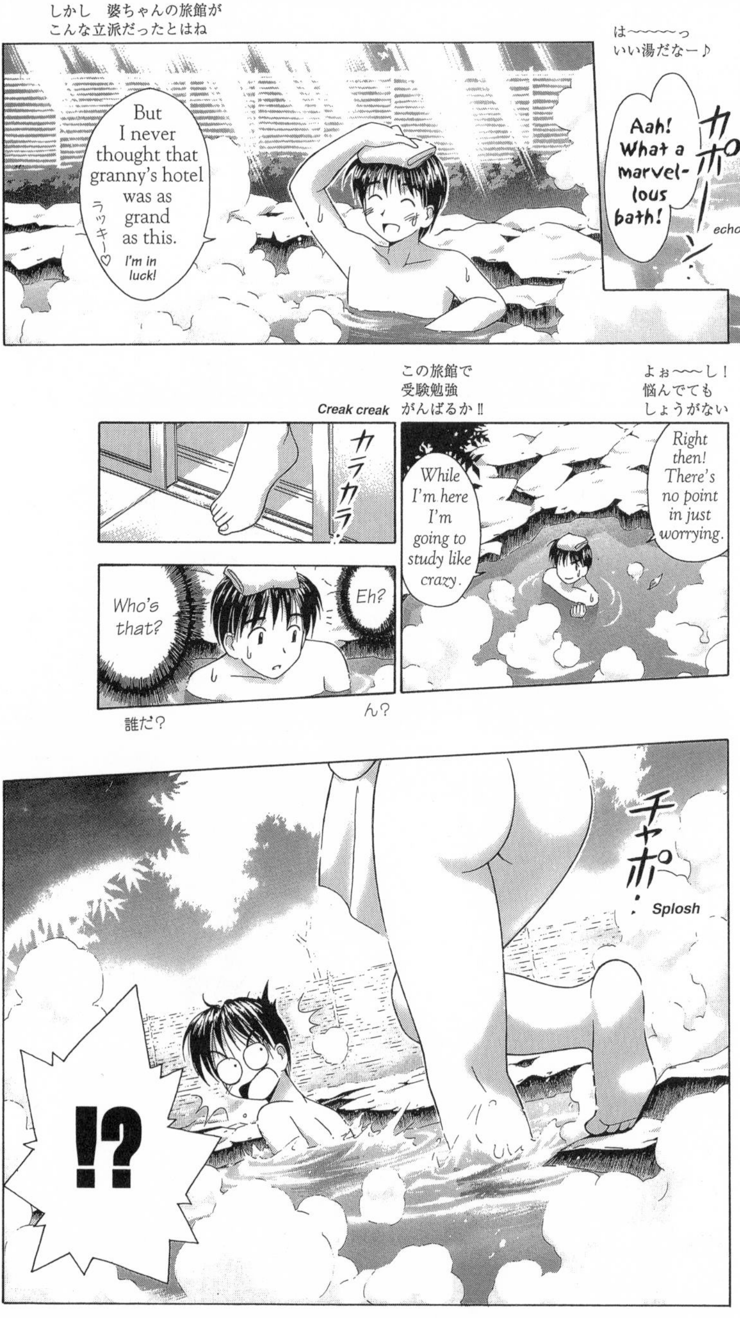
は～～～～っ
いい湯だなー♪
Aah! What a marvellous bath!
カポーン…
echo
しかし　婆ちゃんの旅館が
こんな立派だったとはね
But I never thought that granny's hotel was as grand as this.
ラッキー♡
I'm in luck!
よぉ～～し！
悩んでても
しょうがない
Right then! There's no point in just worrying.
この旅館で
受験勉強
がんばるか!!
While I'm here I'm going to study like crazy.
カラカラ…
Creak creak
Eh?
ん？
Who's that?
誰だ？
チャポ…
Splosh
!?

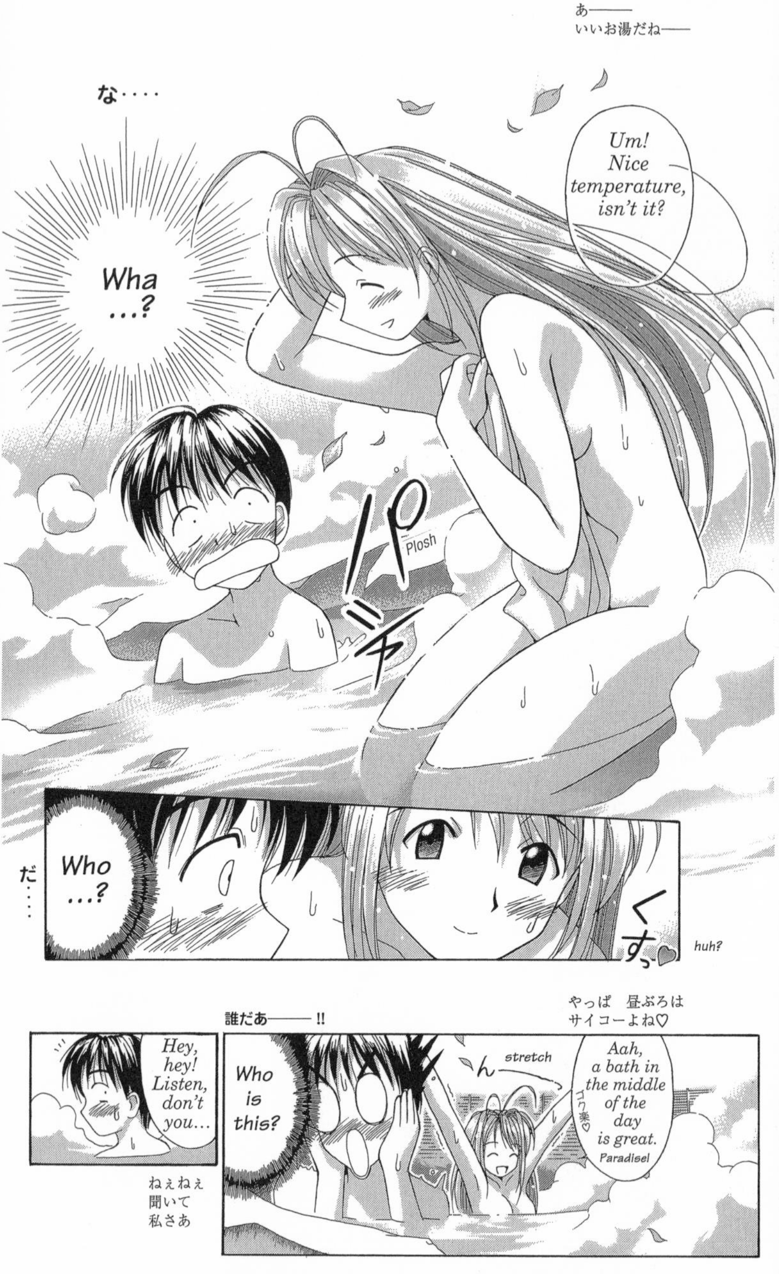
あ——
いいお湯だね——
Um! Nice temperature, isn't it?
な・・・・
Wha …?
Plosh
だ・・・・
Who …?
くすっ♡
huh?
やっぱ　昼ぶろは
サイコーよね♡
Aah, a bath in the middle of the day is great.
ゴク楽♡
Paradise!
ん
stretch
誰だあ——!!
Who is this?
Hey, hey! Listen, don't you…
ねぇねぇ
聞いて
私さあ

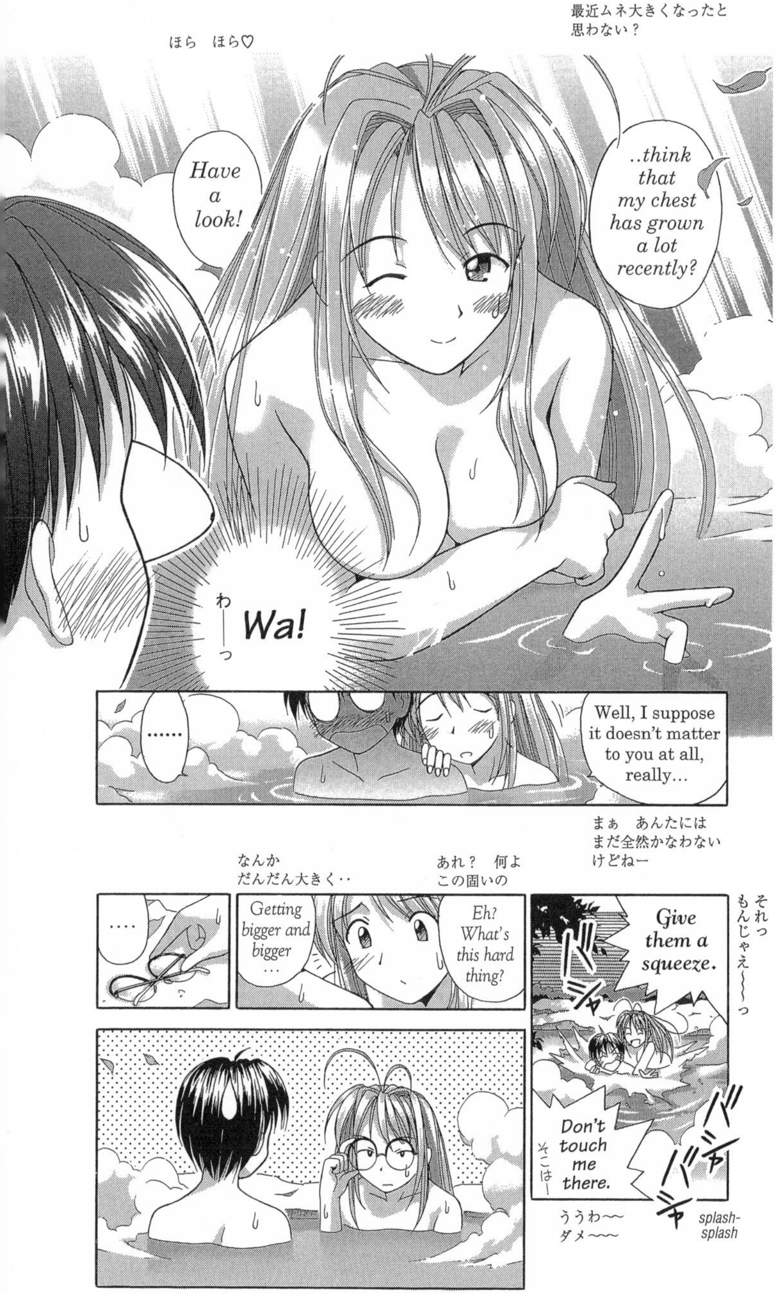
最近ムネ大きくなったと思わない？
..think that my chest has grown a lot recently?
ほら　ほら♡
Have a look!
わ——っ
Wa!
まぁ　あんたには まだ全然かなわない けどねー
Well, I suppose it doesn't matter to you at all, really...
....
それっ もんじゃえ～～っ
Give them a squeeze.
ドシャ
あれ？　何よ この固いの
Eh? What's this hard thing?
なんか だんだん大きく‥
Getting bigger and bigger ...
....
バシャ バシャ
splash-splash
ううわ～～ ダメ～～～
そこは—
Don't touch me there.

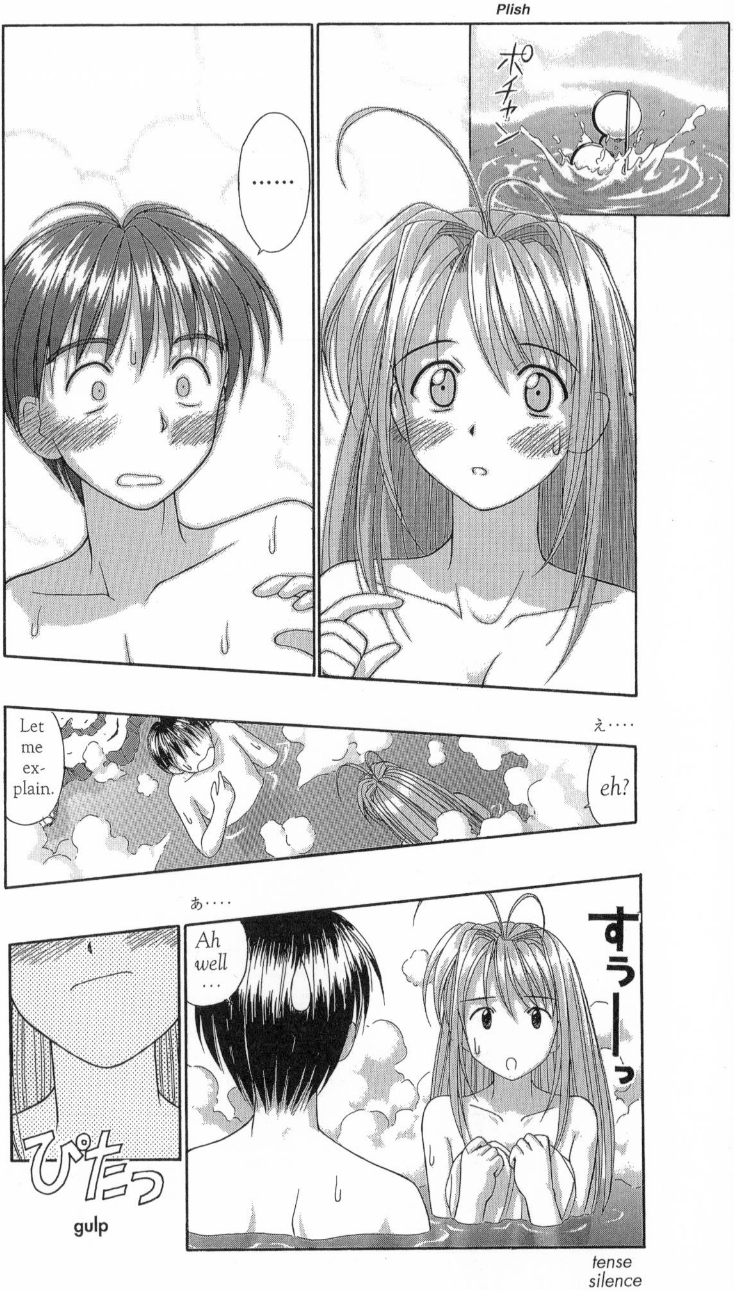
Plish
ポチャン
……
え････
eh?
あのですねぇ
Let me ex-plain.
すぅーーっ
tense silence
あ････
Ah well …
ぴたっ
gulp

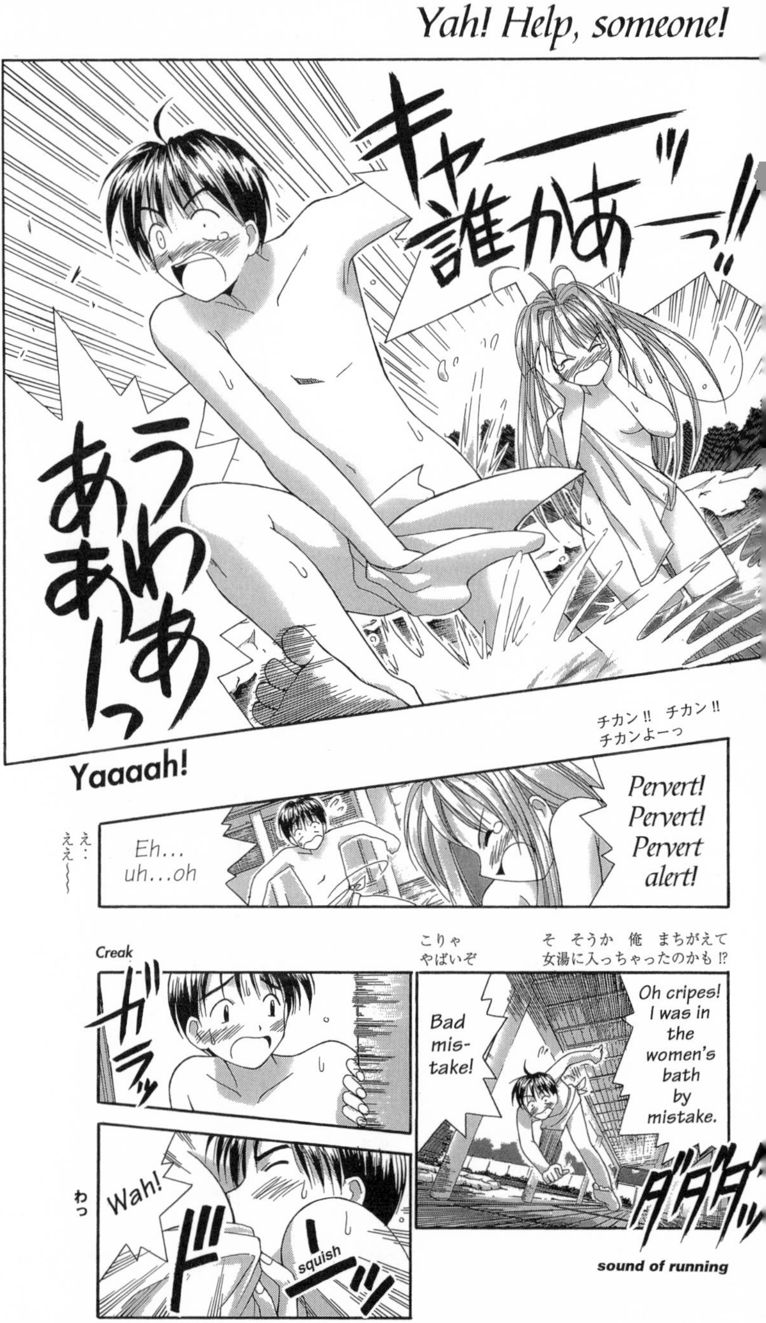
Yah! Help, someone!
キャー誰かあーっ!!
うわあああーっ
Yaaaah!
チカン!! チカン!!
チカンよーっ
Pervert!
Pervert!
Pervert
alert!
え…ええ~~
Eh...
uh...oh
そ そうか 俺 まちがえて
女湯に入っちゃったのかも⁉
Oh cripes!
I was in
the
women's
bath
by
mistake.
こりゃ
やばいぞ
Bad
mis-
take!
ダダダッ
sound of running
Creak
ガラッ
わっ
Wah!
ドーッ
squish

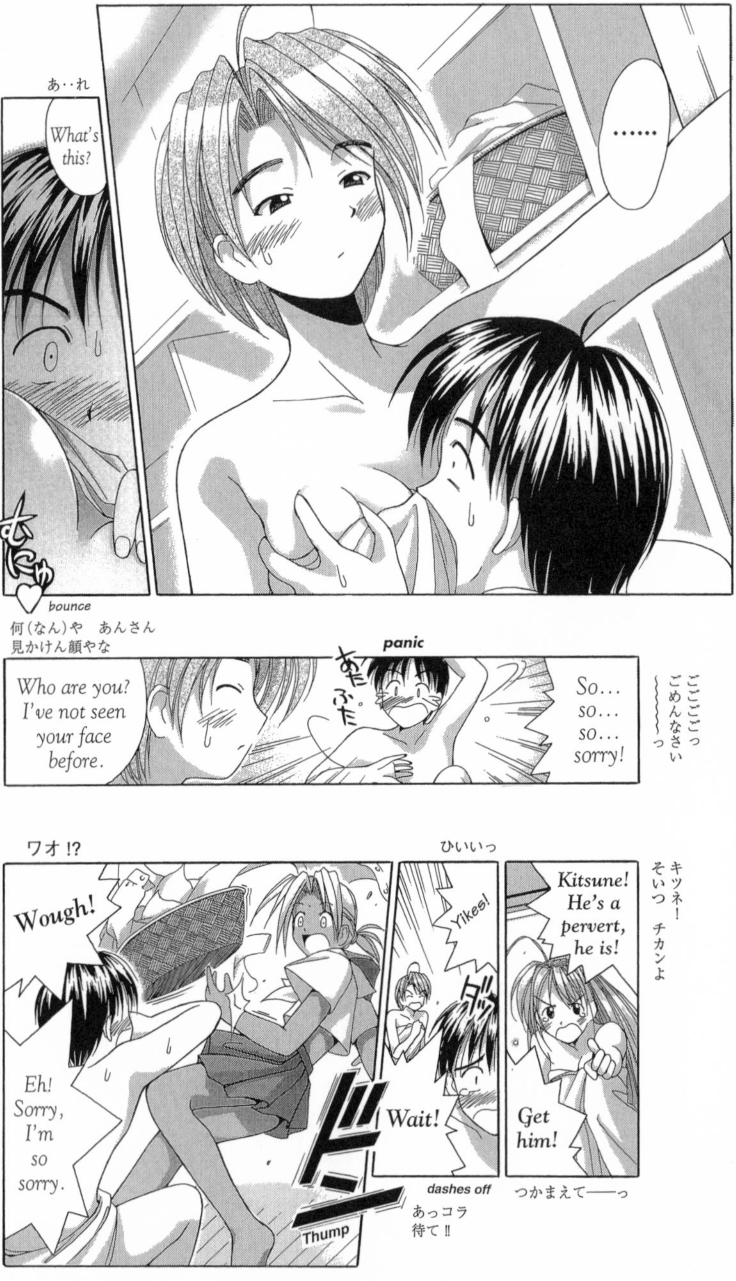
……
あ‥れ
What's this?
むにゅ
bounce
ごごごごっ ごめんなさい〜〜〜〜っ
So… so… so… sorry!
あたふた
panic
何(なん)や　あんさん 見かけん顔やな
Who are you? I've not seen your face before.
キツネ！ そいつ　チカンよ
Kitsune! He's a pervert, he is!
つかまえて――っ
Get him!
ひいいっ
Yikes!
ダッ
dashes off
あっコラ 待て!!
Wait!
ワオ!?
Wough!
あた!?　すみませんっ
Eh! Sorry, I'm so sorry.
ドー
Thump

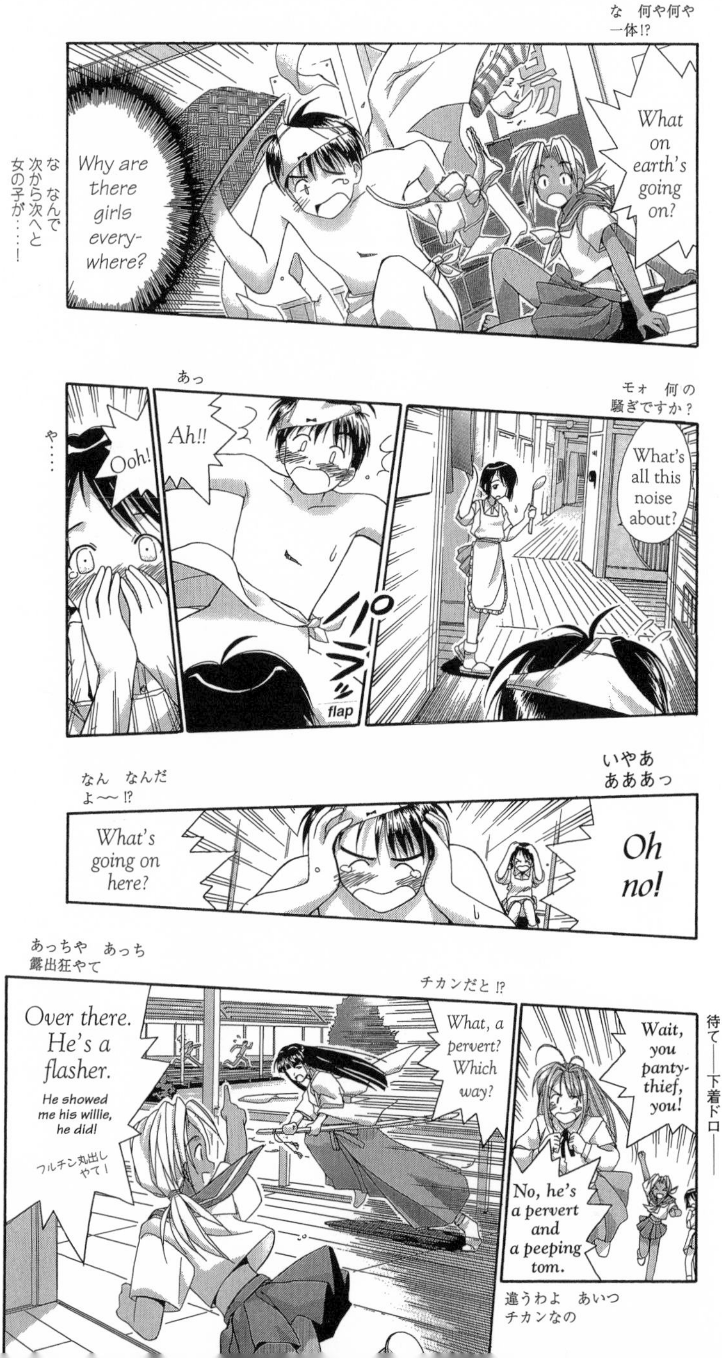
な　何や何や一体!?
What on earth's going on?
な　なんで次から次へと女の子が……!
Why are there girls every-where?
モォ　何の騒ぎですか？
What's all this noise about?
あっ
Ah!!
パラッ
flap
や……
Ooh!
いやあああっ
Oh no!
なん　なんだよ〜!?
What's going on here?
待て――下着ドロ――
Wait, you panty-thief, you!
違うわよ　あいつチカンなの
No, he's a pervert and a peeping tom.
チカンだと!?
What, a pervert? Which way?
あっちや　あっち露出狂やて
Over there. He's a flasher.
He showed me his willie, he did!
フルチン丸出しやて!

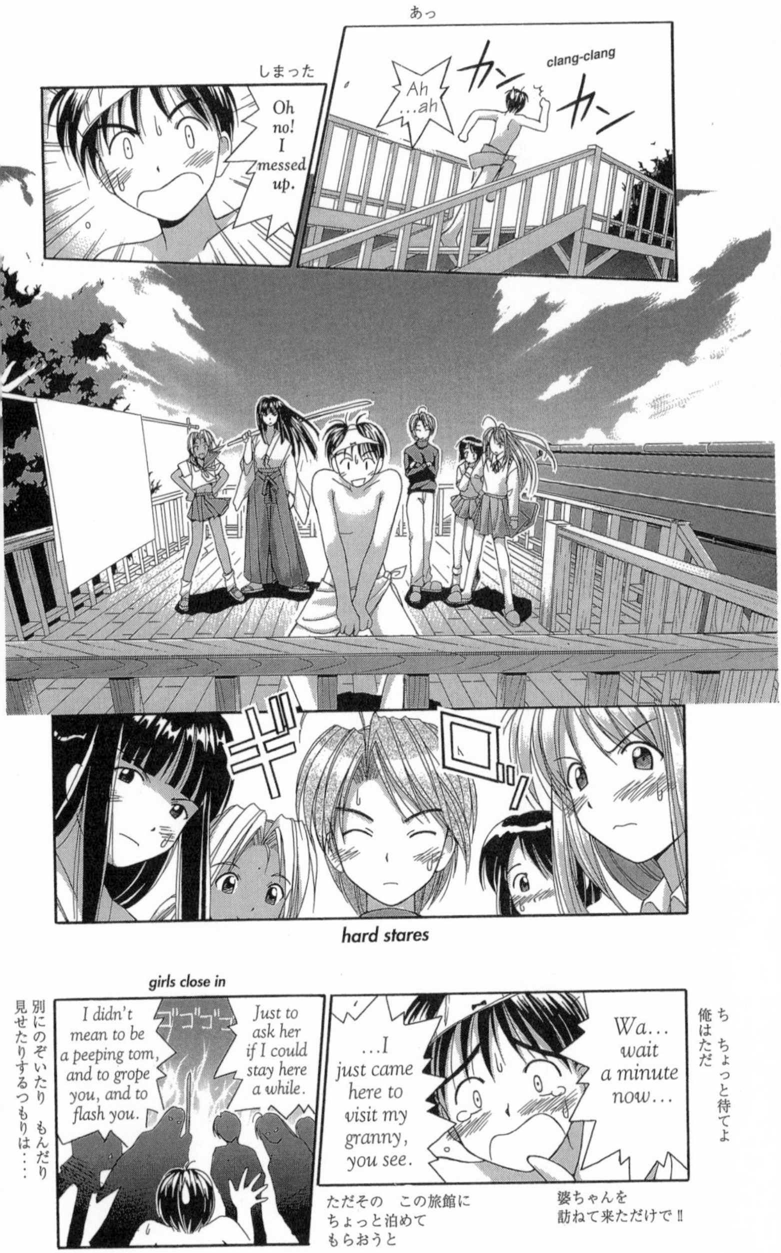
あっ
Ah ...ah
clang-clang
カンカン
しまった
Oh no! I messed up.
ギロッ
hard stares
Wa... wait a minute now...
ち ちょっと待てよ
...I just came here to visit my granny, you see.
俺はただ
婆ちゃんを
訪ねて来ただけで!!
Just to ask her if I could stay here a while.
ただその この旅館に
ちょっと泊めて
もらおうと
I didn't mean to be a peeping tom, and to grope you, and to flash you.
別にのぞいたり もんだり
見せたりするつもりは・・・・
girls close in
ゴゴゴゴ

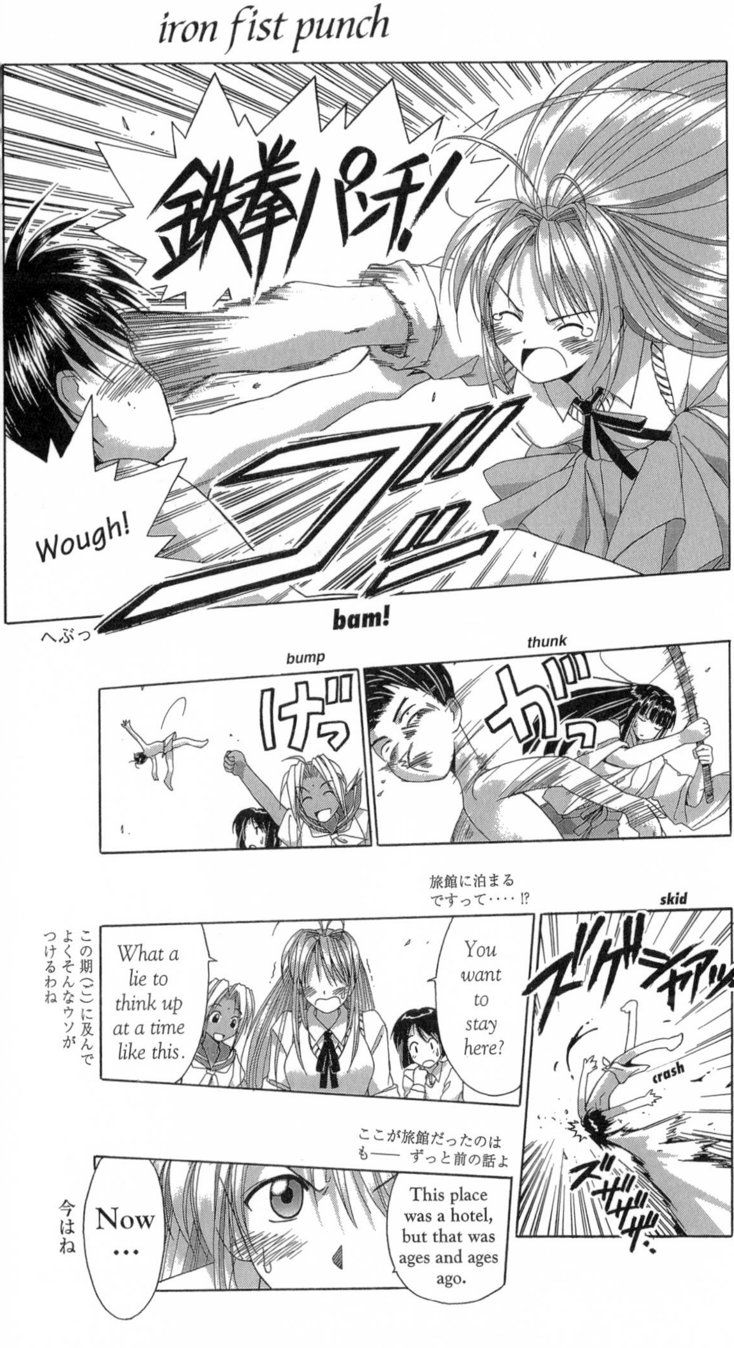
iron fist punch
鉄拳パンチ!
Wough!
bam!
へぶっ
thunk
bump
旅館に泊まるですって…!?
You want to stay here?
この期(ご)に及んでよくそんなウソがつけるわね
What a lie to think up at a time like this.
skid
crash
ここが旅館だったのはも―― ずっと前の話よ
This place was a hotel, but that was ages and ages ago.
今はね
Now ...

男子禁制の
契約アパート！

すなわち
女子寮なのよっ

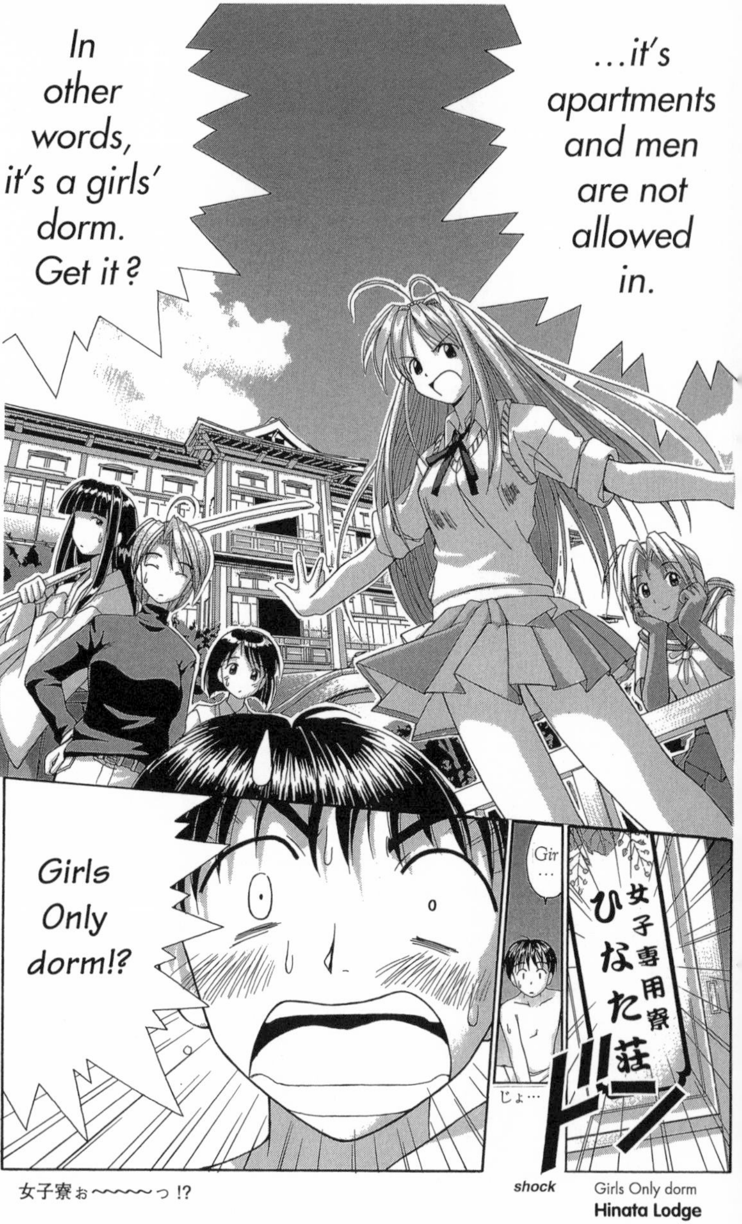
...it's apartments and men are not allowed in.
In other words, it's a girls' dorm. Get it?
Girr...
女子専用寮
ひなた荘
じょ…
Girls Only dorm!?

shock

Girls Only dorm
Hinata Lodge

女子寮ぉ〜〜〜〜っ!?

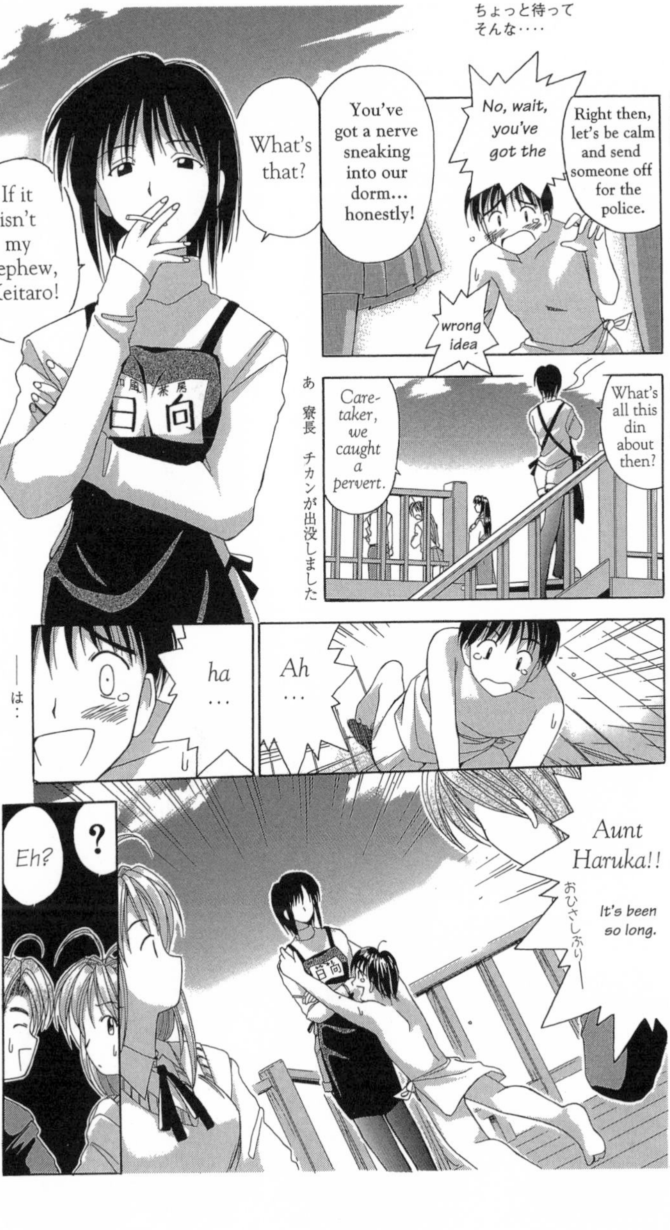
Right then, let's be calm and send someone off for the police.
さぁ おとなしく警察に行ってもらうわよ
No, wait, you've got the
wrong idea
ちがう〜〜う
ちょっと待って そんな‥‥
You've got a nerve sneaking into our dorm… honestly!
うちの寮に忍びこむなんて ええ度胸しとるわ ホンマ
What's that?
ん‥‥？ なんだ
If it isn't my nephew, Keitaro!
おいの景太郎じゃないか
What's all this din about then?
騒々(そうぞう)しいな どうした
Care-taker, we caught a pervert.
あ 寮長 チカンが出没しました
Ah …
あ‥‥!?
ha …
―は‥
Aunt Haruka!!
はるかおばさん!!
It's been so long.
おひさしぶり―
?
Eh?
‥‥え？

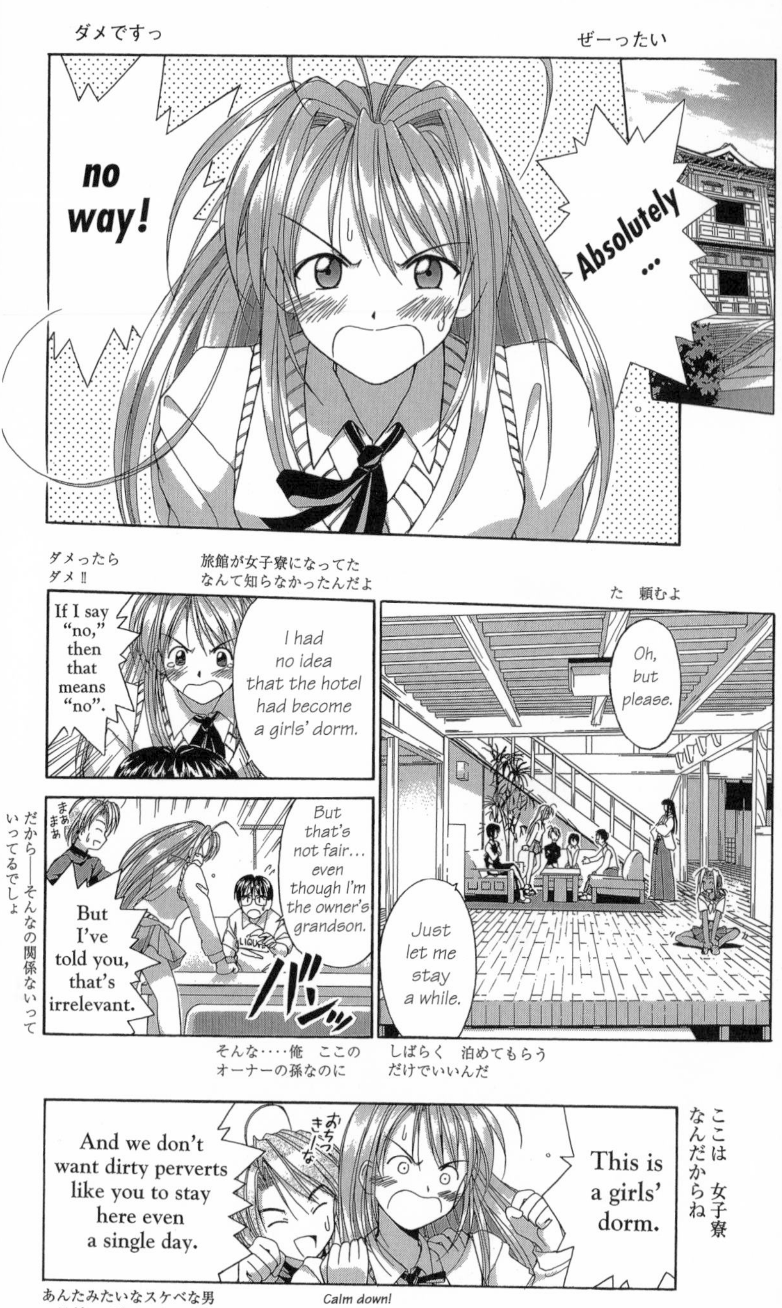
ぜーったい
Absolutely ...
ダメですっ
no way!
旅館が女子寮になってた
なんて知らなかったんだよ
I had no idea that the hotel had become a girls' dorm.
ダメったら
ダメ!!
If I say "no," then that means "no".
そんな‥‥俺　ここの
オーナーの孫なのに
But that's not fair... even though I'm the owner's grandson.
まあまあ
だから――そんなの関係ないって
いってるでしょ
But I've told you, that's irrelevant.
た　頼むよ
Oh, but please.
しばらく　泊めてもらう
だけでいいんだ
Just let me stay a while.
ここは　女子寮
なんだからね
This is a girls' dorm.
おちつきーな
Calm down!
あんたみたいなスケベな男
一日だって泊めるわけにはいかないのよ
And we don't want dirty perverts like you to stay here even a single day.

さんざん　ハレンチな
行為をしでかして

あまつさえ　まだ中１の
しのぶちゃんに　あんなもん見せて！

だいたい　人の裸みたり
胸もんだり　下着盗んだり

――変なトラウマに
なったら　どーすんのよ!!

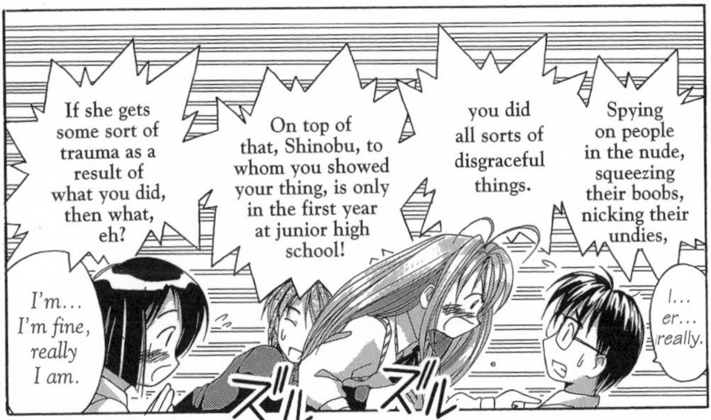

Spying on people in the nude, squeezing their boobs, nicking their undies,
you did all sorts of disgraceful things.
On top of that, Shinobu, to whom you showed your thing, is only in the first year at junior high school!
If she gets some sort of trauma as a result of what you did, then what, eh?
I... er... really.
I'm... I'm fine, really I am.
ズル ズル

leaning in threateningly

そ　そんな!!

あ　あの私
平気ですから

ち　小さくて
よく見えなかったし
全然気にしてませんから

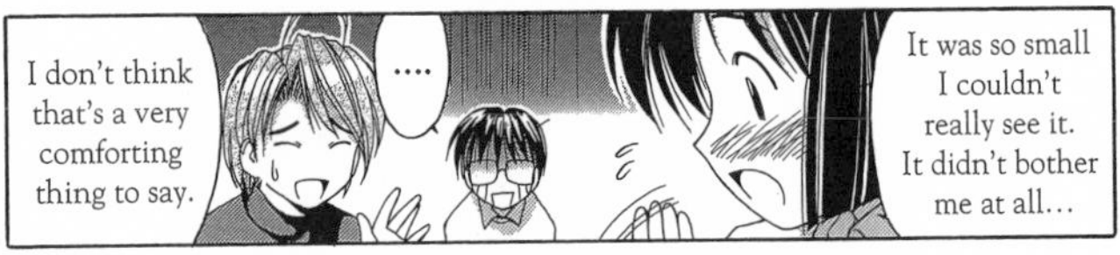

It was so small I couldn't really see it. It didn't bother me at all...
....
I don't think that's a very comforting thing to say.

あんさん　あんさん
なぐさめに
なってへんで

でも　まいったな　婆ちゃんを頼って
来たからお金も持ってないし・・・

screech-yell

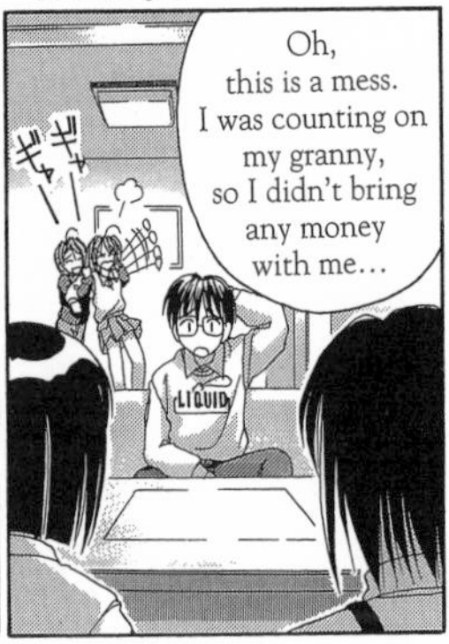

Oh, this is a mess. I was counting on my granny, so I didn't bring any money with me...
ギャ ギャ
LIQUID

そうだ　婆ちゃんは
どこにいるの？

たのめば
きっと・・・・

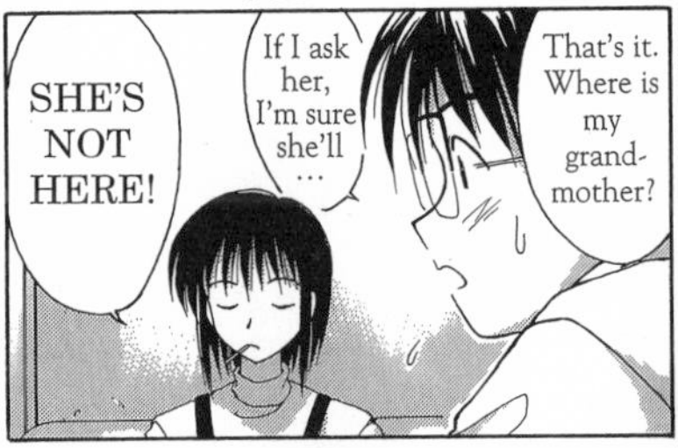

That's it. Where is my grand-mother?
If I ask her, I'm sure she'll ...
SHE'S NOT HERE!

――いないよ

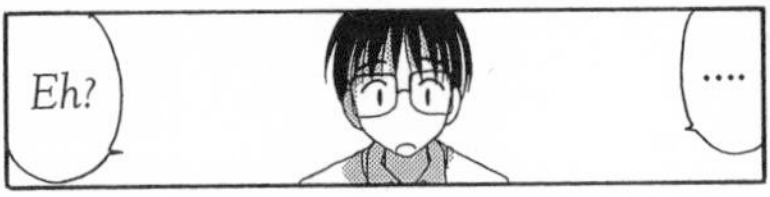

....
Eh?

え？

一年以上前に　世界一周旅行
行ったきりでな

たま～～に　FAXが
来るぐらいなのさ

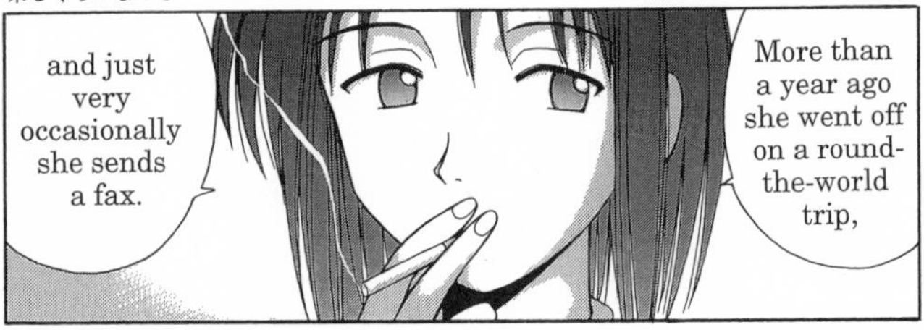

More than a year ago she went off on a round-the-world trip,
and just very occasionally she sends a fax.

世界一周旅行!?

いいトシして
新しい恋の出会い
もとめてとかいってね

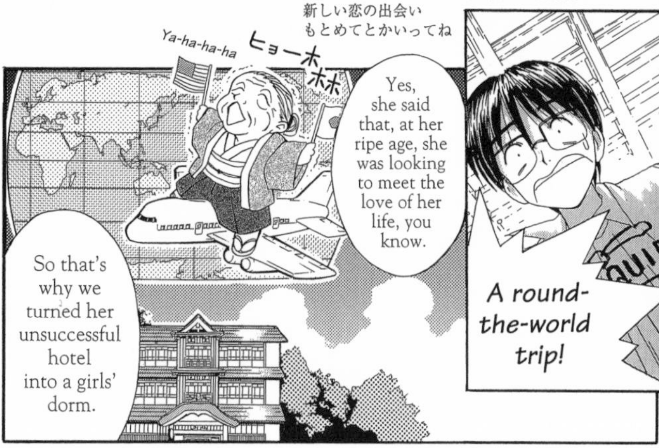
A round-the-world trip!
Yes, she said that, at her ripe age, she was looking to meet the love of her life, you know.
ヒョーホホホ
Ya-ha-ha-ha
So that's why we turned her unsuccessful hotel into a girls' dorm.

だからそれを機に　はやらない旅館から
女子寮に切りかえたわけだ

そ・・・・
そうですか

婆ちゃんは
いないんですか・・・・

あ～～あ
なんてこった

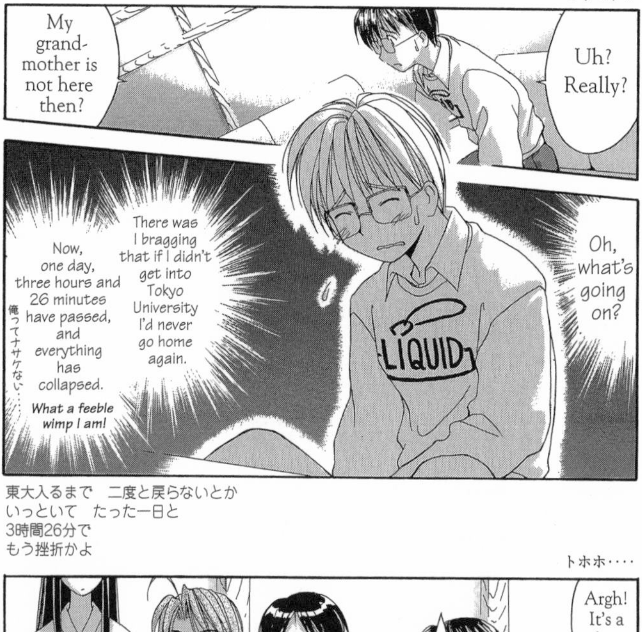
Uh? Really?
My grand-mother is not here then?
Oh, what's going on?
There was I bragging that if I didn't get into Tokyo University I'd never go home again.
Now, one day, three hours and 26 minutes have passed, and everything has collapsed.
俺ってナサケない・・・
What a feeble wimp I am!

東大入るまで　二度と戻らないとか
いっといて　たった一日と
3時間26分で
もう挫折かよ

トホホ・・・・

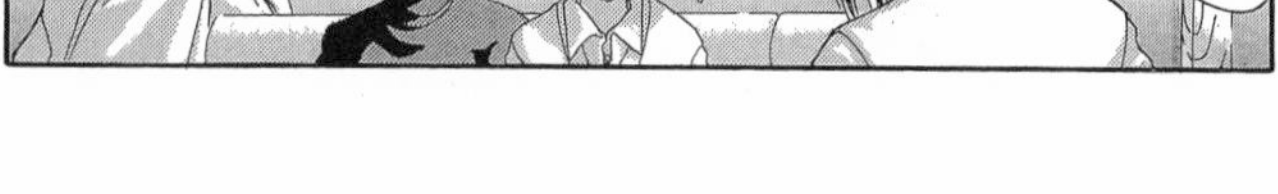
Argh! It's a big mess.

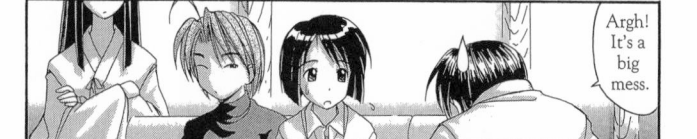

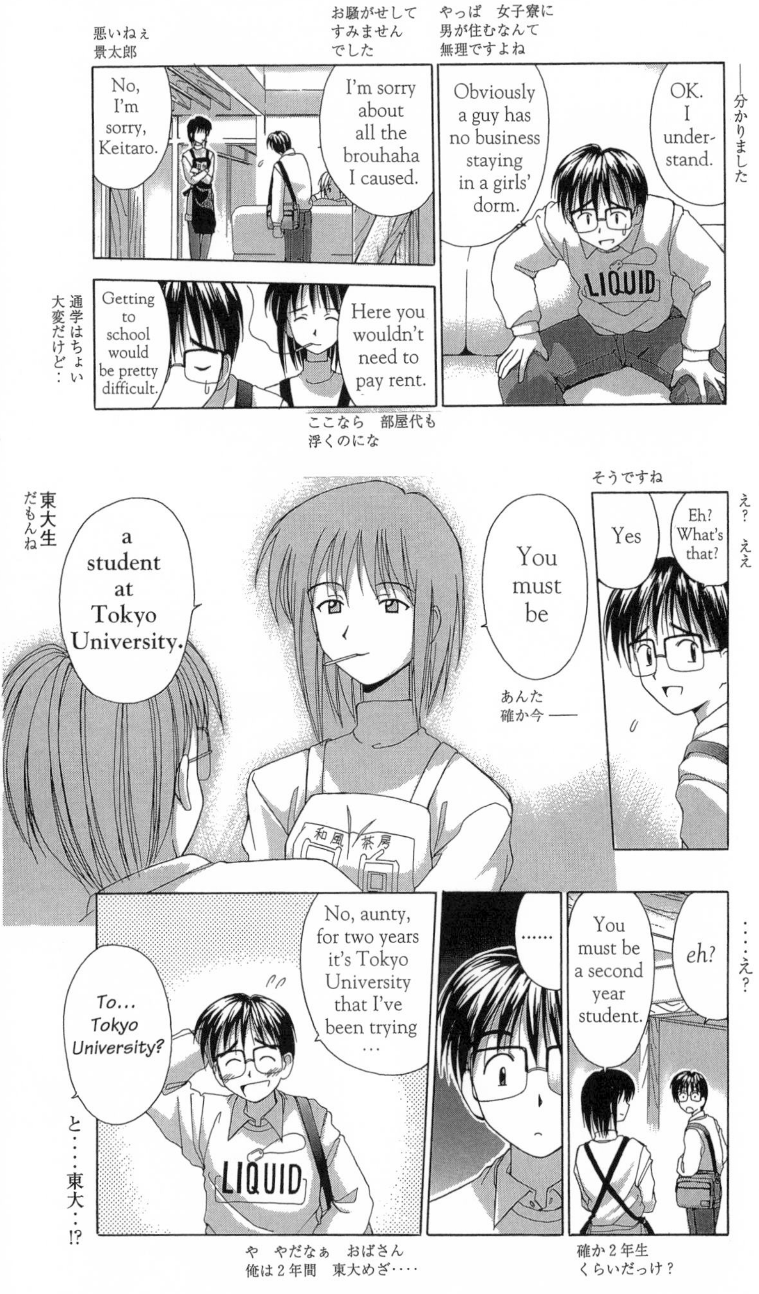
──分かりました
OK. I under-stand.
Obviously a guy has no business staying in a girls' dorm.
やっぱ 女子寮に 男が住むなんて 無理ですよね
I'm sorry about all the brouhaha I caused.
お騒がせして すみません でした
No, I'm sorry, Keitaro.
悪いねぇ 景太郎
Here you wouldn't need to pay rent.
ここなら 部屋代も 浮くのにな
Getting to school would be pretty difficult.
通学はちょい 大変だけど‥
え？ ええ
Eh? What's that?
Yes
そうですね
You must be
あんた 確か今──
a student at Tokyo University.
東大生 だもんね
‥‥え？
eh?
You must be a second year student.
確か2年生 くらいだっけ？
......
No, aunty, for two years it's Tokyo University that I've been trying …
To… Tokyo University?
と‥‥東大‥!?
や やだなぁ おばさん 俺は2年間 東大めざ‥‥

東京大学 !?

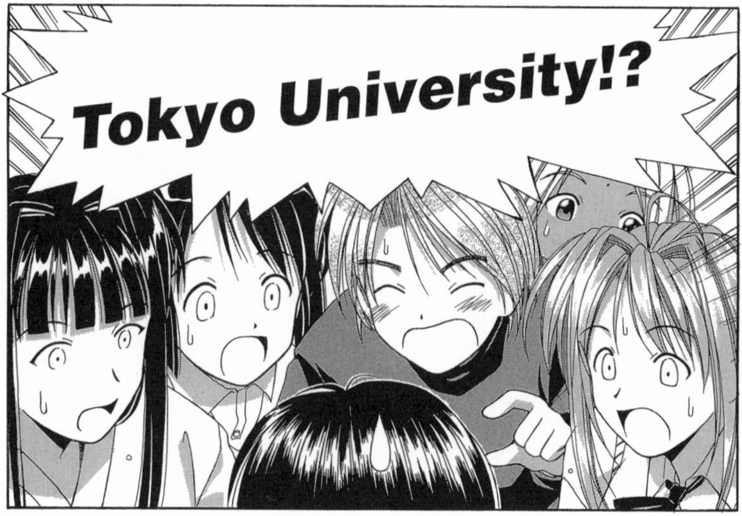
Tokyo University!?

は・・・・

はあ？

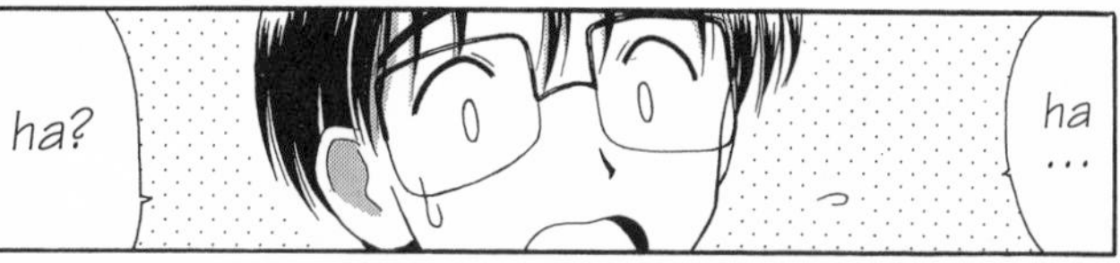
ha
...
ha?

あんた　東大生
やったんか !!

(scraping of chairs)

す・・・・　すごいやん
〜〜〜〜っ !!

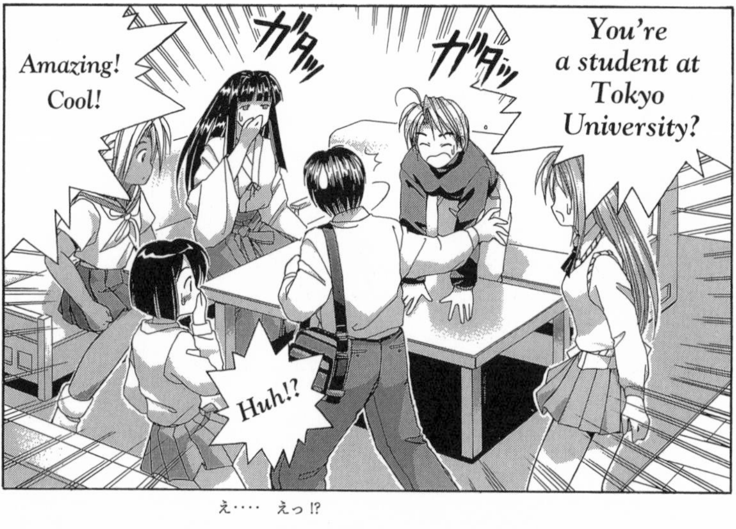
You're a student at Tokyo University?
ガタッ
ガタッ
Amazing! Cool!
Huh!?

え・・・・　えっ !?

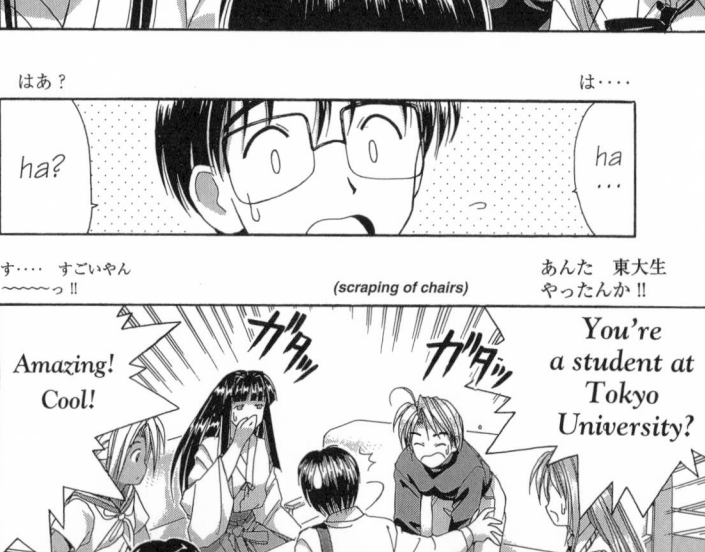

ちょ　ちょっ

う～～む
人は見かけに
よらないと
言うが‥‥

い　いや
俺は‥‥

トーダイて
何や？
食いモンか？

と　東大生だろうが
スケベはスケベ
なんじゃないの？

なに言うとんのや
天下の東大やで!!

ホンマやで
こんなさえない顔して!!

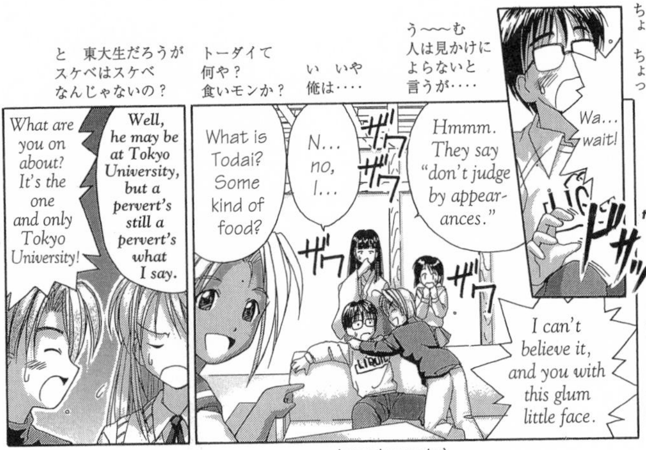

Wa… wait!
thump
Hmmm. They say "don't judge by appearances."
N… no, I…
What is Todai? Some kind of food?
Well, he may be at Tokyo University, but a pervert's still a pervert's what I say.
What are you on about? It's the one and only Tokyo University!
I can't believe it, and you with this glum little face.
(amazed murmuring)

やっぱアレか　東大つーたら
かなり偏差値必要なんやろ

え？

うーん
まあ今だと

偏差値69　センター試験で
700点ぐらいは必要かなぁ

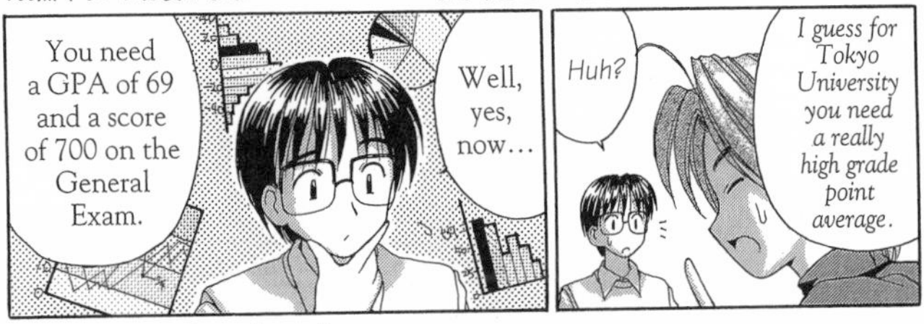

I guess for Tokyo University you need a really high grade point average.
Huh?
Well, yes, now…
You need a GPA of 69 and a score of 700 on the General Exam.

聞いたか!?
偏差値69やて!!

すごーい
69――!?

な
トーダイって
うまいの？

ちょっと
聞いてよ
俺は‥‥

で　あんさん
学部は　どこなん？

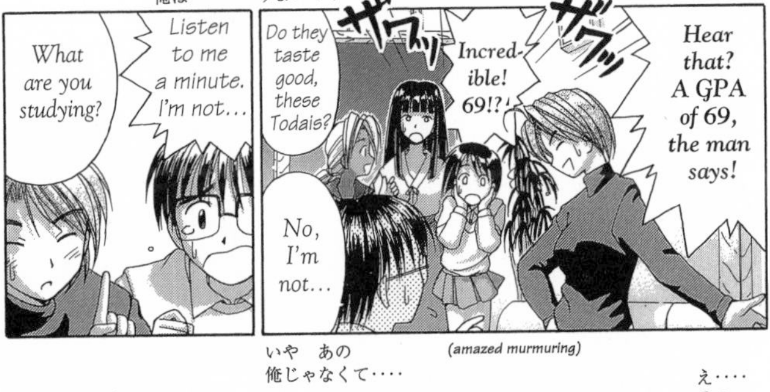

Hear that? A GPA of 69, the man says!
Incred-ible! 69!?!
Do they taste good, these Todais?
No, I'm not…
Listen to me a minute. I'm not…
What are you studying?
(amazed murmuring)

いや　あの
俺じゃなくて‥‥

え‥‥
その‥

一応　法学部を‥‥

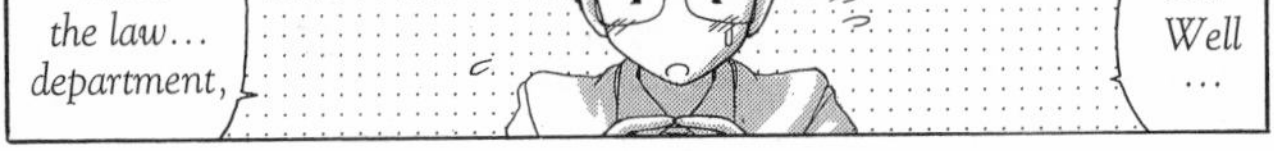

Eh? Well …
…it's the law… department,

聞いたか !?
東大の法やで！

····ねらって
るんだけど

まいったな〜〜
俺　本当は２浪で
しかも偏差値48なのに····

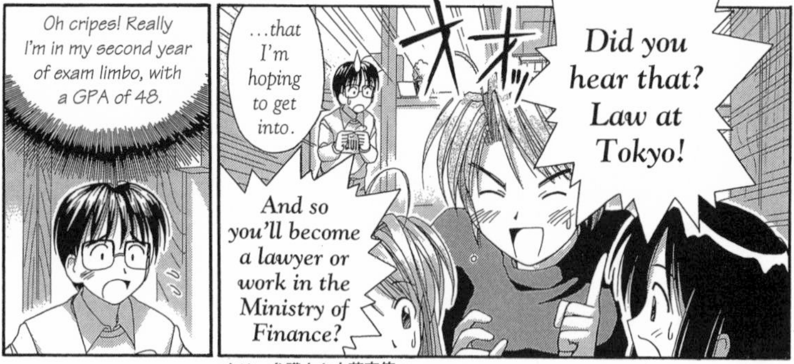
Did you hear that? Law at Tokyo!
Ooh!
And so you'll become a lawyer or work in the Ministry of Finance?
...that I'm hoping to get into.
Oh cripes! Really I'm in my second year of exam limbo, with a GPA of 48.

末は　弁護士か大蔵官僚って
やっちゃ !!

まさか　このさえない男が
東大の法科とはなぁ

しかもこの寮のオーナーの孫って
からには資産家のボンボンやで

clap そや

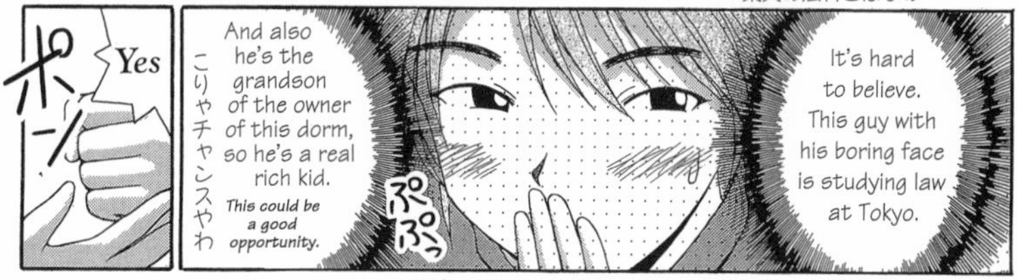
It's hard to believe. This guy with his boring face is studying law at Tokyo.
ぷぷっ
And also he's the grandson of the owner of this dorm, so he's a real rich kid.
こりゃチャンスやわ
This could be a good opportunity.
Yes

giggle

どやみんな !!　ここはひとつ
センセをおいてやろやないか !!

え····
ええ〜〜 !?

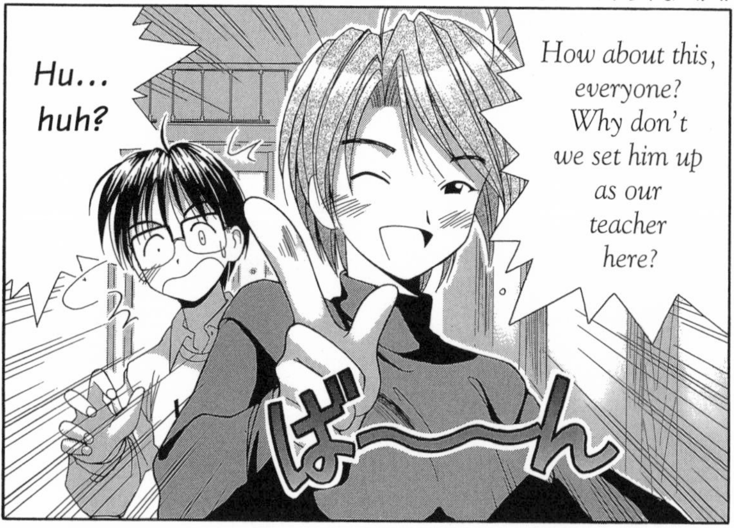
How about this, everyone? Why don't we set him up as our teacher here?
Hu... huh?
ば〜〜ん

もちろん　ここは
女子寮やから
条件ありや

滞在中もう一度
さっきみたいなスケベな事したら
即刻（そっこく）退寮ってのでどや？

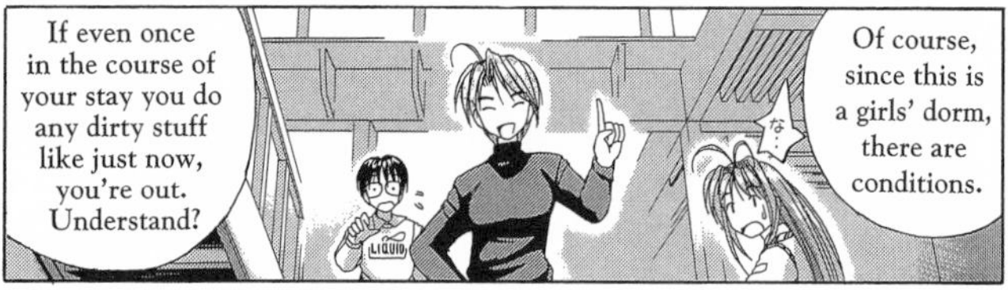
Of course, since this is a girls' dorm, there are conditions.
な…
If even once in the course of your stay you do any dirty stuff like just now, you're out. Understand?
LIQUID

うむ
異議なし
Wha...?
I'm for it.
え!?
ちょっと
キツネ！

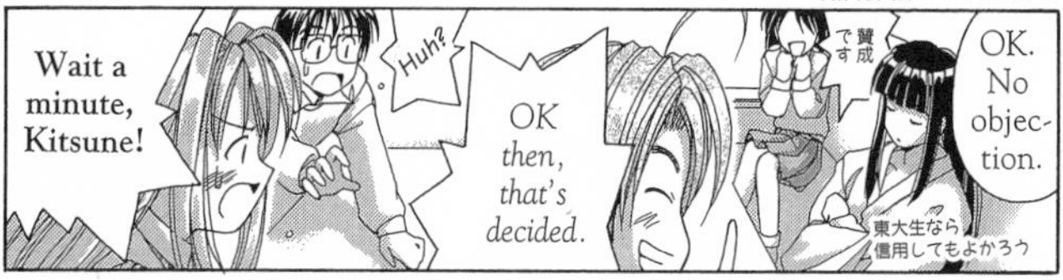
OK. No objec-tion.
賛成です
東大生なら
信用してもよかろう
OK then, that's decided.
Huh?
Wait a minute, Kitsune!

If he's a Tokyo University student
it's OK to trust him.
よっしゃ
じゃあ　決まりや

ここは女子寮なのよ！
そんなの
勝手に決めないでよ！

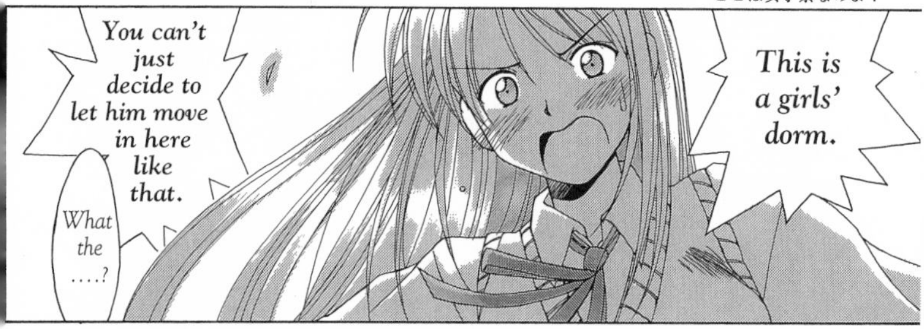
This is a girls' dorm.
You can't just decide to let him move in here like that.
What the .....?

あれ〜〜〜？

何や　成瀬川
婆ちゃんに会えず悲しんでる青年を
このまま　外へほっぽり出す気か？

「袖振り合うも他生（たしょう）の縁」
ここで追い出すのは
少し情（じょう）に欠けるのでは？
えぇ

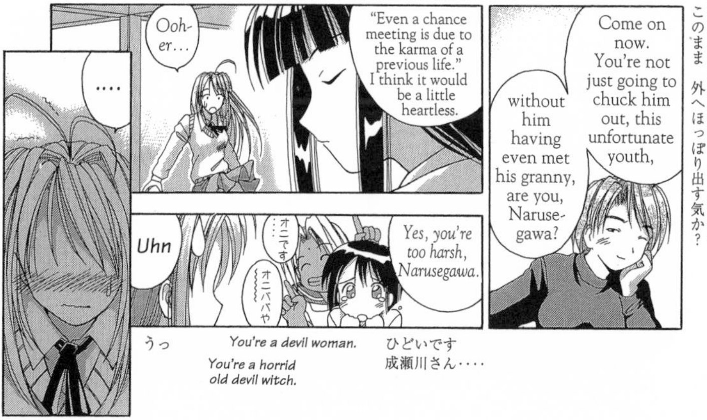
Come on now. You're not just going to chuck him out, this unfortunate youth,
without him having even met his granny, are you, Naruse-gawa?
"Even a chance meeting is due to the karma of a previous life." I think it would be a little heartless.
Ooh-er...
....
Yes, you're too harsh, Narusegawa.
オニです…
オニババや〜
Uhn

ひどいです
成瀬川さん‥‥
You're a devil woman.
You're a horrid
old devil witch.
うっ

分かったわよ

とりあえず
歓迎って事に
してあげるわ

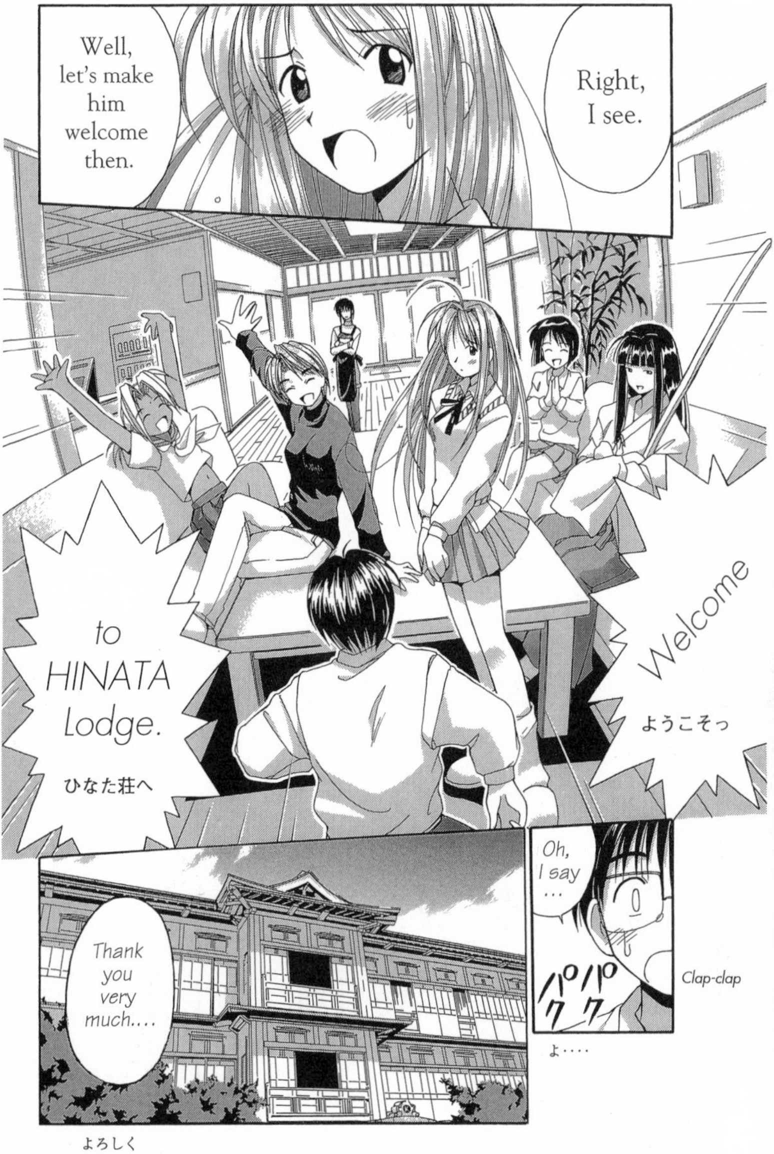
Right, I see.
Well, let's make him welcome then.
Welcome
ようこそっ
to HINATA Lodge.
ひなた荘へ
Oh, I say …
パクパク
Clap-clap
Thank you very much....

よ‥‥

よろしく
お願いします‥‥

Caretaker's Room

なーーんか
やっかいなことに
なっちゃったなぁ

はあ〜〜

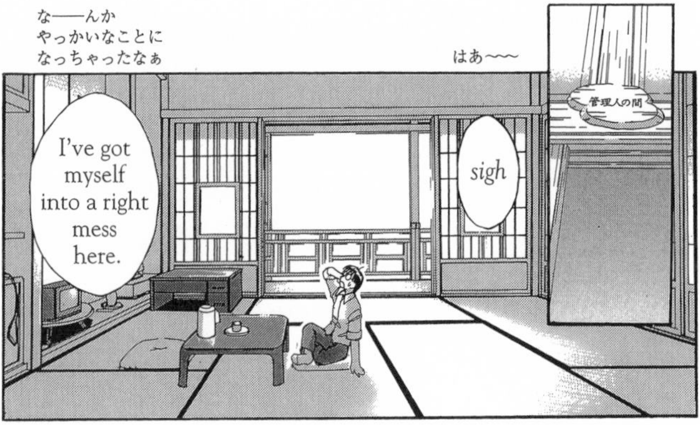

管理人の間
sigh
I've got myself into a right mess here.

どうしよう
みんな完璧（かんぺき）に
かんちがいしてるよ〜〜

俺は東大狙ってるだけで
東大生でも何（なん）でもないのに

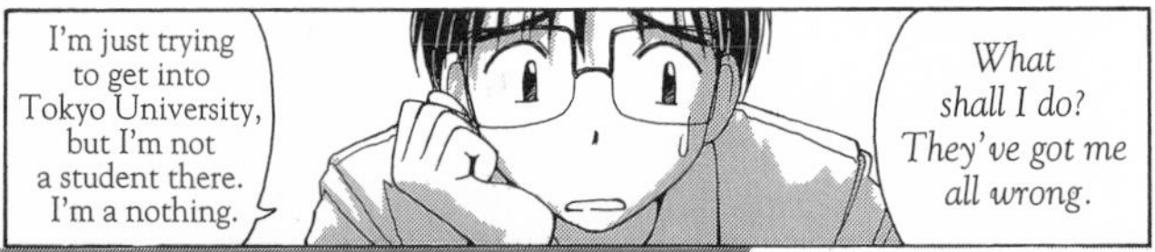

What shall I do? They've got me all wrong.
I'm just trying to get into Tokyo University, but I'm not a student there. I'm a nothing.

ふう

ん？

お——

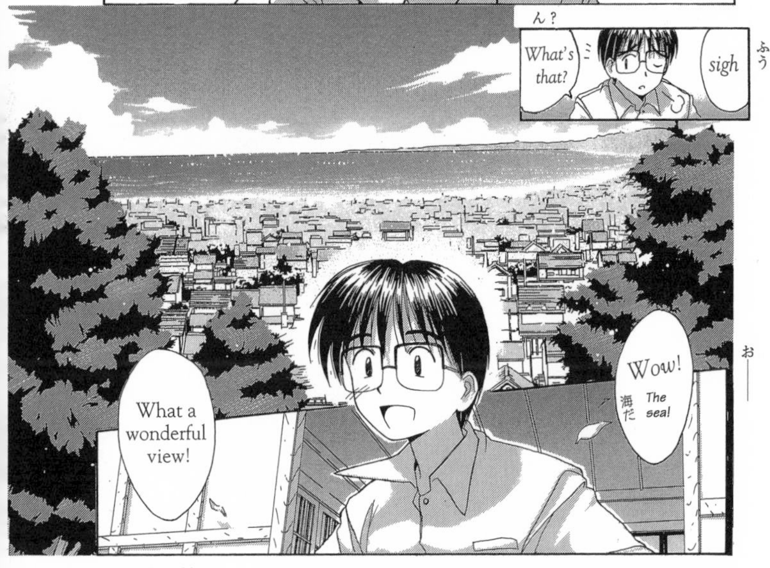

sigh
What's that?
Wow!
海だ The sea!
What a wonderful view!

いい眺めだなぁ

しっかし やっぱ
東大って名前は
効くんだなぁ〜〜〜

〜〜〜女の子と
こんなに話したの
何年ぶりだろ

If I reckon the time.... from when I spoke to HER, the girl of my memories,

it's 15 years. Yes, it's been a special day.

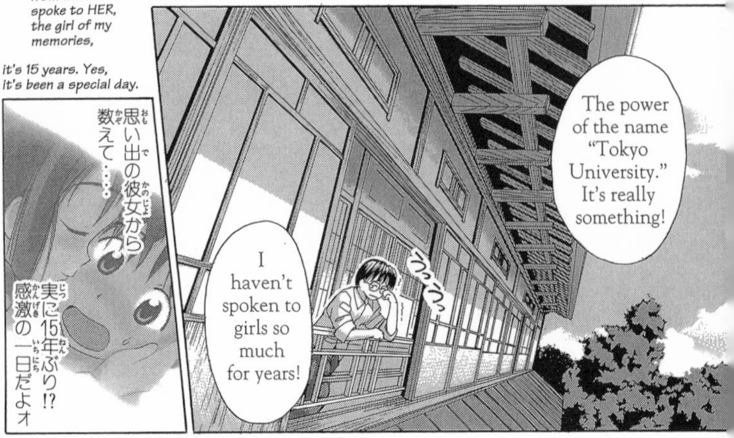

The power of the name "Tokyo University." It's really something!
I haven't spoken to girls so much for years!
思い出の彼女から数えて・・・・
実に15年ぶり!? 感激の一日だよォ

(weeping for joy)

—— 誰？
思い出の彼女って

うわあ —— っ

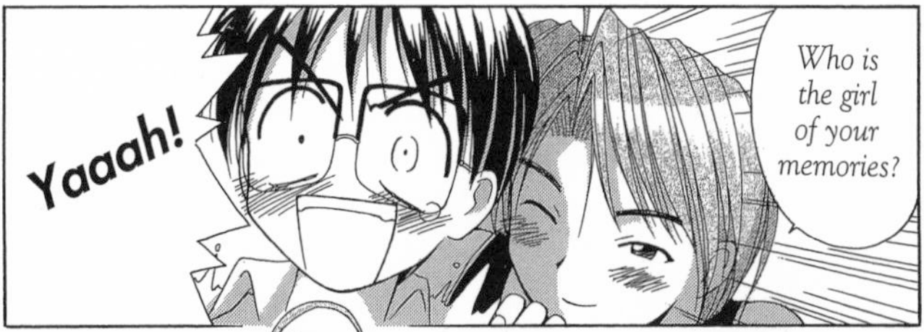

Who is the girl of your memories?
Yaaah!

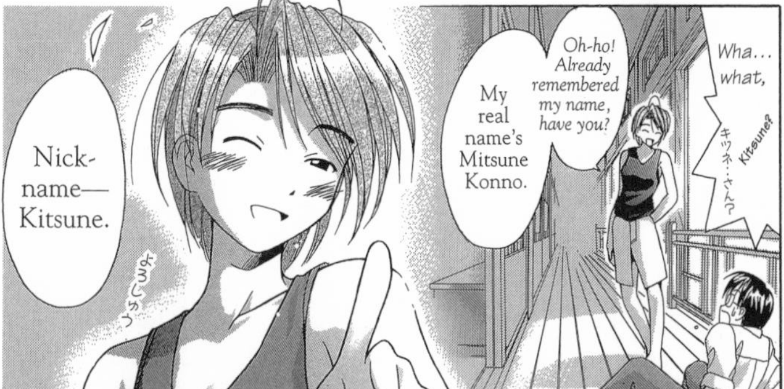

Wha… what,
キツネ…さん?
Kitsune?
Oh-ho! Already remembered my name, have you?
My real name's Mitsune Konno.
Nick-name—Kitsune.
よろしゅう

な・・・・なな

お もう名前
おぼえて
くれたんか
ウチの名前は紺野みつね！

通称
キツネや

Take it easy!

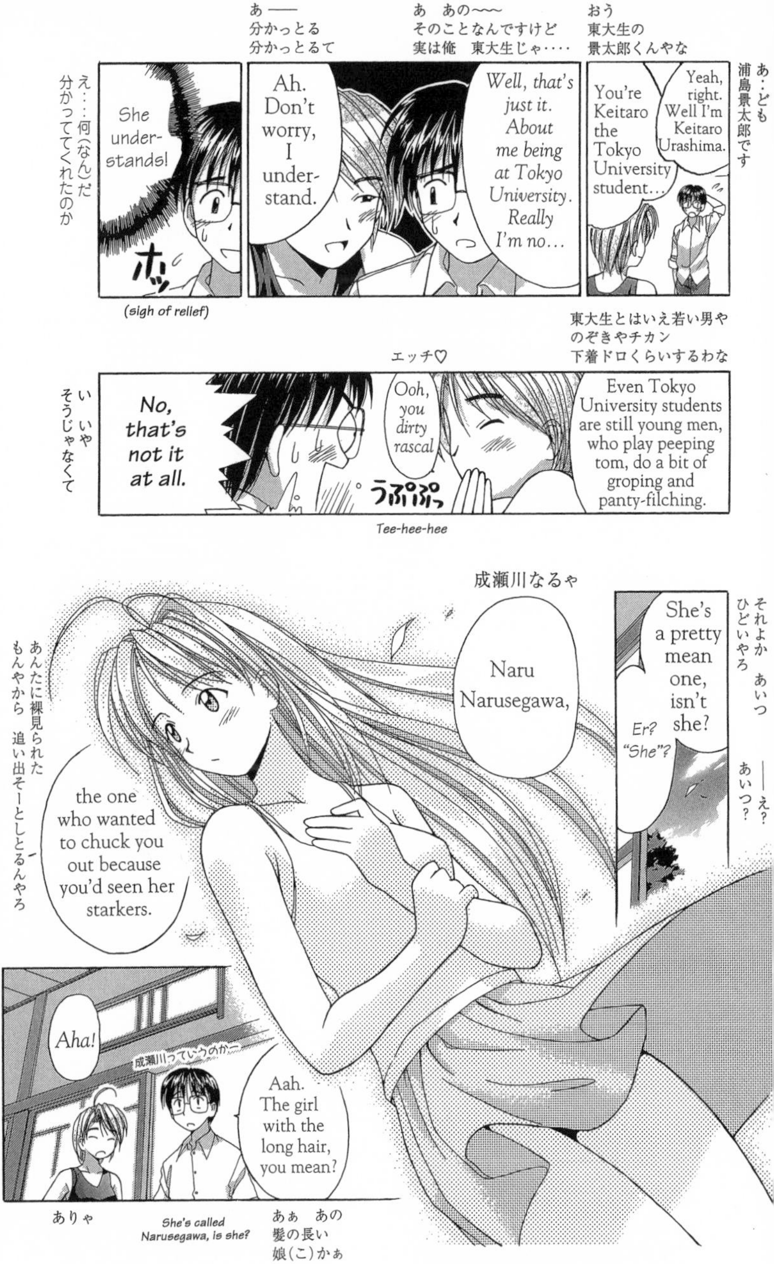
おう
東大生の
景太郎くんやな
You're Keitaro the Tokyo University student…
あ…ども
浦島景太郎です
Yeah, right. Well I'm Keitaro Urashima.
あ あの〜〜
そのことなんですけど
実は俺 東大生じゃ‥‥
Well, that's just it. About me being at Tokyo University. Really I'm no…
あ——
分かっとる
分かっとるて
Ah. Don't worry, I understand.
え…何(なん)だ
分かっててくれたのか
She understands!
ホッ
(sigh of relief)
東大生とはいえ若い男や
のぞきやチカン
下着ドロくらいするわな
Even Tokyo University students are still young men, who play peeping tom, do a bit of groping and panty-filching.
エッチ♡
Ooh, you dirty rascal
うぷぷっ
Tee-hee-hee
い いや
そうじゃなくて
No, that's not it at all.
それよか あいつ
ひどいやろ
She's a pretty mean one, isn't she?
——え?
あいつ?
Er? "She"?
成瀬川なるゃ
Naru Narusegawa,
あんたに裸見られた
もんやから 追い出そーとしとるんやろ
the one who wanted to chuck you out because you'd seen her starkers.
ありゃ
Aha!
成瀬川っていうのかー
She's called Narusegawa, is she?
あぁ あの
髪の長い
娘(こ)かぁ
Aah. The girl with the long hair, you mean?

景太郎クンは

髪の毛長い方が
好きなん？

え　いえ　別にそんな
ことないよ・・・・

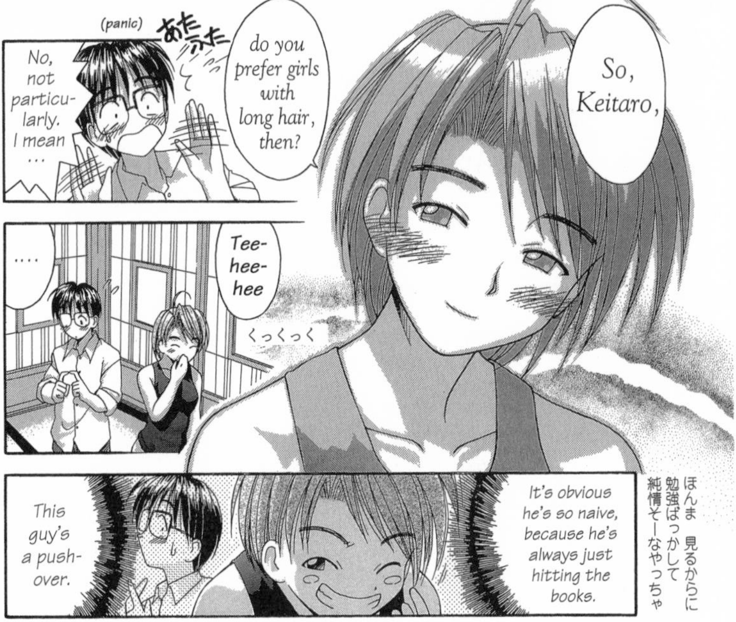

So, Keitaro,
do you prefer girls with long hair, then?
(panic)
No, not particu-larly. I mean …
Tee-hee-hee
….
It's obvious he's so naive, because he's always just hitting the books.
This guy's a push-over.

ほんま　見るからに
勉強ばっかして
純情そーなやっちゃ

こりゃ　イチコロ
楽勝やで

なぁ景太郎クン
彼女とか　おるん？

——え!?
い　いや
そんな俺　彼女なんて

そーか!!
よかったわァ

実は
ウチな・・・・

東大生の彼氏
もつの　ずっと
夢やったんや

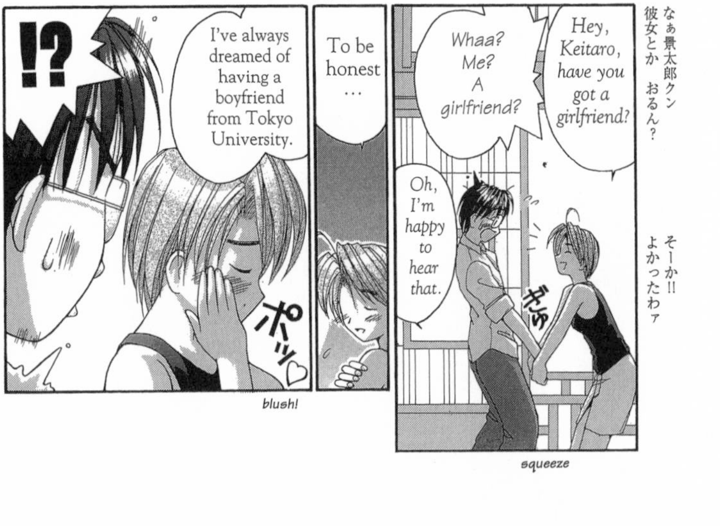

Hey, Keitaro, have you got a girlfriend?
Whaa? Me? A girlfriend?
Oh, I'm happy to hear that.
squeeze
To be honest …
I've always dreamed of having a boyfriend from Tokyo University.
!?
blush!

・・・・え
な・・・・っ!?

いや　もちろんな　相手の
気持ちも聞かずに　こんなん
言うのもアレなんやけどォ

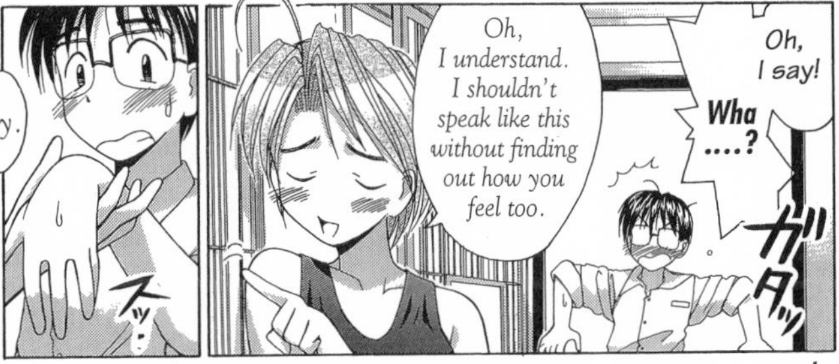
Oh,
I say!
Wha
....?
Oh,
I understand.
I shouldn't
speak like this
without finding
out how you
feel too.
Hey.

crash

(lifts his hand)

なぁ

ウチのこと・・・・
どう思う？

ぷくく
チョロ〜〜ッ

な　どっ
どどど‥

どどどど
どうって!?

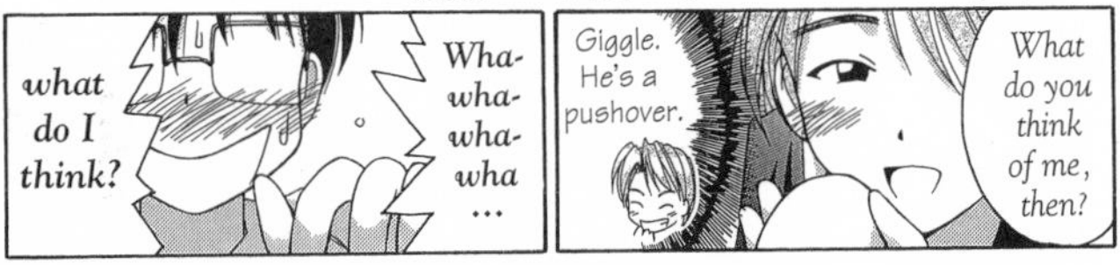
What
do you
think
of me,
then?
Giggle.
He's a
pushover.
Wha-
wha-
wha-
wha
...
what
do I
think?

ほら　ウチの
胸のたかなり

ぺぇ

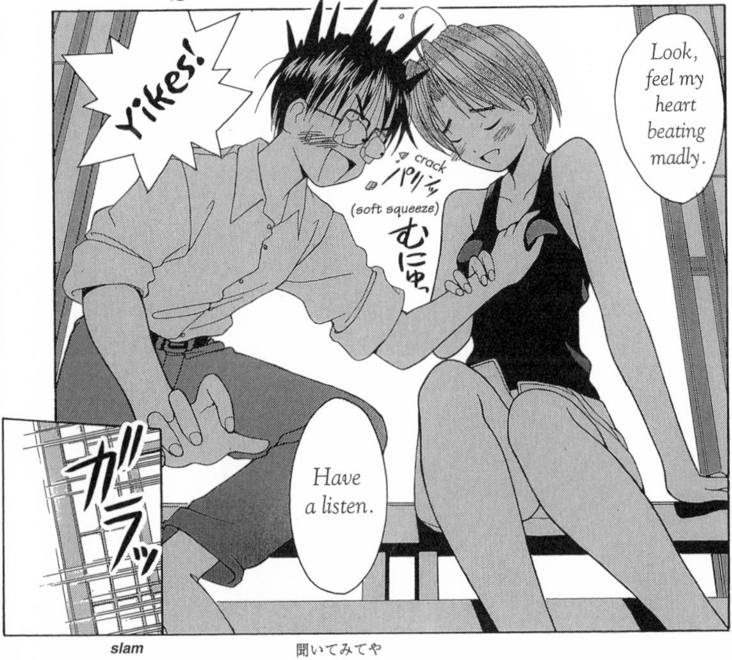
Look,
feel my
heart
beating
madly.
Yikes!
crack
(soft squeeze)
Have
a listen.

slam

聞いてみてや

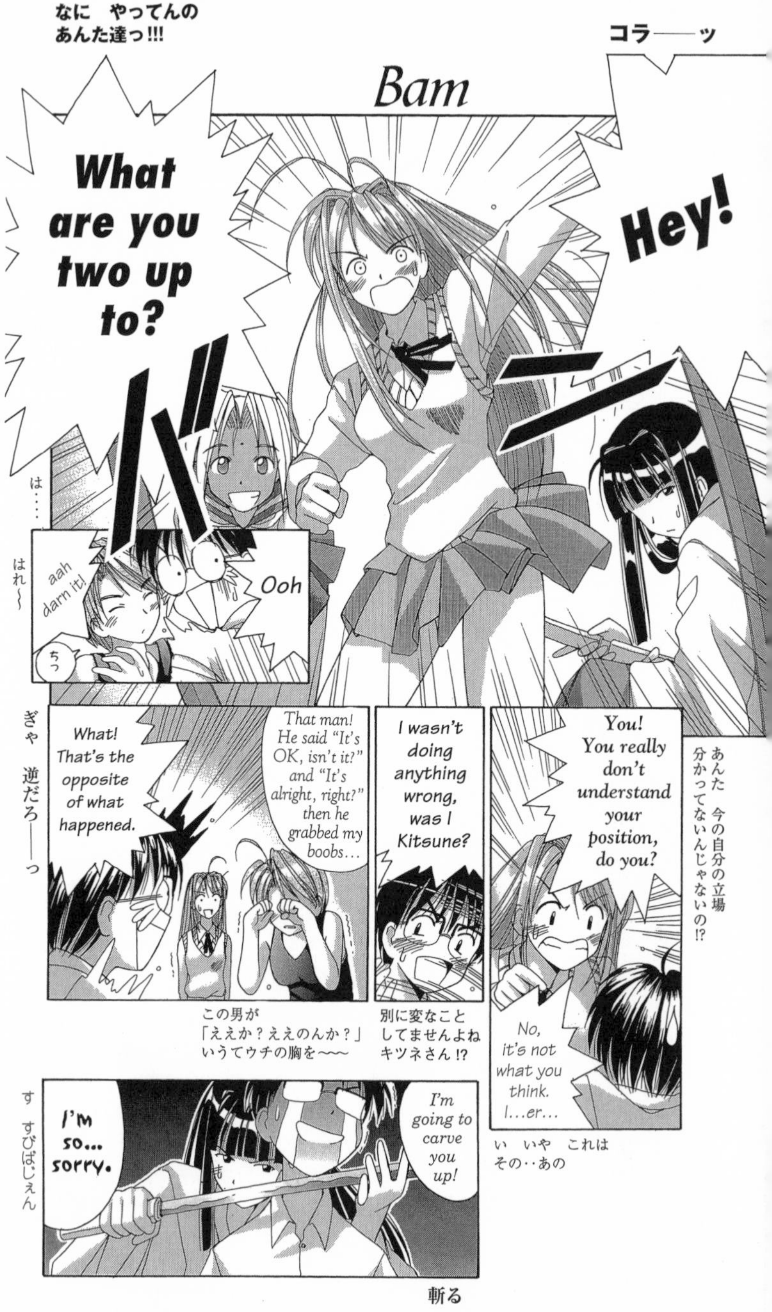

Hey!
コラ――ッ
Bam
What are you two up to?
なに　やってんの
あんた達っ!!!
Ooh
aah darn it!
はれ～
ちっ
は‥‥
You! You really don't understand your position, do you?
あんた　今の自分の立場
分かってないんじゃないの!?
I wasn't doing anything wrong, was I Kitsune?
別に変なこと
してませんよね
キツネさん!?
That man! He said "It's OK, isn't it?" and "It's alright, right?" then he grabbed my boobs…
この男が
「ええか？ええのんか？」
いうてウチの胸を～～
What! That's the opposite of what happened.
ぎゃ　逆だろ――っ
No, it's not what you think. I…er…
い　いや　これは
その‥あの
I'm going to carve you up!
斬る
I'm so… sorry.
す　すびばじぇん

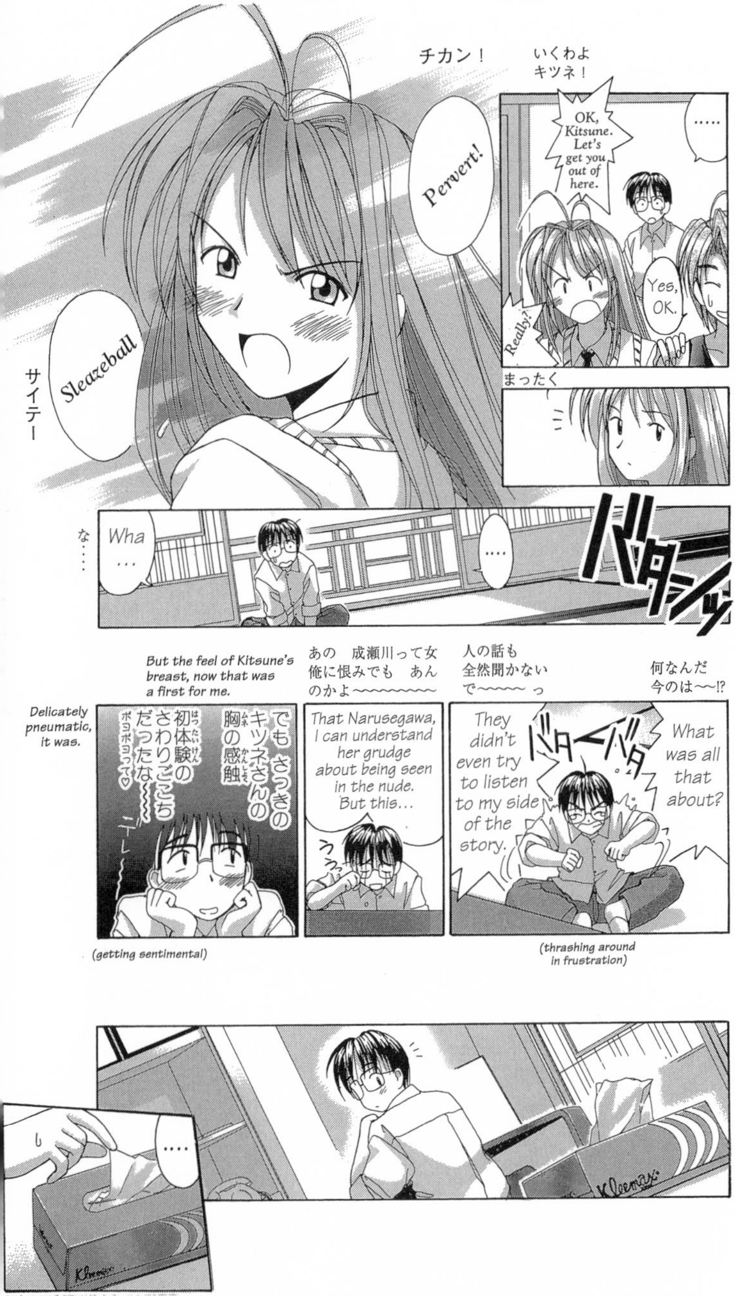
いくわよ
キツネ！
OK, Kitsune. Let's get you out of here.
.....
Yes, OK.
へいへい
Really?
まったく
チカン！
Pervert!
サイテー
Sleazeball
バタンッ
....
Wha ...
な……
何なんだ
今のは～～!?
What was all that about?
バタ＜バタ
人の話も
全然聞かない
で～～～～っ
They didn't even try to listen to my side of the story.
(thrashing around in frustration)
あの　成瀬川って女
俺に恨みでも　あん
のかよ～～～～～～～
That Narusegawa, I can understand her grudge about being seen in the nude. But this…
But the feel of Kitsune's breast, now that was a first for me.
でもさっきのキツネさんの胸の感触
初体験のさわりごこちだったな～～
ボヨボヨって♡
Delicately pneumatic, it was.
デレ～
(getting sentimental)
....
し

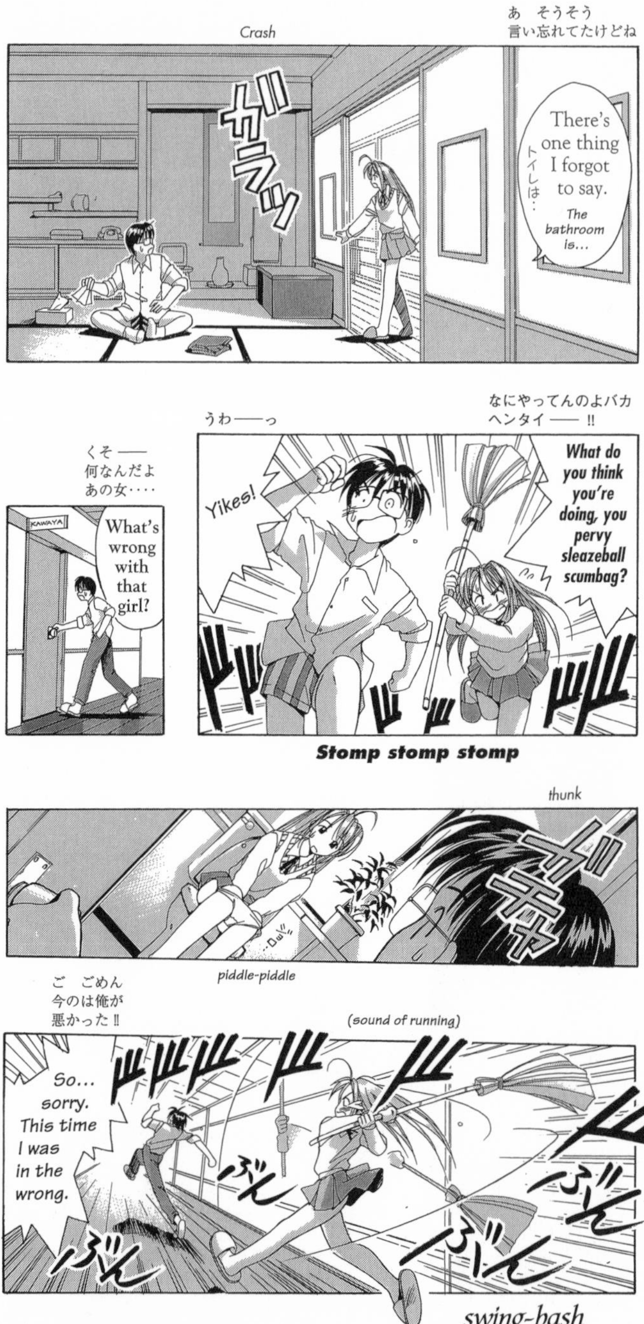
あ　そうそう
言い忘れてたけどね
There's one thing I forgot to say.
トイレは・・
The bathroom is...
Crash
なにやってんのよバカ
ヘンタイ―― !!
What do you think you're doing, you pervy sleazeball scumbag?
うわ――っ
Yikes!
Stomp stomp stomp
くそ――
何なんだよ
あの女・・・・
What's wrong with that girl?
KAWAYA
thunk
piddle-piddle
ご　ごめん
今のは俺が
悪かった !!
So... sorry. This time I was in the wrong.
(sound of running)
ぶん
swing-bash

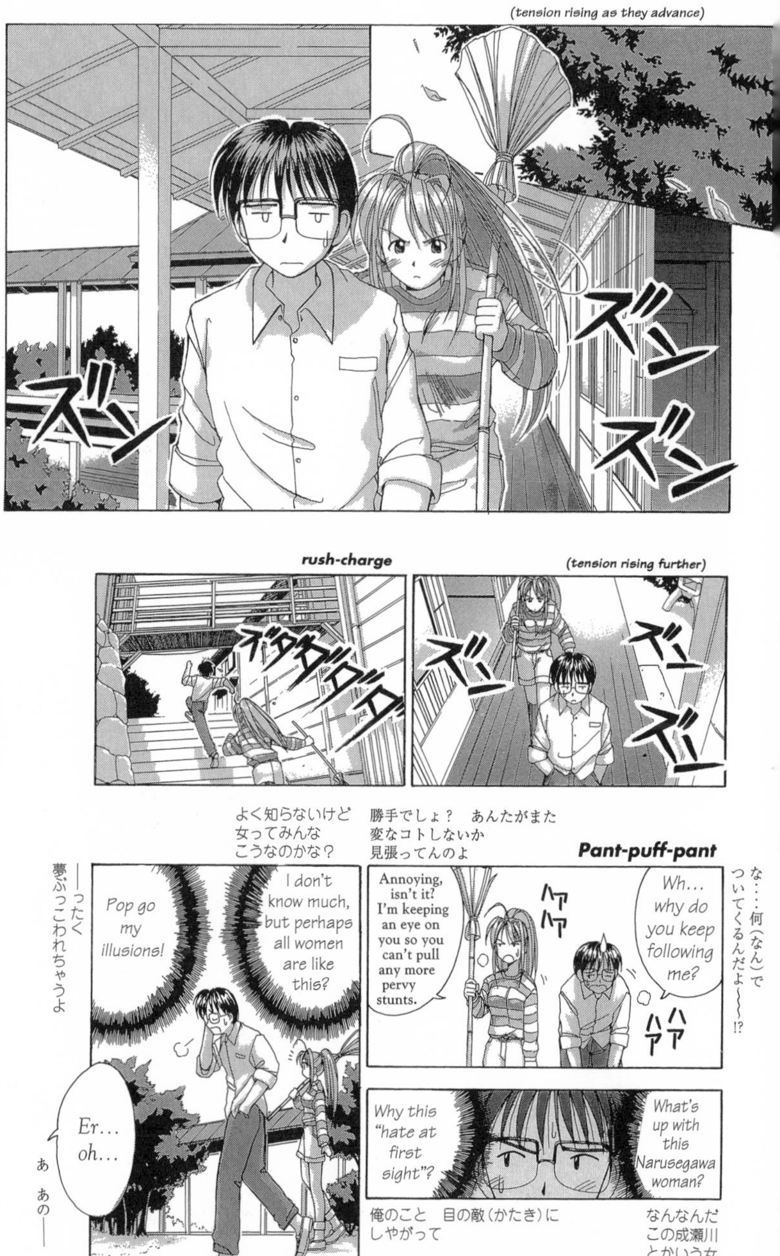
(tension rising as they advance)
ズーン
ズーン
ズーン
(tension rising further)
ズーン
ズーン
ズーン
rush-charge
ダダダダダダ
Pant-puff-pant
Wh… why do you keep following me?
な…何(なん)でついてくるんだよ~~~!?
ハァ
ハァ
ハァ
ハァ
Annoying, isn't it? I'm keeping an eye on you so you can't pull any more pervy stunts.
勝手でしょ? あんたがまた変なコトしないか見張ってんのよ
What's up with this Narusegawa woman?
なんなんだ この成瀬川とかいう女
Why this "hate at first sight"?
俺のこと 目の敵(かたき)にしやがって
I don't know much, but perhaps all women are like this?
よく知らないけど 女ってみんな こうなのかな?
Pop go my illusions!
—ったく 夢ぶっこわれちゃうよ
Er… oh…
あ あの——

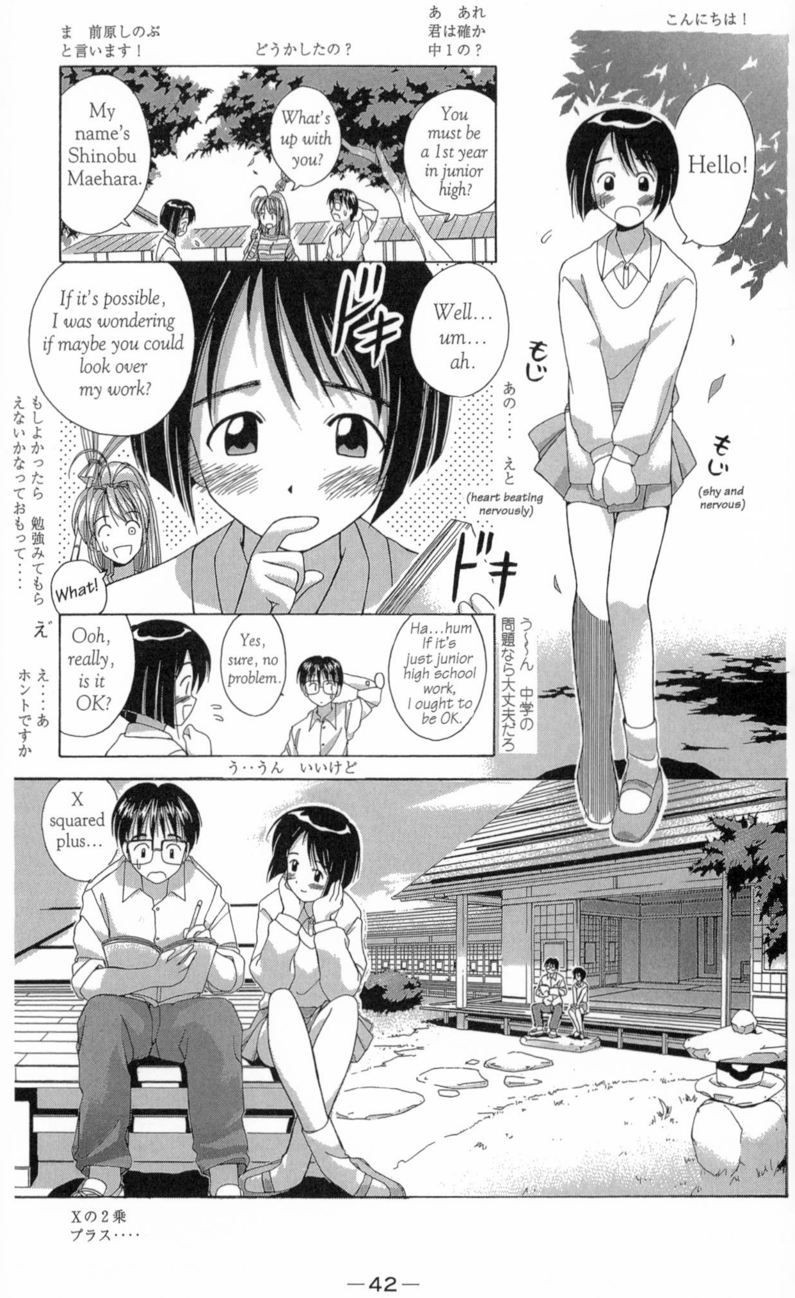
Hello!
もじ
もじ
(shy and nervous)
You must be a 1st year in junior high?
What's up with you?
My name's Shinobu Maehara.
Well… um… ah.
ドキ
ドキ
(heart beating nervously)
If it's possible, I was wondering if maybe you could look over my work?
What!
Ha…hum If it's just junior high school work, I ought to be OK.
Yes, sure, no problem.
Ooh, really, is it OK?
X squared plus…

こんにちは！

あ　あれ
君は確か
中１の？

どうかしたの？

ま　前原しのぶ
と言います！

あの‥‥　えと

もしよかったら　勉強みてもら
えないかなっておもって‥‥

え

う〜ん　中学の
問題なら大丈夫だろ

う‥うん　いいけど

え‥‥あ
ホントですか

Xの２乗
プラス‥‥

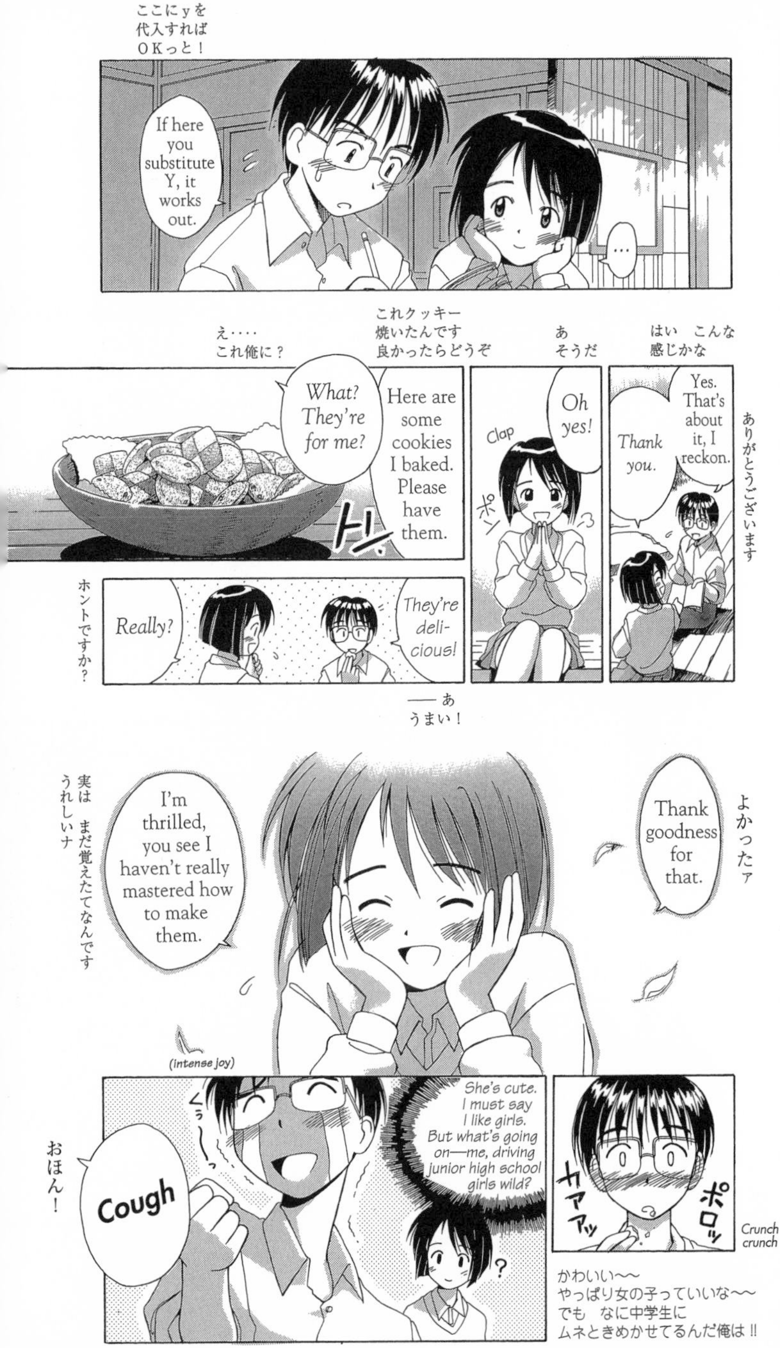
ここにyを
代入すれば
ＯＫっと！
If here you substitute Y, it works out.
…
これクッキー
焼いたんです
良かったらどうぞ
Here are some cookies I baked. Please have them.
え・・・・
これ俺に？
What? They're for me?
あ
そうだ
Oh yes!
Clap
ポン
はい　こんな
感じかな
Yes. That's about it, I reckon.
ありがとうございます
Thank you.
ホントですか？
Really?
They're deli-cious!
──あ
うまい！
実は　まだ覚えたてなんです
うれしいナ
I'm thrilled, you see I haven't really mastered how to make them.
よかったァ
Thank goodness for that.
(intense joy)
くぅ～～っ
She's cute. I must say I like girls. But what's going on—me, driving junior high school girls wild?
おほん！
Cough
?
カァアァッ
ポロッ
Crunch crunch
かわいい～～
やっぱり女の子っていいな～～
でも　なに中学生に
ムネときめかせてるんだ俺は !!

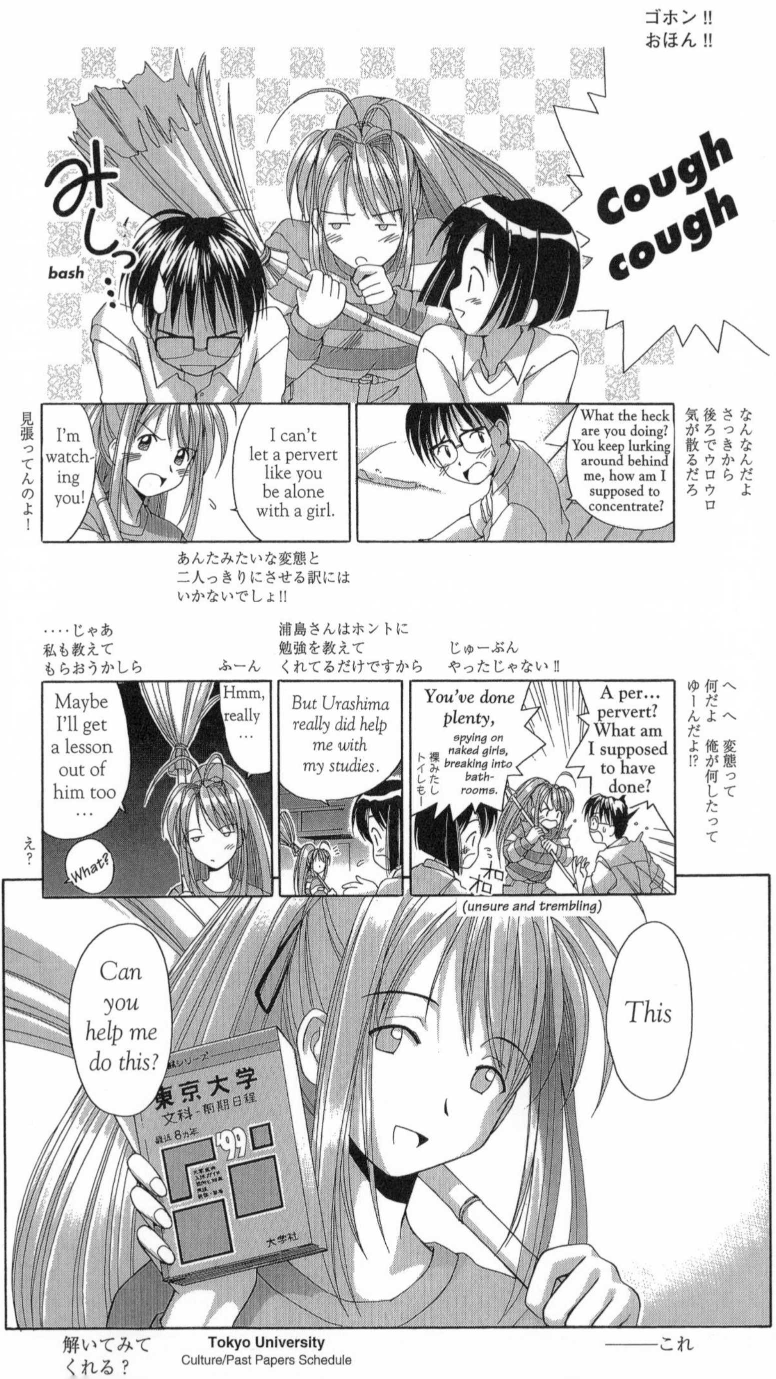
ゴホン!!
おほん!!
Cough cough
みしっ
bash
なんなんだよ さっきから後ろでウロウロ気が散るだろ
What the heck are you doing? You keep lurking around behind me, how am I supposed to concentrate?
あんたみたいな変態と二人っきりにさせる訳にはいかないでしょ!!
I can't let a pervert like you be alone with a girl.
見張ってんのよ!
I'm watching you!
へへ 変態って何だよ 俺が何したってゆーんだよ!?
A per... pervert? What am I supposed to have done?
じゅーぶん やったじゃない!!
You've done plenty,
裸みたし トイレも一
spying on naked girls, breaking into bathrooms.
(unsure and trembling)
浦島さんはホントに勉強を教えてくれてるだけですから
But Urashima really did help me with my studies.
ふーん
Hmm, really ...
・・・じゃあ 私も教えてもらおうかしら
Maybe I'll get a lesson out of him too ...
え?
What?
——これ
This
解いてみてくれる?
Can you help me do this?
東京大学
Tokyo University
Culture/Past Papers Schedule

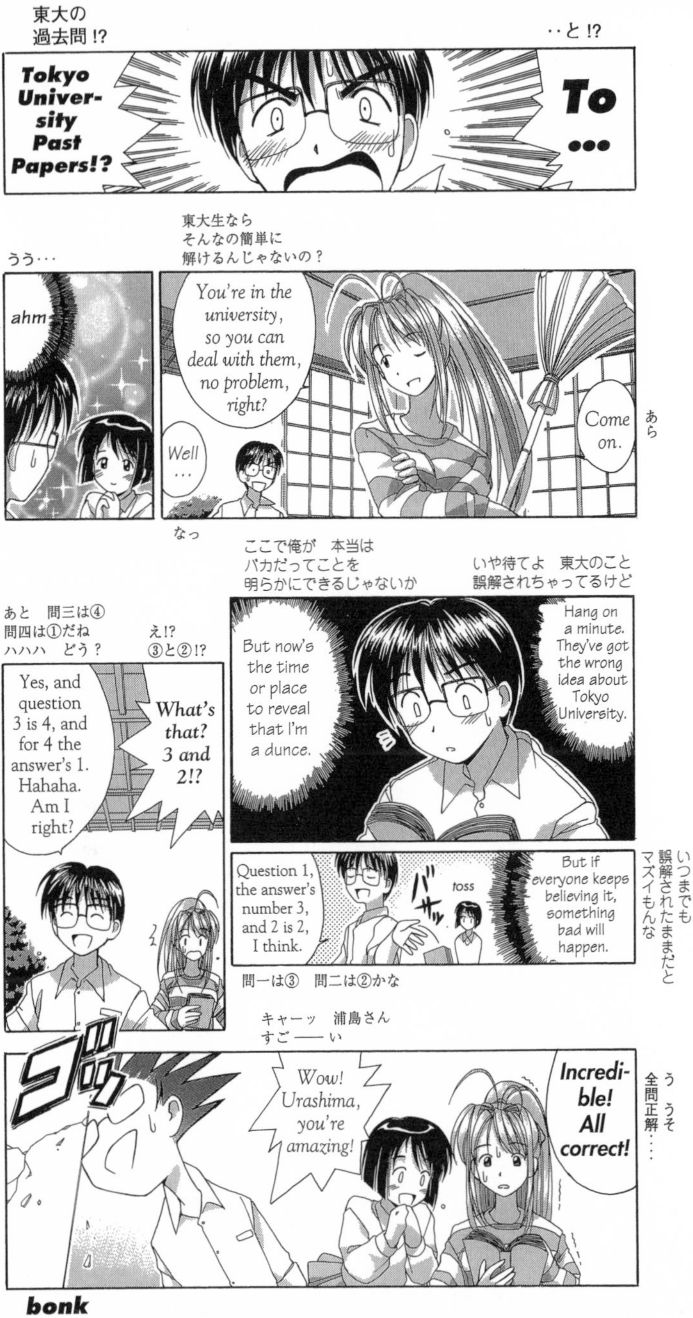

・・と!?
東大の
過去問!?
To ...
Tokyo University Past Papers!?
東大生なら
そんなの簡単に
解けるんじゃないの？
あら
Come on.
You're in the university, so you can deal with them, no problem, right?
Well ...
なっ
うう・・・
ahm
いや待てよ　東大のこと
誤解されちゃってるけど
Hang on a minute. They've got the wrong idea about Tokyo University.
ここで俺が　本当は
バカだってことを
明らかにできるじゃないか
But now's the time or place to reveal that I'm a dunce.
いつまでも
誤解されたままだと
マズイもんな
But if everyone keeps believing it, something bad will happen.
toss
問一は③　問二は②かな
Question 1, the answer's number 3, and 2 is 2, I think.
え!?
③と②!?
What's that? 3 and 2!?
あと　問三は④
問四は①だね
ハハハ　どう？
Yes, and question 3 is 4, and for 4 the answer's 1. Hahaha. Am I right?
う　うそ
全問正解・・・
Incredible! All correct!
キャーッ　浦島さん
すご――い
Wow! Urashima, you're amazing!
bonk

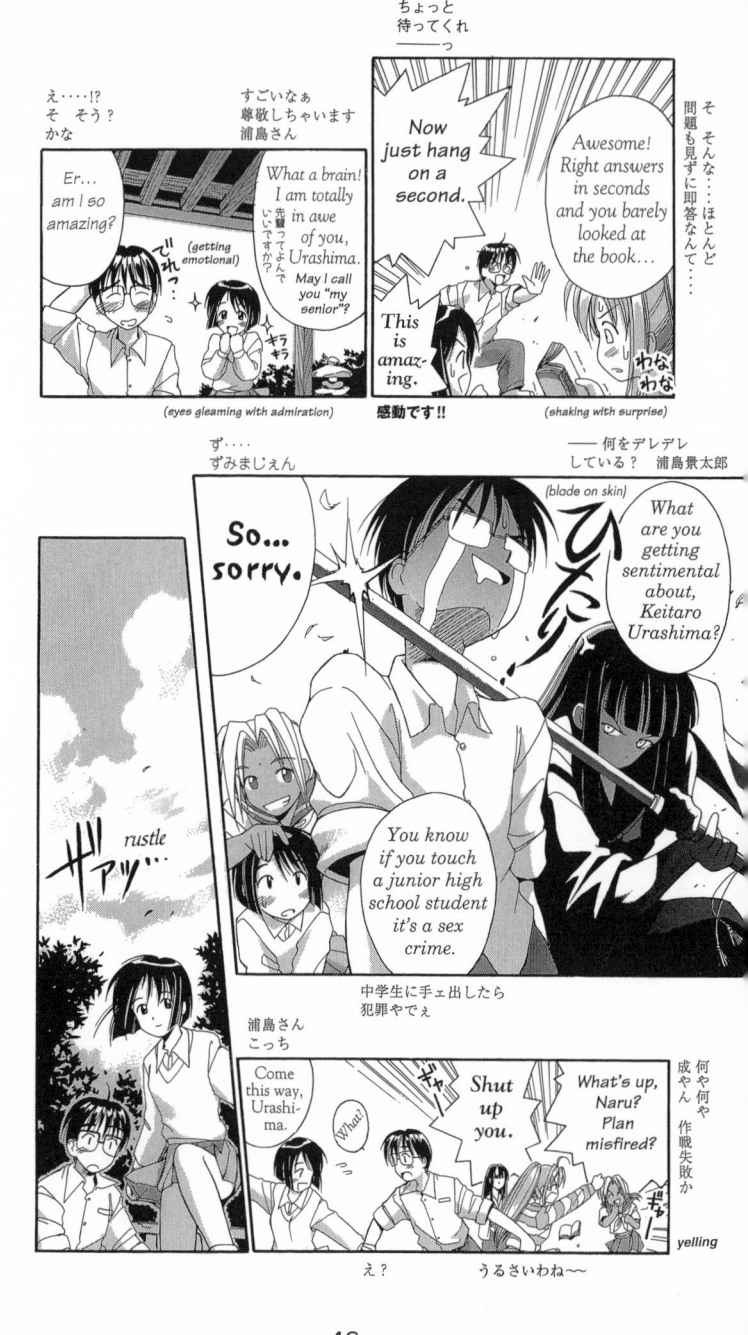

そ　そんな‥‥ほとんど
問題も見ずに即答なんて‥‥

ちょっと
待ってくれ
――っ

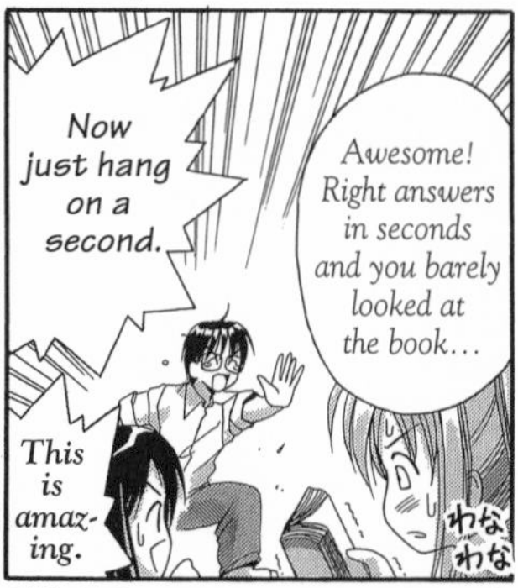
Awesome! Right answers in seconds and you barely looked at the book…
Now just hang on a second.
This is amazing.
わなわな

感動です!!

(shaking with surprise)

すごいなぁ
尊敬しちゃいます
浦島さん

え‥‥!?
そ　そう？
かな

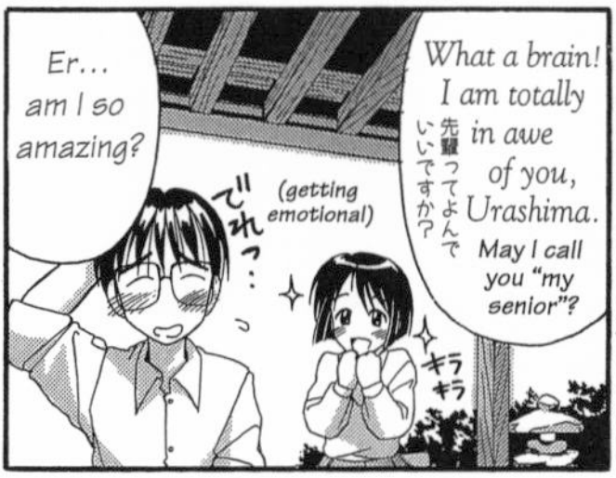
What a brain! I am totally in awe of you, Urashima.
先輩ってよんでいいですか？
May I call you "my senior"?
キラキラ
(getting emotional)
でれっ‥
Er… am I so amazing?

(eyes gleaming with admiration)

―― 何をデレデレ
している？　浦島景太郎

ず‥‥
ずみまじぇん

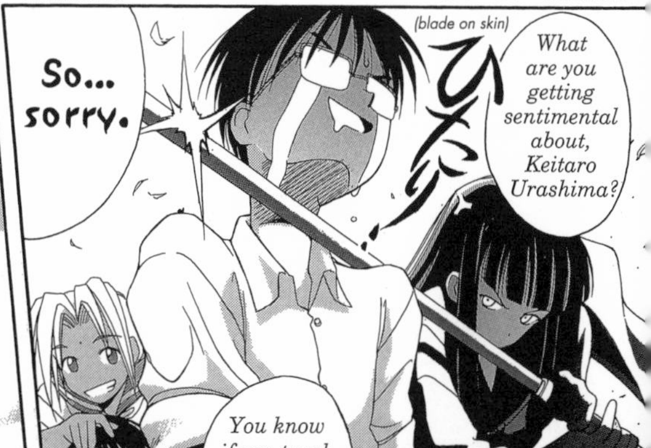
What are you getting sentimental about, Keitaro Urashima?
(blade on skin)
ひたり
So... sorry.
You know if you touch a junior high school student it's a sex crime.

中学生に手ェ出したら
犯罪やでぇ

何や何や
成やん　作戦失敗か

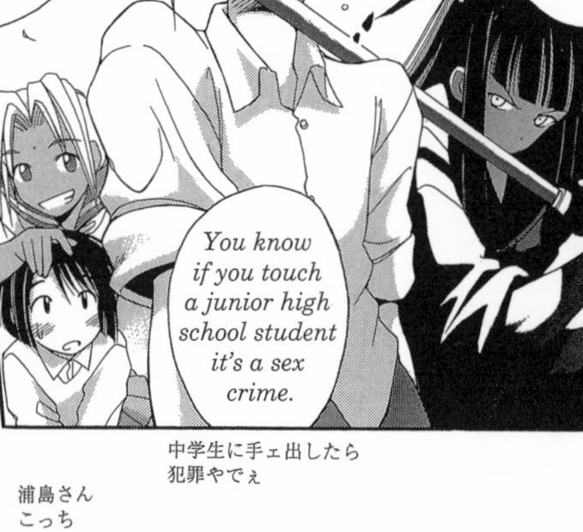
What's up, Naru? Plan misfired?
ギャー
Shut up you.
ギャー
What?
Come this way, Urashima.

yelling

うるさいわね～

え？

浦島さん
こっち

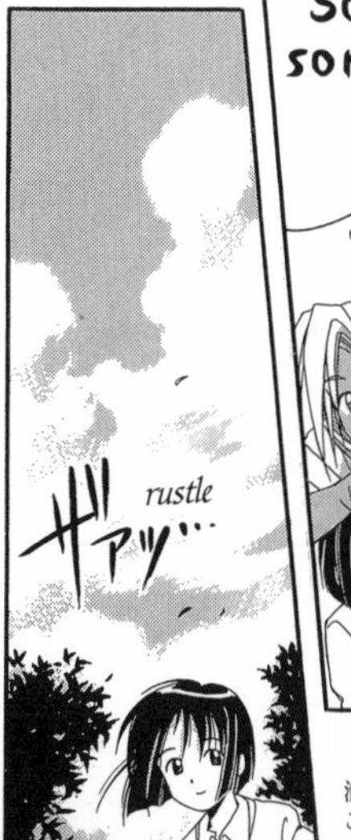
ザアッ‥
rustle

うわぁ

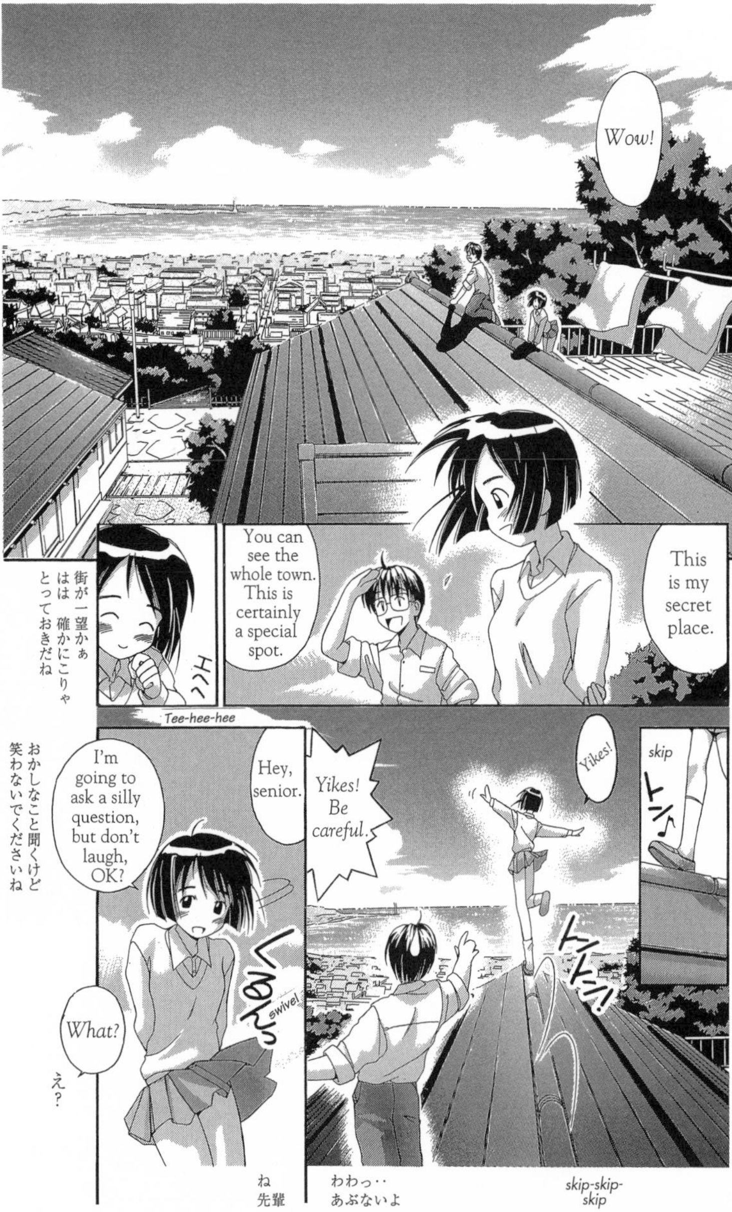

Wow!
This is my secret place.
You can see the whole town. This is certainly a special spot.
Tee-hee-hee
skip
Yikes!
Yikes! Be careful.
skip-skip-skip
Hey, senior.
I'm going to ask a silly question, but don't laugh, OK?
swivel
What?

場所なんです

街が一望かぁ
はは　確かにこりゃ
とっておきだね

……っと

わわっ‥
あぶないよ

ね
先輩

おかしなこと聞くけど
笑わないでくださいね

え？

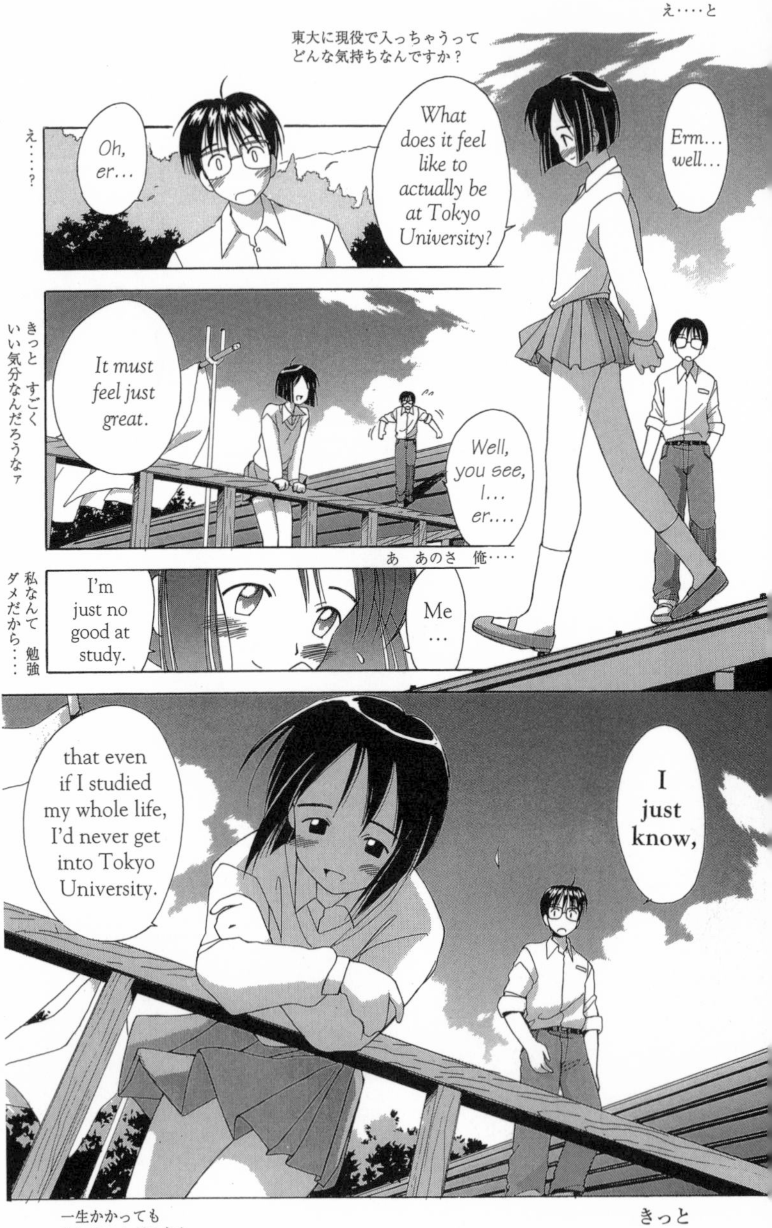
え・・・・と
Erm… well…
東大に現役で入っちゃうって
どんな気持ちなんですか？
What does it feel like to actually be at Tokyo University?
え・・・・？
Oh, er…
Well, you see, I… er….
あ　あのさ　俺・・・・
きっと　すごく
いい気分なんだろうなァ
It must feel just great.
Me …
私なんて　勉強
ダメだから・・・・
I'm just no good at study.
きっと
I just know,
一生かかっても
入れないんだろうな
東大なんて・・・・
that even if I studied my whole life, I'd never get into Tokyo University.

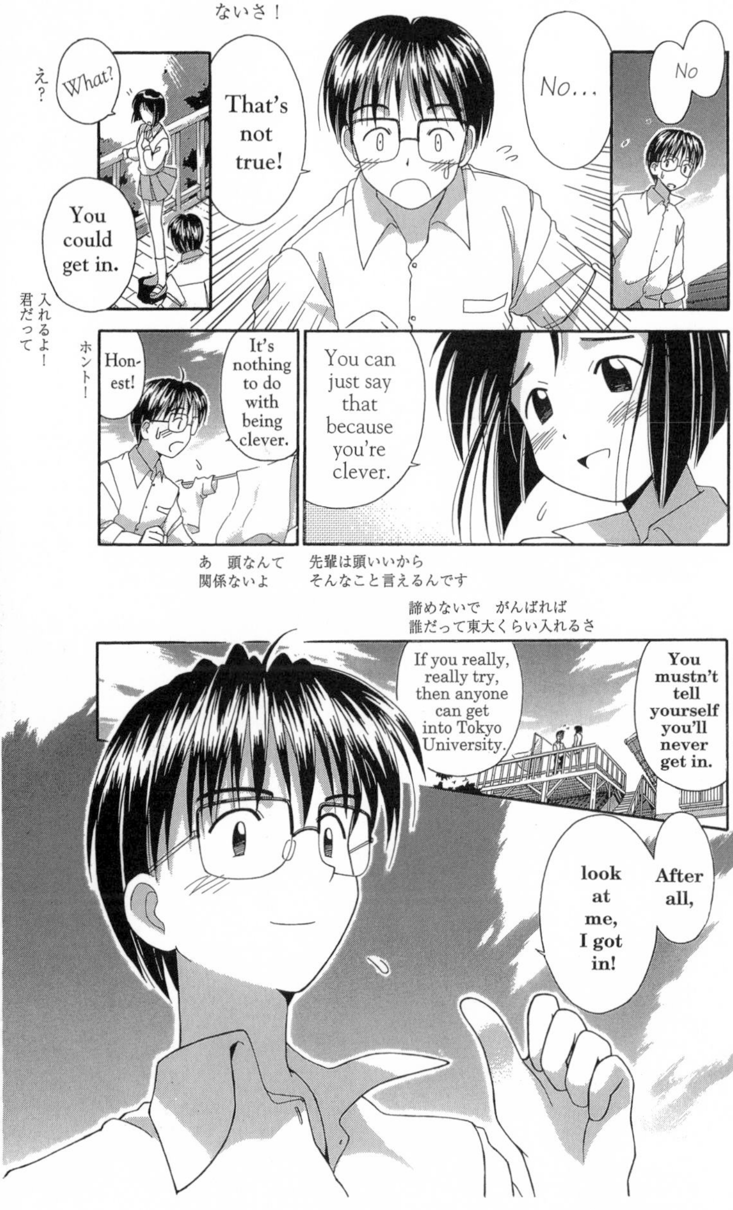
No
No...
That's not true!
What?
You could get in.
You can just say that because you're clever.
Hon-est!
It's nothing to do with being clever.
You mustn't tell yourself you'll never get in.
If you really, really try, then anyone can get into Tokyo University.
After all, look at me, I got in!

そ····
そんな····
そんなこと ないさ！
え？
君だって 入れるよ！
先輩は頭いいから そんなこと言えるんです
ホント！
あ 頭なんて 関係ないよ
はじめからダメだなんて 決めつけちゃいけないよ
諦めないで がんばれば 誰だって東大くらい入れるさ
何せ 俺にだって 入れたんだもの

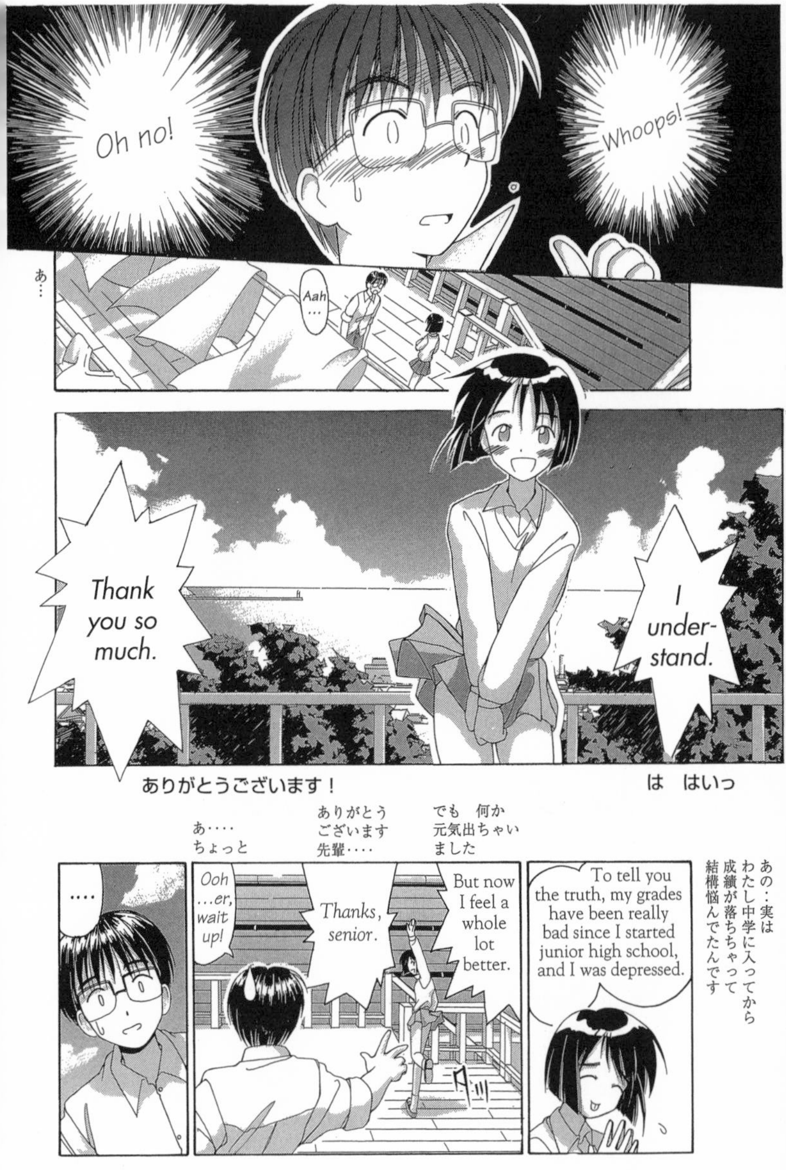

あ!?
Whoops!
ヤバ!?
Oh no!
あ…
Aah …
は　はいっ
I under-stand.
ありがとうございます！
Thank you so much.
あの…実は　わたし中学に入ってから　成績が落ちちゃって　結構悩んでたんです
To tell you the truth, my grades have been really bad since I started junior high school, and I was depressed.
でも　何か　元気出ちゃいました
But now I feel a whole lot better.
ありがとう　ございます　先輩‥‥
Thanks, senior.
あ‥‥　ちょっと
Ooh …er, wait up!
‥‥

やっちまった——っ

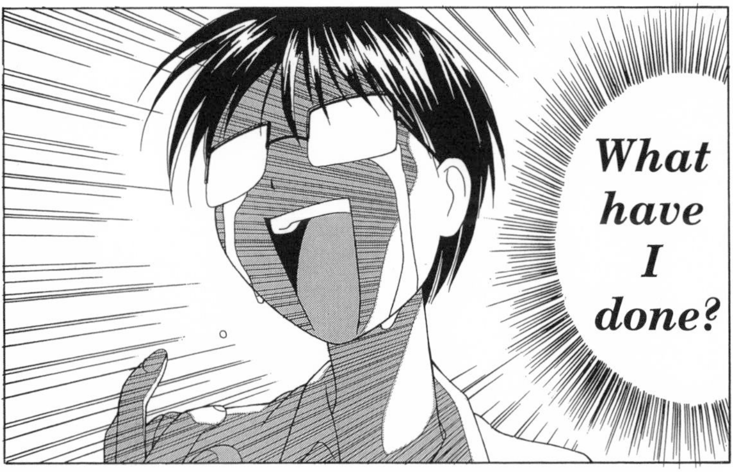
What have I done?

はあ——
どうしよう

流れとはいえ　自分から積極的に
誤解を大ウソに
レベルアップさせちゃった

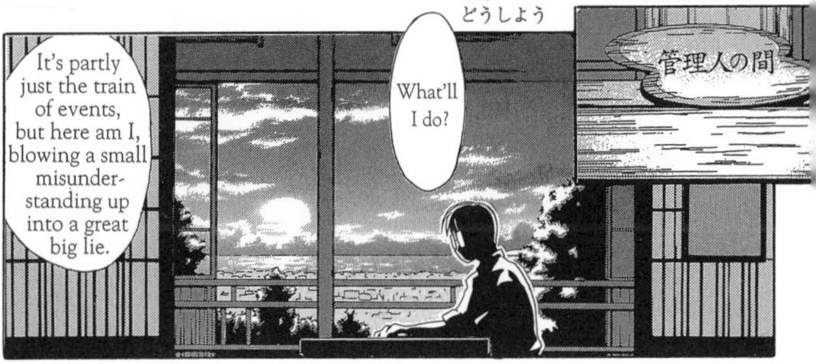
Caretaker's Room
管理人の間
What'll I do?
It's partly just the train of events, but here am I, blowing a small misunder-standing up into a great big lie.

ありがとう
ございます

まいったな····
まさかこんなことに
なるなんて

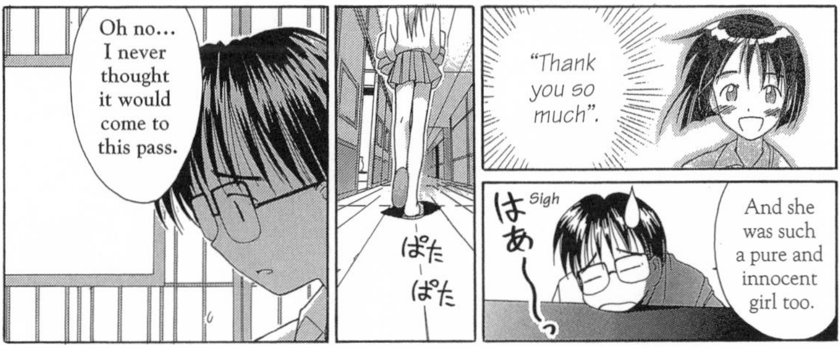
"Thank you so much".
Oh no… I never thought it would come to this pass.
ぱた
ぱた
(sound of footsteps)
はあ〜〜っ
Sigh
And she was such a pure and innocent girl too.

——しかも
あんな純真
そうな子に

東大生でも
何でもないのに

(steps stop)

本当は　俺‥‥

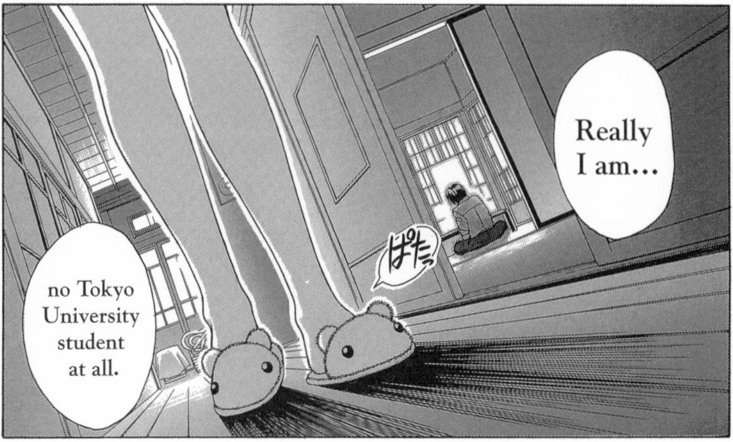
Really I am...
ぱたっ
no Tokyo University student at all.

今日みたいなラッキーは
もう二度とないだろうからな

——とにかく　こうなった以上
絶対バレないようにしなきゃ

東大生として　ある程度の問題は

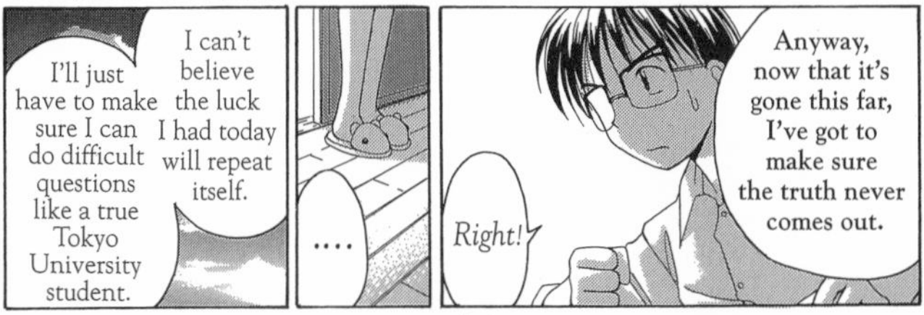
Anyway, now that it's gone this far, I've got to make sure the truth never comes out.
Right!
....
I can't believe the luck I had today will repeat itself.
I'll just have to make sure I can do difficult questions like a true Tokyo University student.

うん！

よぉ———し
まずは彼女達が置いていった
東大の赤本からいってみよう

え〜と‥‥

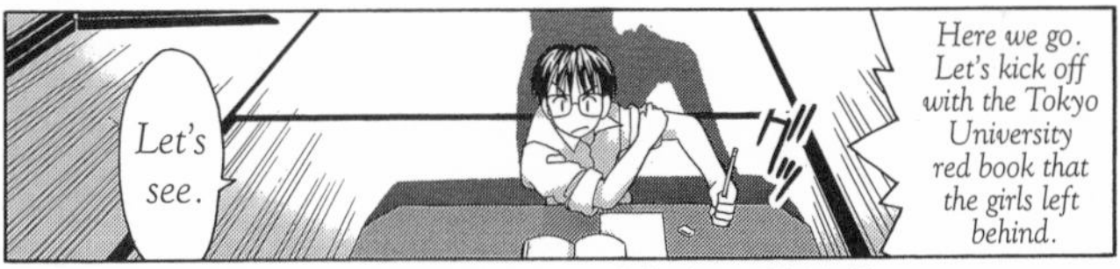
Here we go. Let's kick off with the Tokyo University red book that the girls left behind.
グッ
Let's see.

OK! (grabs pencil decisively)

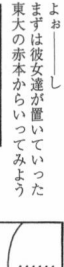

うーん

え〜〜と
次から

つ　次は‥‥

次‥‥

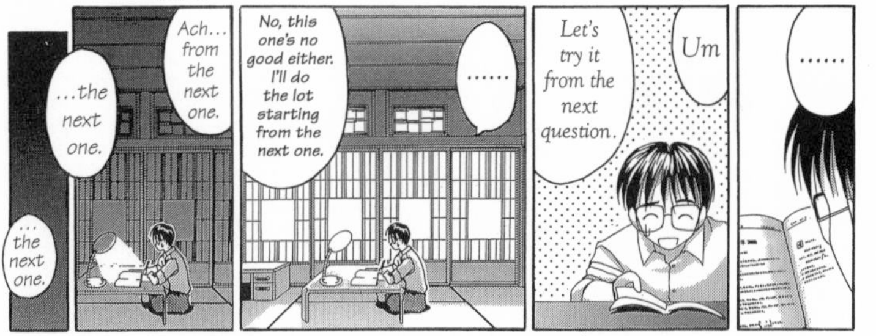
......
Um
Let's try it from the next question.
......
No, this one's no good either. I'll do the lot starting from the next one.
Ach... from the next one.
...the next one.
...the next one.

ま　コレも　いいか
次から全部　解いていこう

つ　次の
問題からいって
みようかな

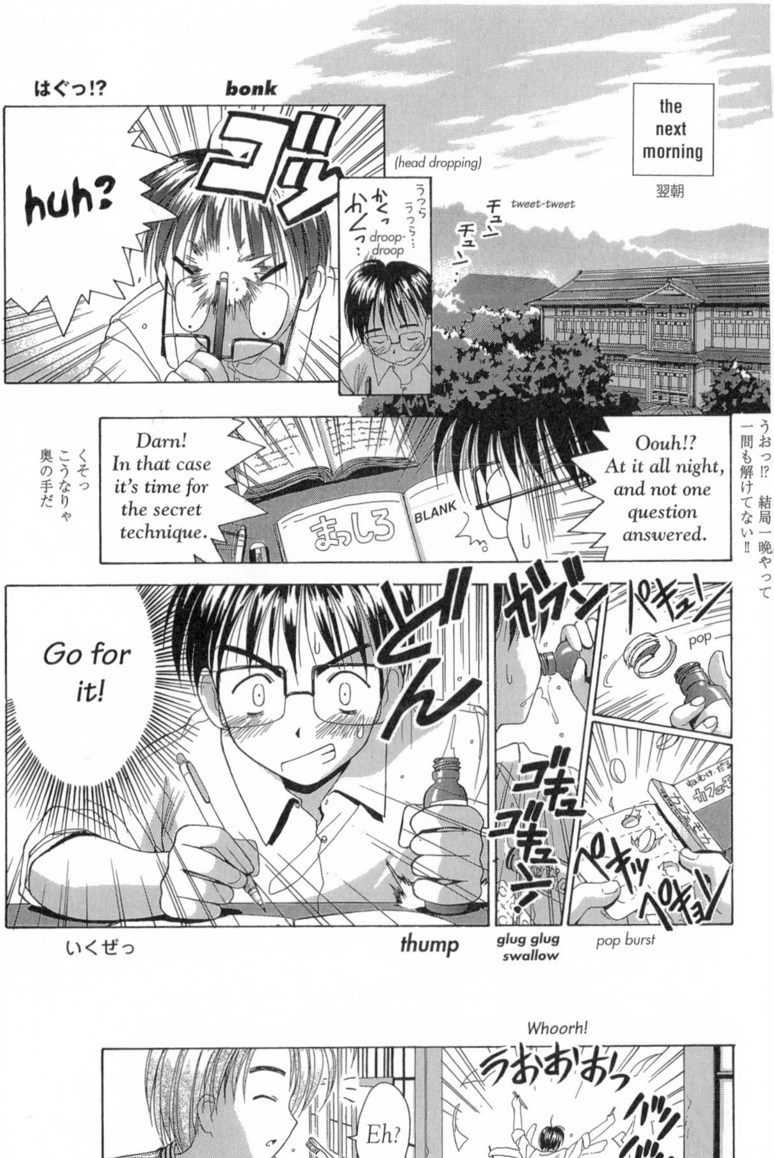
the next morning
翌朝
チュン チュン…
tweet-tweet
うつら うつら…
かくっ かくっ…
droop-droop
(head dropping)
ゴン
bonk
はぐっ!?
huh?
Oouh!? At it all night, and not one question answered.
うおっ!? 結局一晩やって一問も解けてない!!
まっしろ
BLANK
Darn! In that case it's time for the secret technique.
くそっ こうなりゃ奥の手だ
パキュ
pop
ペキッ ペキョ
pop burst
ゴキュ ゴキュ…
glug glug swallow
ガブン
どん
thump
Go for it!
いくぜっ
うおおおっ
Whoorh!
ババッ
Swish swish
Eh?
およ?

さすがやな
こないな朝早(はよ)
から猛勉強してるで

ほ――

あ
オーッス

おはよう
ございます

tweet-tweet

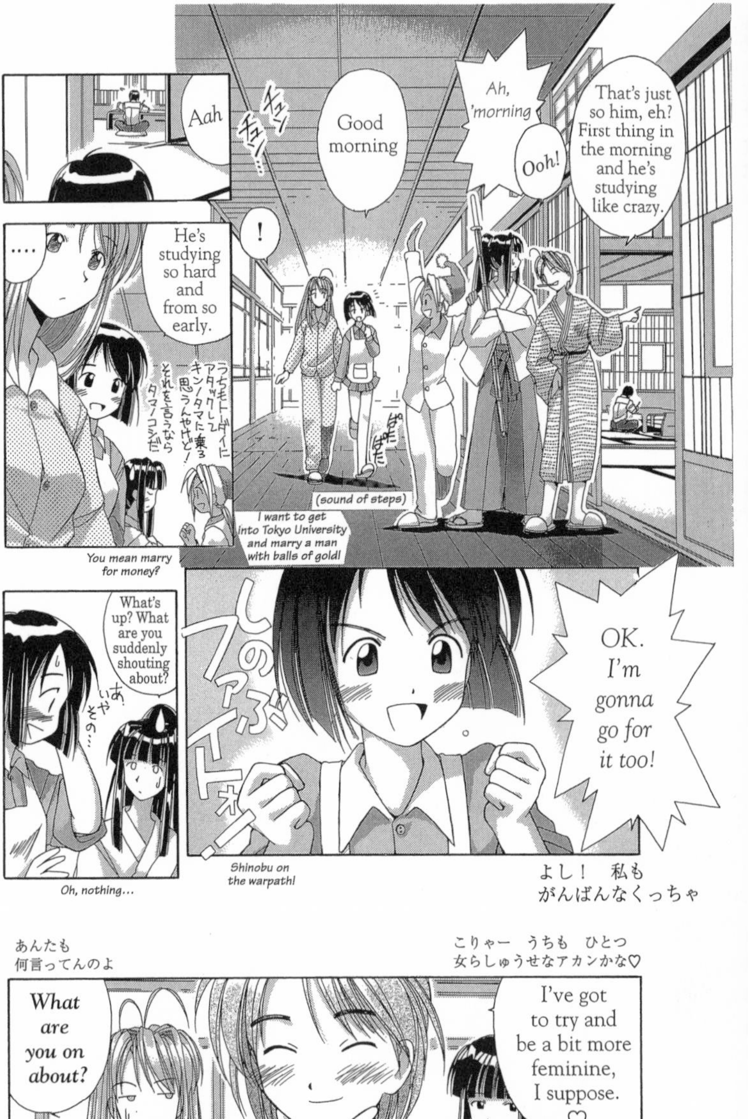
That's just so him, eh? First thing in the morning and he's studying like crazy.
Ooh!
Ah, 'morning
Good morning
チュン チュン…
Aah
!
He's studying so hard and from so early.
....
うちもトーダイにアタックしてキンノタマに乗ろ思うんやけど!
それを言うならタマノコシだ
ぱた ぱた
(sound of steps)
I want to get into Tokyo University and marry a man with balls of gold!
OK. I'm gonna go for it too!
しのぶファイトォー!
What's up? What are you suddenly shouting about?
あ! いや その…
I've got to try and be a bit more feminine, I suppose. ♡
What are you on about?

わあー♡

先輩　こんなに早くから
がんばってるんですねぇ

You mean marry for money?

どうした?
いきなり大声だして?

Oh, nothing…

Shinobu on the warpath!

よし!　私も
がんばんなくっちゃ

こりゃー　うちも　ひとつ
女らしゅうせなアカンかな♡

あんたも
何言ってんのよ

—— いや
何(なん)やあの男が
来てから

この寮の雰囲気
ちょい明るなったと
思わんか？

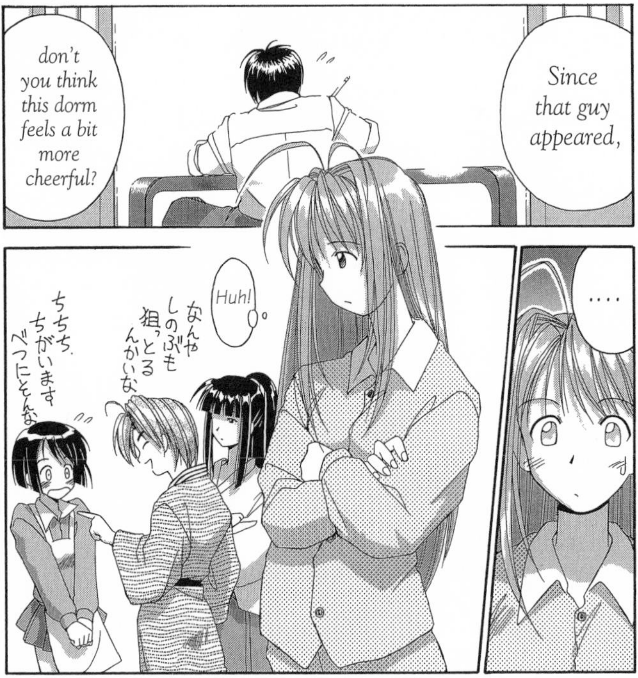
Since that guy appeared,
don't you think this dorm feels a bit more cheerful?
....
Huh!
なんや しのぶも 狙っとる んかいな
ちちち ちがいます べつにそんな
ふーん

Uh…eh.
No, not really.

Shinobu,
you're after him too,
then?

できたっ
で！

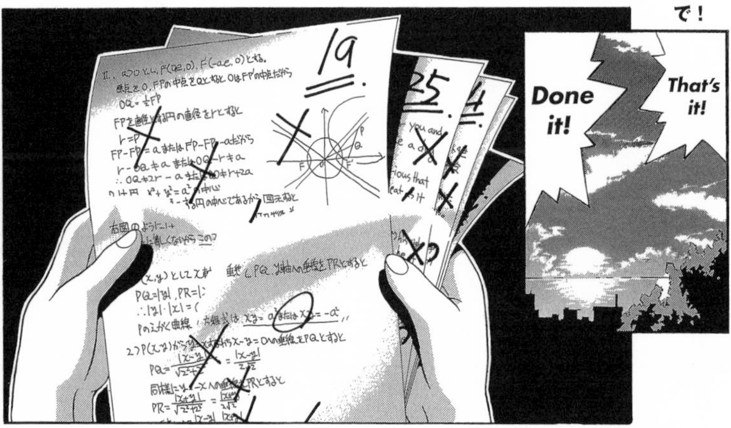
19
25
4
Done it!
That's it!

これが簡単に解けるなら
今頃ホントに東大生の
はずだもんな‥‥

そ‥‥そりゃ
そうか

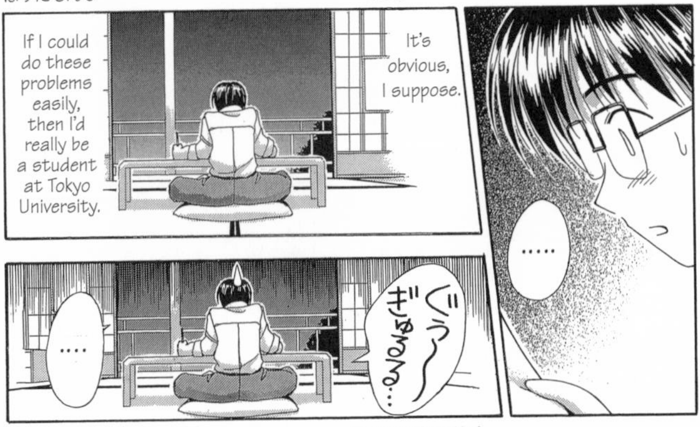
If I could do these problems easily, then I'd really be a student at Tokyo University.
It's obvious, I suppose.
.....
....
ぐぅ~ぎゅるるる…
(his stomach rumbles)

俺なんか
格好つけても
だめじゃん!

あ――
やめた　やめた!!

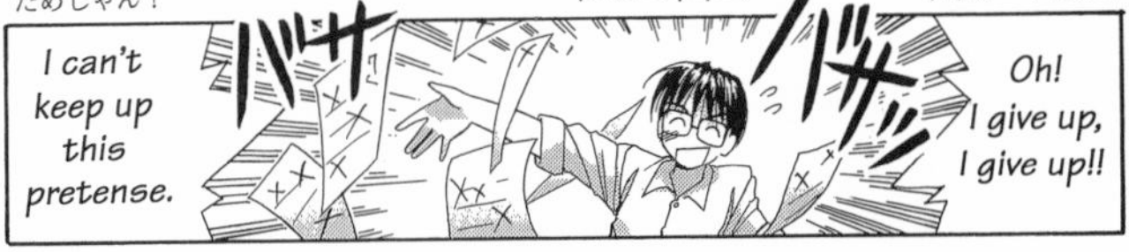
(swish of paper)
I can't keep up this pretense.
バサ
バサッ
Oh! I give up, I give up!!

しょうがないから
実家にでも帰って‥‥

さてと　ボロが出る前に
こっそりここを
抜け出すとするか

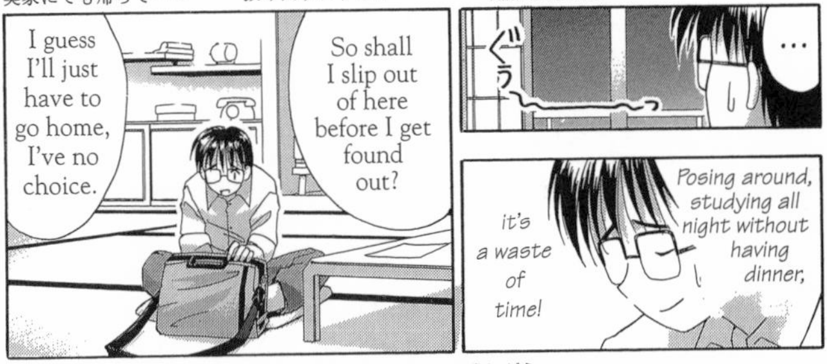
I guess I'll just have to go home, I've no choice.
So shall I slip out of here before I get found out?
rumble-rumble
ぐぅ~
...
Posing around, studying all night without having dinner,
it's a waste of time!

な――んか　いっちょまえに
飯も食わずに
徹夜なんかして

我ながら
無駄骨(むだぼね)だったな

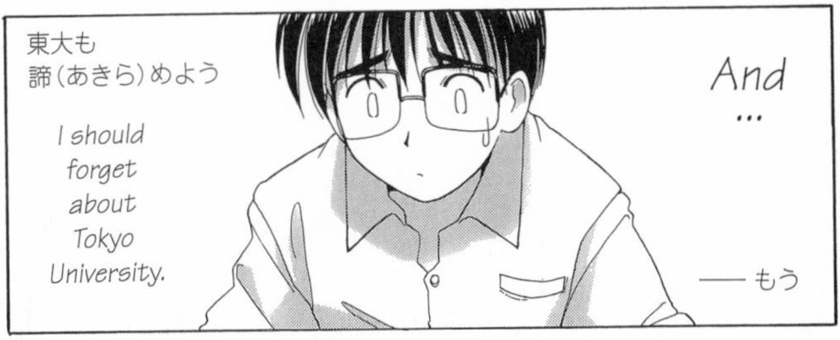
東大も
諦(あきら)めよう
I should forget about Tokyo University.
And ...
――もう

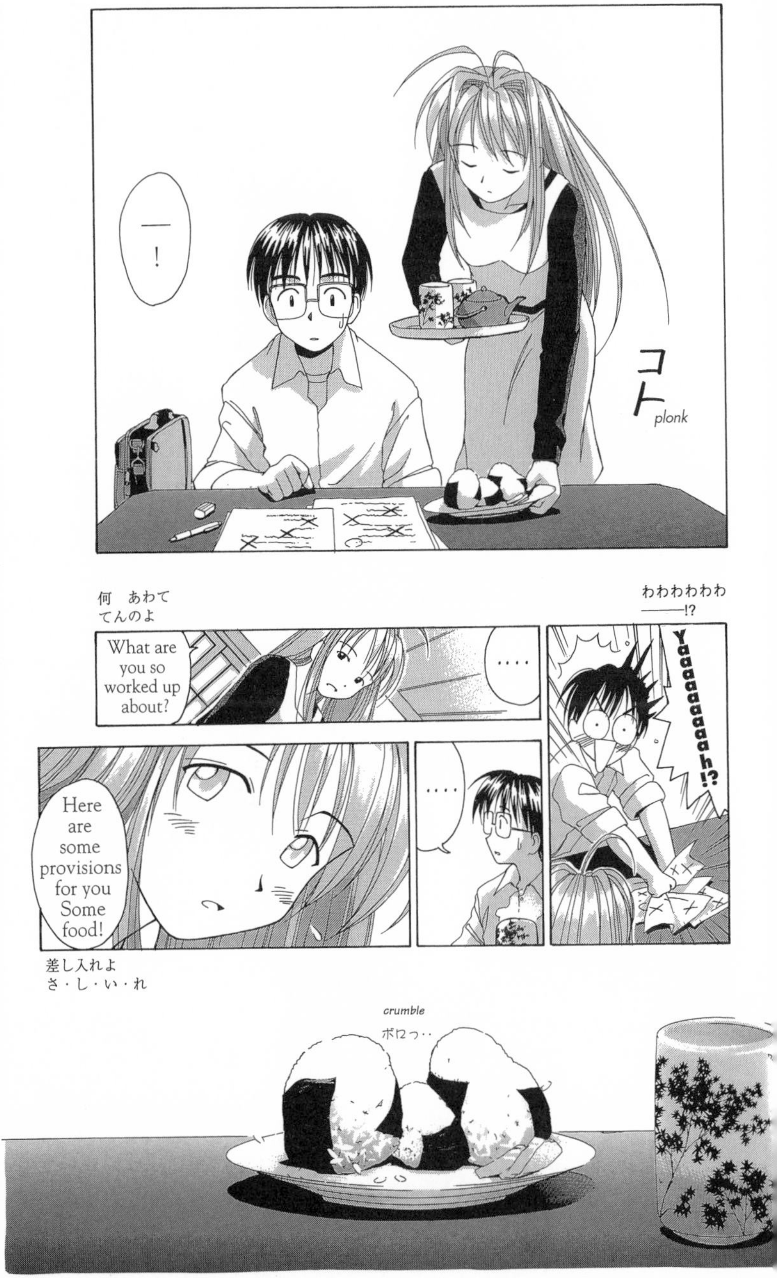
—!
コト
plonk
わわわわわわ——!?
Yaaaaaaaah!?
何 あわて てんのよ
What are you so worked up about?
....
....
差し入れよ さ・し・い・れ
Here are some provisions for you Some food!
crumble
ボロっ・・

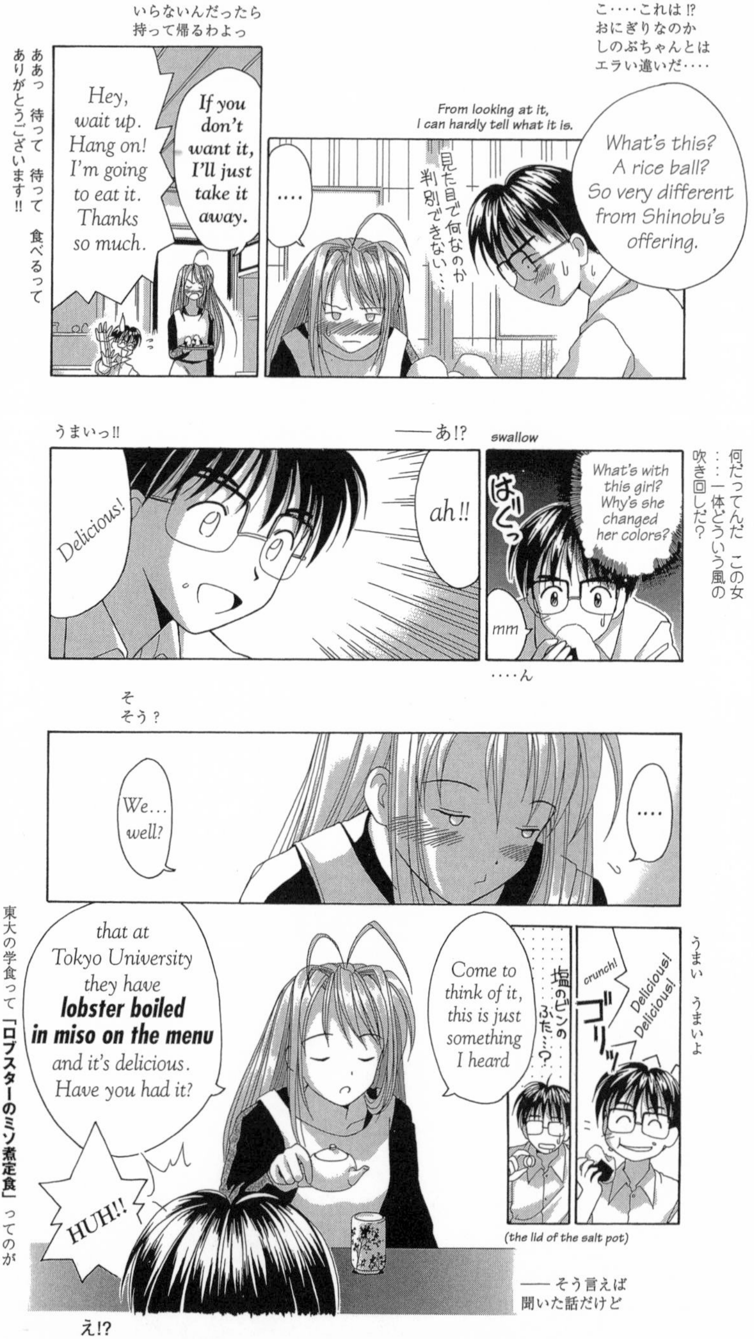

こ・・・・これは⁉
おにぎりなのか
しのぶちゃんとは
エラい違いだ・・・・
What's this? A rice ball? So very different from Shinobu's offering.
From looking at it, I can hardly tell what it is.
見た目で何なのか判別できない・・・
....
いらないんだったら持って帰るわよっ
If you don't want it, I'll just take it away.
ああっ 待って 待って 食べるって ありがとうございます!!
Hey, wait up. Hang on! I'm going to eat it. Thanks so much.
swallow
何だってんだ この女 ・・・一体どういう風の吹き回しだ？
What's with this girl? Why's she changed her colors?
はぐっ
mm
・・・・ん
——あ!?
ah!!
うまいっ!!
Delicious!
....
そ そう？
We... well?
うまい うまいよ
crunch!
ゴリッ
Delicious! Delicious!
塩のビンのふた・・・？
(the lid of the salt pot)
——そう言えば 聞いた話だけど
Come to think of it, this is just something I heard
東大の学食って「ロブスターのミソ煮定食」ってのがすごくおいしいんだってね 食べたことある？
that at Tokyo University they have **lobster boiled in miso on the menu** and it's delicious. Have you had it?
HUH!!
え!?

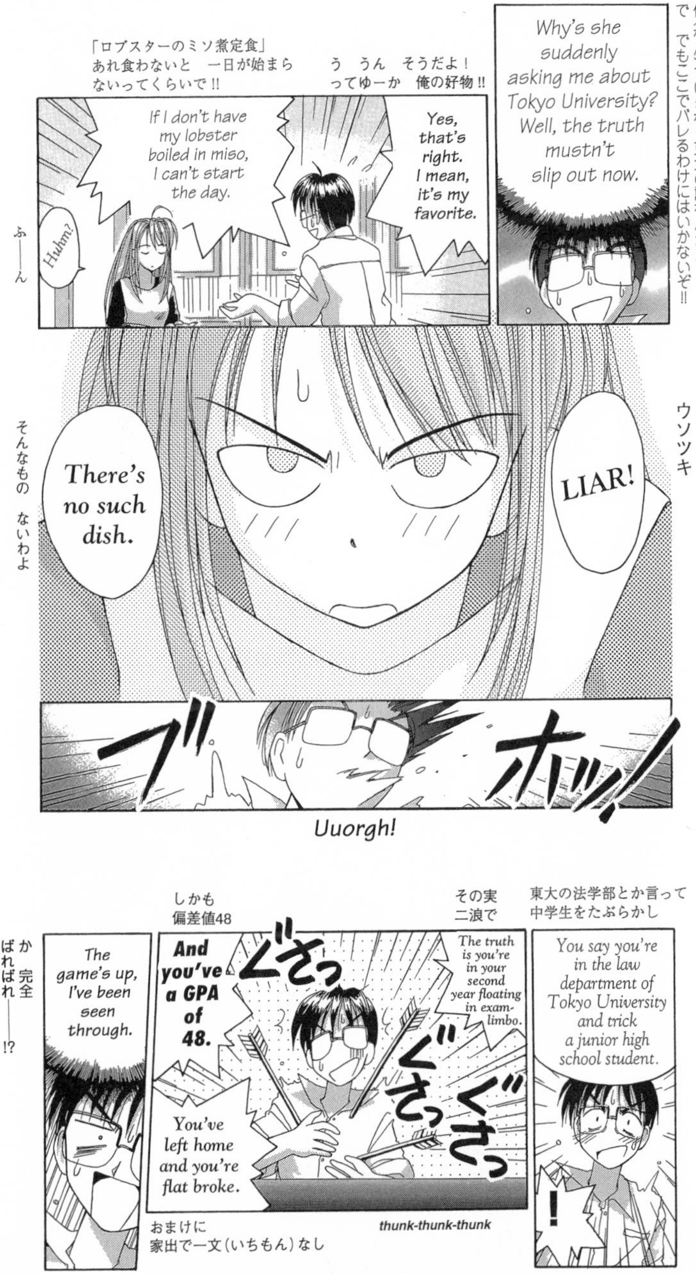
何(なん)でいきなり東大の話なんか!? でもここでバレるわけにはいかないぞ!!
Why's she suddenly asking me about Tokyo University? Well, the truth mustn't slip out now.
う うん そうだよ! ってゆーか 俺の好物!!
Yes, that's right. I mean, it's my favorite.
「ロブスターのミソ煮定食」 あれ食わないと 一日が始まら ないってくらいで!!
If I don't have my lobster boiled in miso, I can't start the day.
ふ―――ん
Huhm?
ウソツキ
LIAR!
そんなもの ないわよ
There's no such dish.
ブホッ!
Uuorgh!
東大の法学部とか言って 中学生をたぶらかし
You say you're in the law department of Tokyo University and trick a junior high school student.
!
その実 二浪で
The truth is you're in your second year floating in exam-limbo.
しかも 偏差値48
And you've a GPA of 48.
ぐさっ ぐさっ ぐさっ
おまけに 家出で一文(いちもん)なし
You've left home and you're flat broke.
thunk-thunk-thunk
完全 ばればれ―――!?
The game's up, I've been seen through.

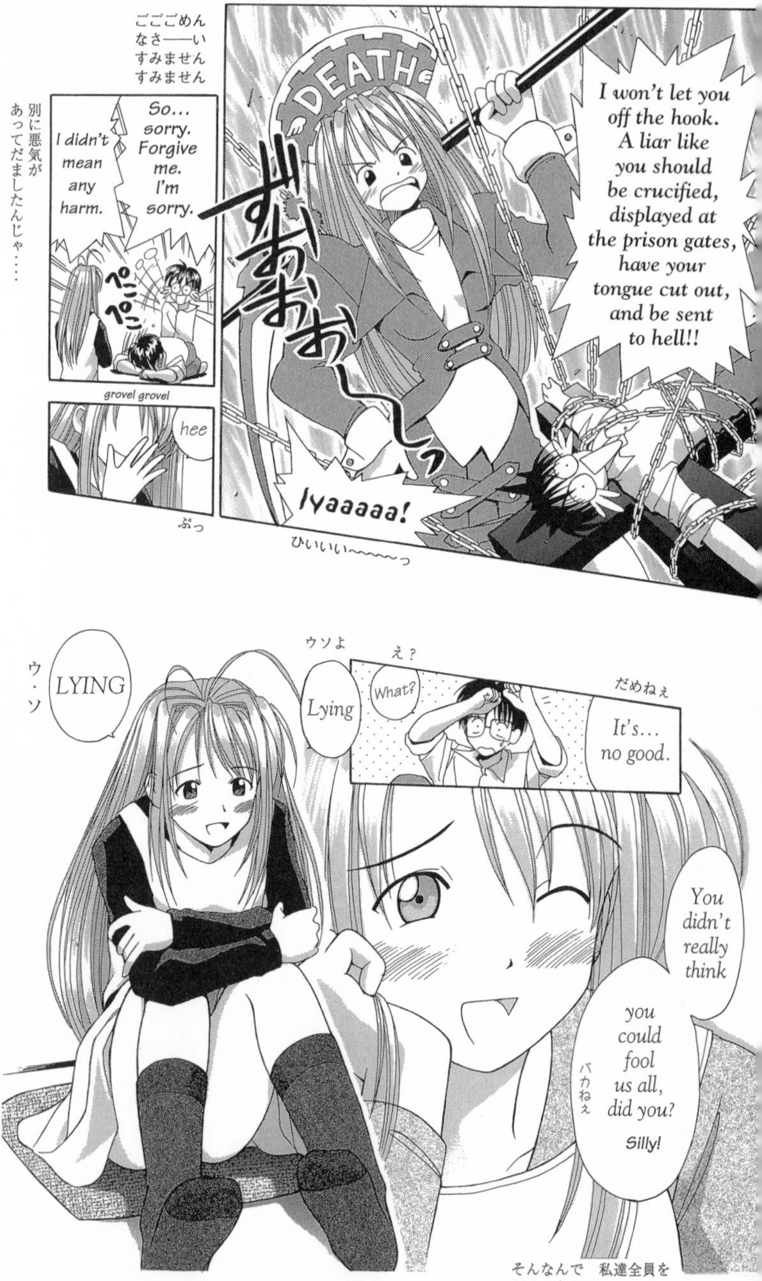
はっきり言って許せないわ
あんたみたいなウソツキ
はりつけ　獄門　舌切って地獄行きよ——!!
(she looms over him)
I won't let you off the hook. A liar like you should be crucified, displayed at the prison gates, have your tongue cut out, and be sent to hell!!
Iyaaaaa!
ひいいい〜〜〜〜っ
ごごごめん
なさ——い
すみません
すみません
So… sorry. Forgive me. I'm sorry.
別に悪気が
あってだましたんじゃ……
I didn't mean any harm.
ぺこぺこ
grovel grovel
hee
ぷっ
ウ・ソ
LYING
ウソよ
Lying
え？
What?
だめねぇ
It's… no good.
そんなんで　私達全員を
だまそうと思ったわけ？
You didn't really think you could fool us all, did you?
バカねぇ
Silly!

――見逃して
あげるよ　今回は

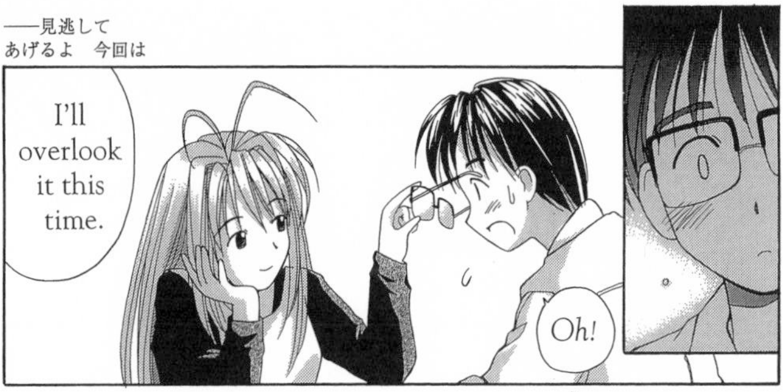

Oh!
I'll overlook it this time.

あ

しのぶちゃん
喜んでたわよ

あの子
ここんとこずっと
元気なかったんだけど

あんたのおかげで
元気出てきたみたい！

「がんばれば必ずできる」
私もがんばんなきゃって

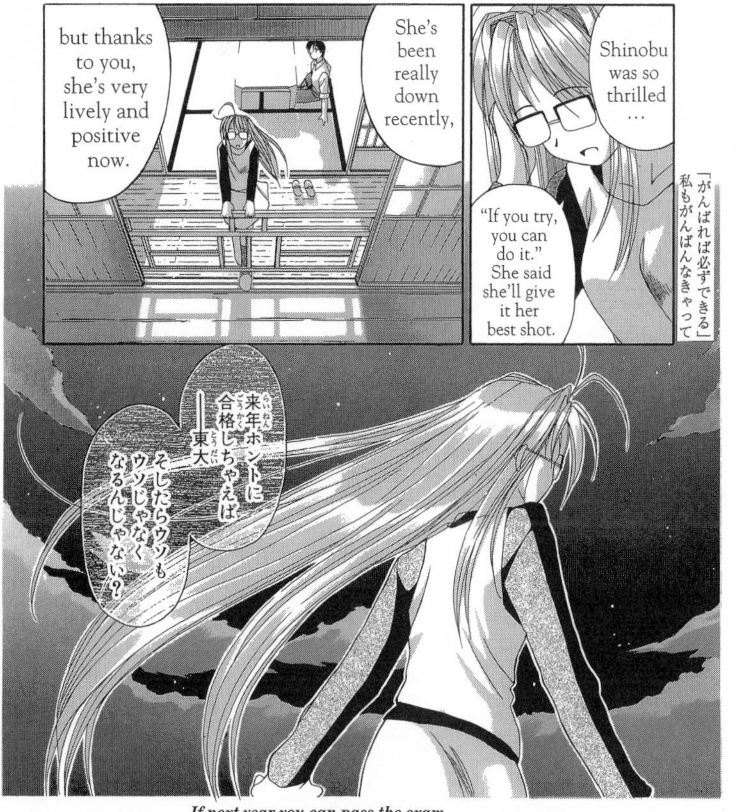

Shinobu was so thrilled …
"If you try, you can do it." She said she'll give it her best shot.
She's been really down recently,
but thanks to you, she's very lively and positive now.
来年ホントに合格しちゃえば――東大
そしたらウソもウソじゃなくなるんじゃない？

If next year you can pass the exam, then it's Tokyo University for you.

And then your lie stops being a lie.

がんばれば
必ずできる

諦(あきら)めないで
やってみなよ

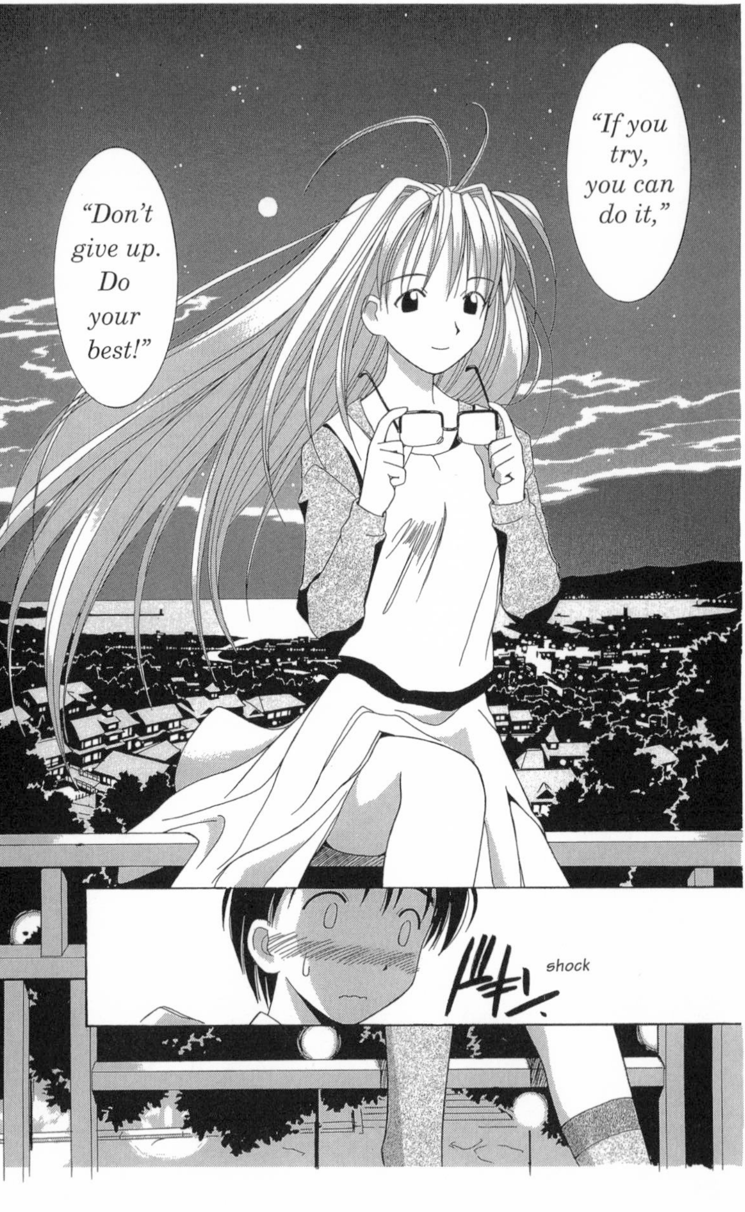
"If you try, you can do it,"
"Don't give up. Do your best!"
ドキン
shock

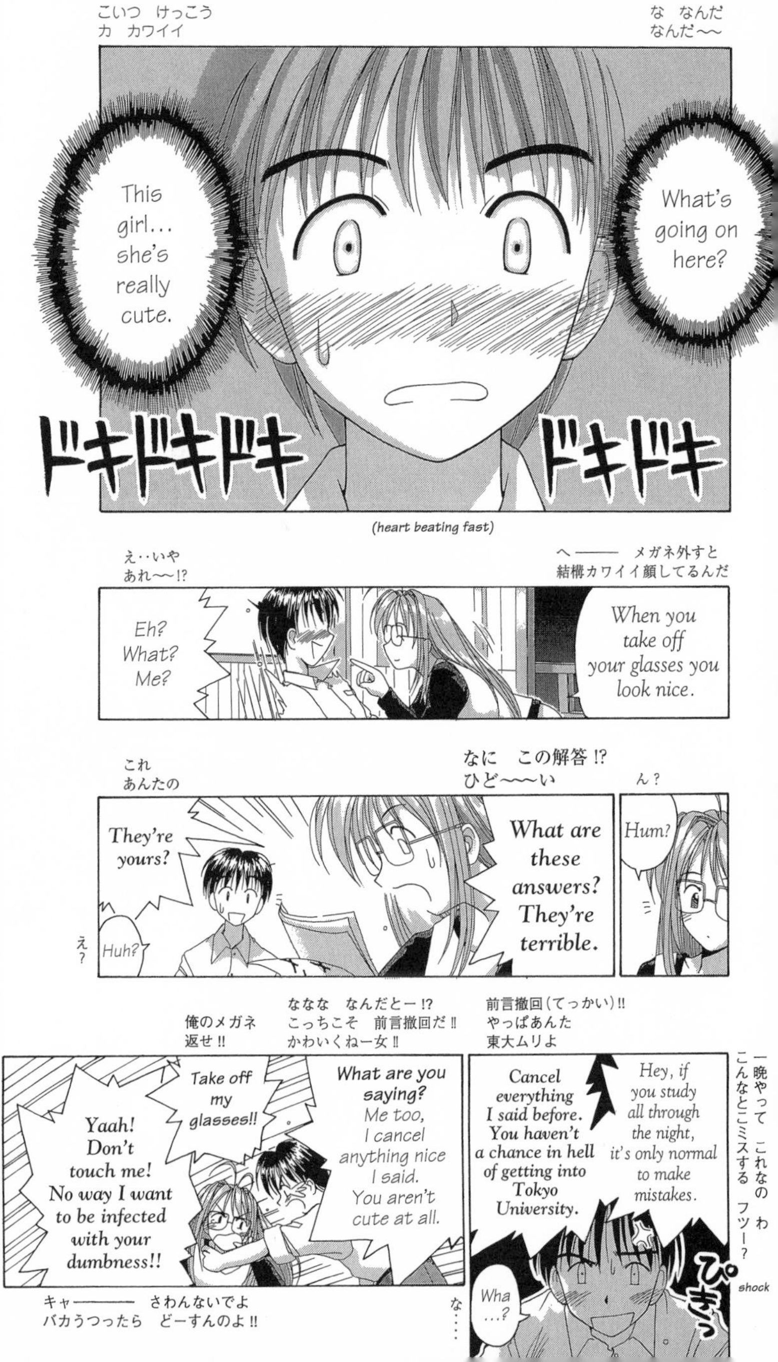
な なんだ
なんだ〜〜
What's going on here?
こいつ けっこう
カ カワイイ
This girl… she's really cute.
ドキドキドキ
ドキドキ
(heart beating fast)
へ―― メガネ外すと
結構カワイイ顔してるんだ
When you take off your glasses you look nice.
え‥いや
あれ〜〜!?
Eh? What? Me?
ん？
Hum?
なに この解答!?
ひど〜〜い
What are these answers? They're terrible.
これ
あんたの
They're yours?
え？
Huh?
一晩やって これなの わ
こんなとこミスする フツー？
Hey, if you study all through the night, it's only normal to make mistakes.
前言撤回(てっかい)!!
やっぱあんた
東大ムリよ
Cancel everything I said before. You haven't a chance in hell of getting into Tokyo University.
ぴきっ
shock
な‥‥
Wha …?
ななな なんだとー!?
こっちこそ 前言撤回だ!!
かわいくねー女!!
What are you saying? Me too, I cancel anything nice I said. You aren't cute at all.
俺のメガネ
返せ!!
Take off my glasses!!
キャ―――― さわんないでよ
バカうつったら どーすんのよ!!
Yaah! Don't touch me! No way I want to be infected with your dumbness!!

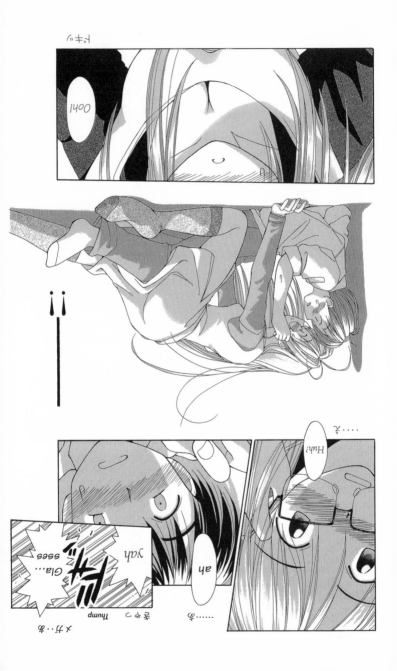

ドキッ

1400

！！

あ‥‥

Thump
どきっ
yah

Gla‥‥
sses

あ‥‥

Huh!?

え‥‥

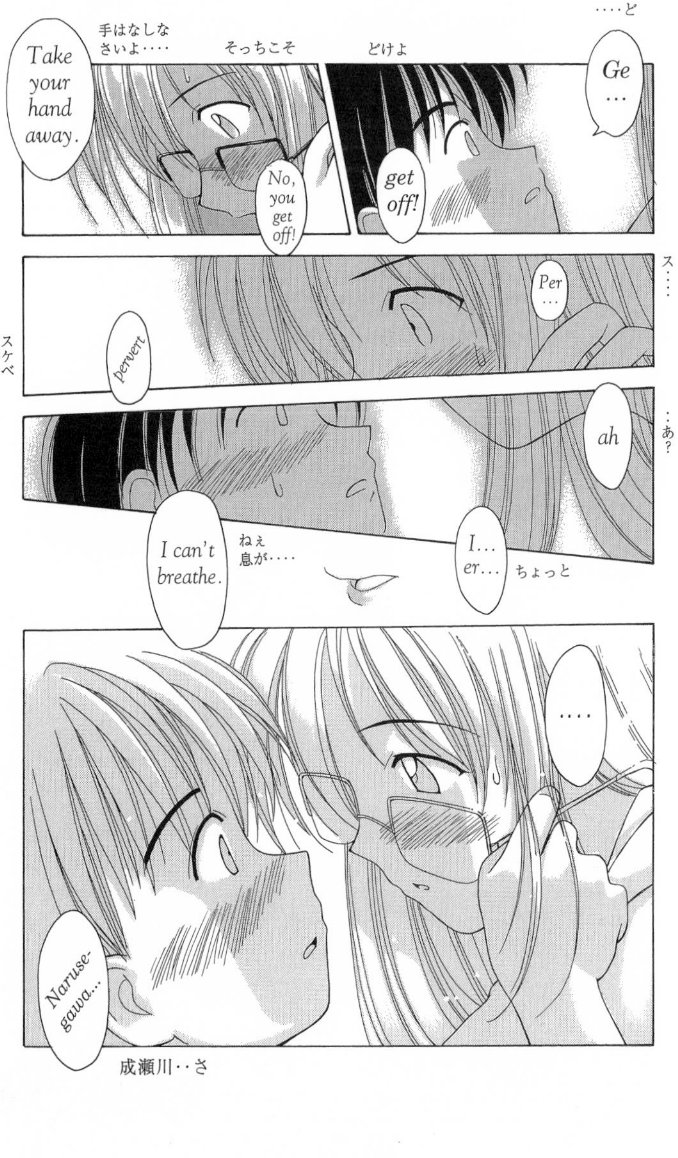
····ど
Ge …
どけよ
get off!
そっちこそ
No, you get off!
手はなしなさいよ····
Take your hand away.
ス····
Per …
スケベ
pervert
··あ?
ah
ちょっと
I… er…
ねぇ息が····
I can't breathe.
····
Naruse-gawa...
成瀬川··さ

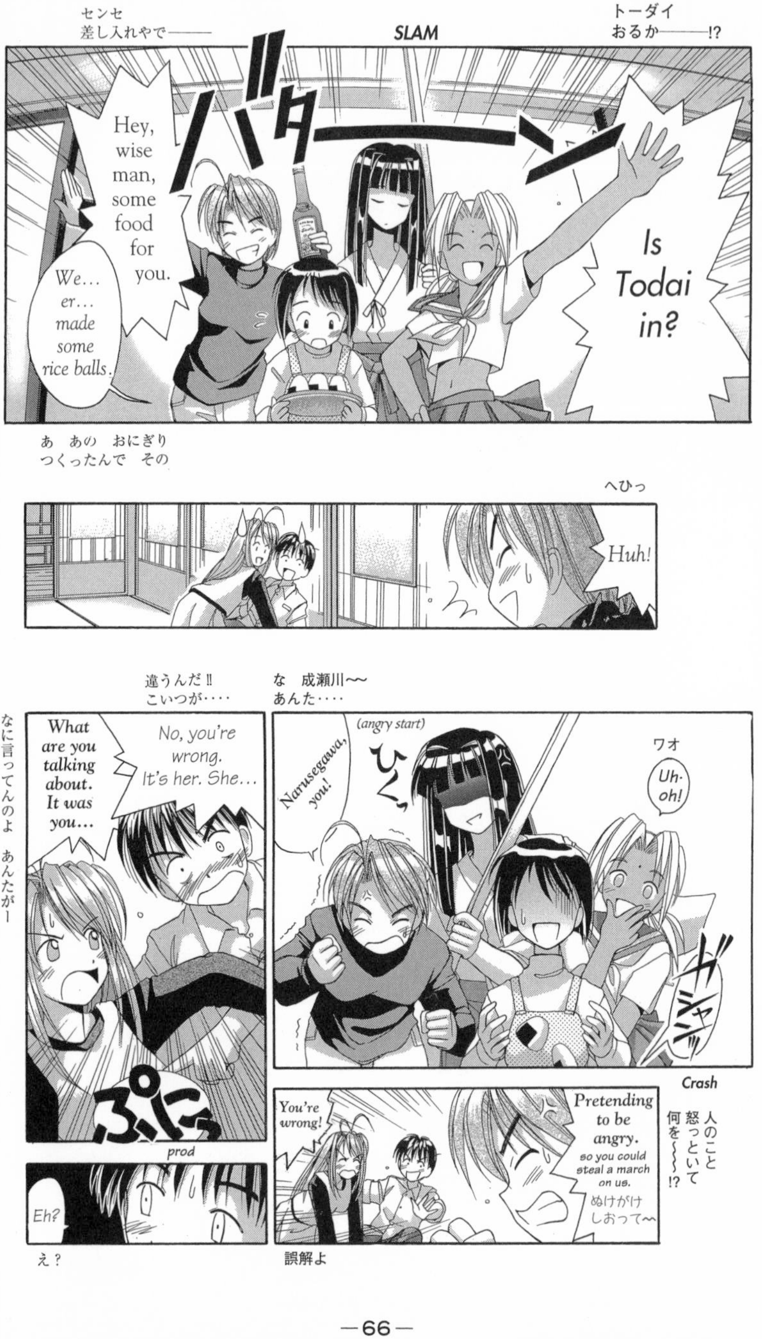
トーダイ
おるか———!?
SLAM
センセ
差し入れやで———
Is Todai in?
Hey, wise man, some food for you.
We… er… made some rice balls.
あ あの おにぎり
つくったんで その
へひっ
Huh!
な 成瀬川~~
あんた・・・・
(angry start)
Narusegawa, you!
ワオ
Uh-oh!
Crash
違うんだ!!
こいつが・・・・
なに言ってんのよ あんたがー
What are you talking about. It was you…
No, you're wrong. It's her. She…
prod
Eh?
え?
人のこと
怒っといて
何を~~!?
Pretending to be angry.
so you could steal a march on us.
ぬけがけ
しおって~
You're wrong!
誤解よ

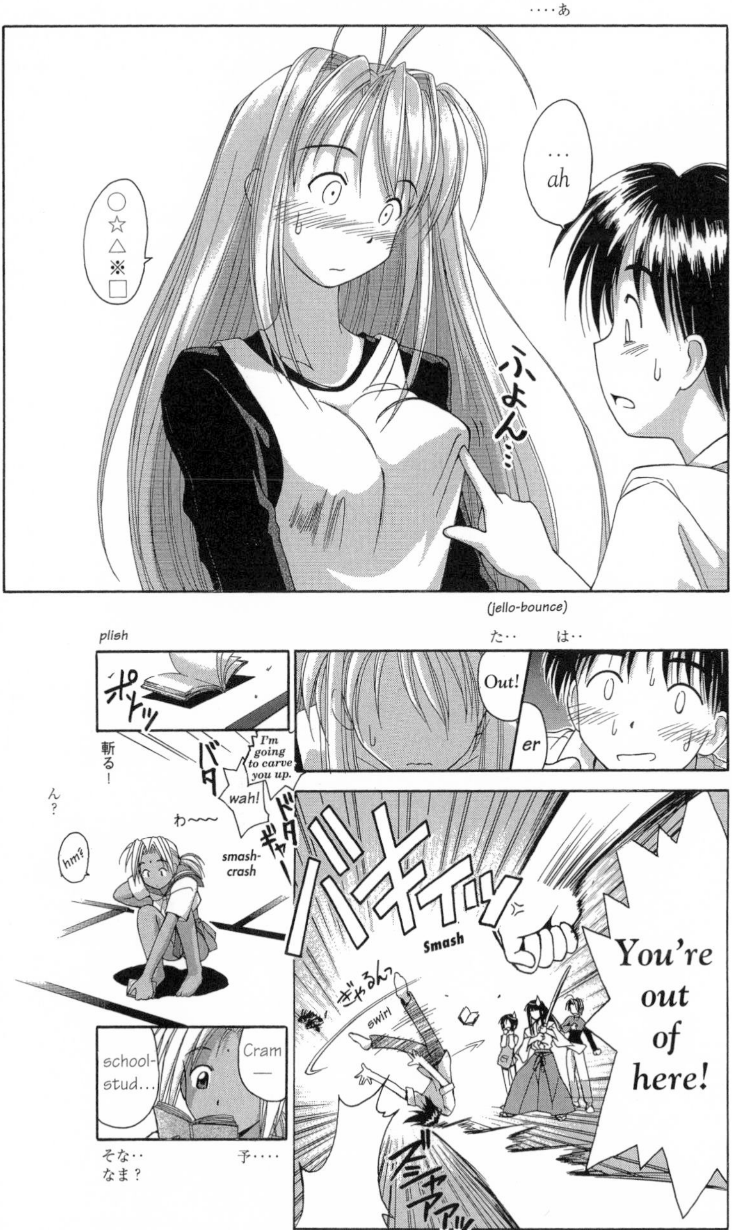
・・・・あ
…ah
○☆△※□
ふよん…
(jello-bounce)
は・・
た・・
Out!
er
plish
ポトッ
斬る！
I'm going to carve you up.
バタ
wah!
わ～～
ん？
hm!?
ドタ
ギャ
smash-crash
バキィッ
Smash
You're out of here!
ぎゃるんっ
swirl
ズシャアァッ
zoot
退寮――――――っ!!
Cram—
school-stud…
予・・・・
そな・・なま？

なあ

よ そなこうなま と しょう
予備校生徒証て何や？

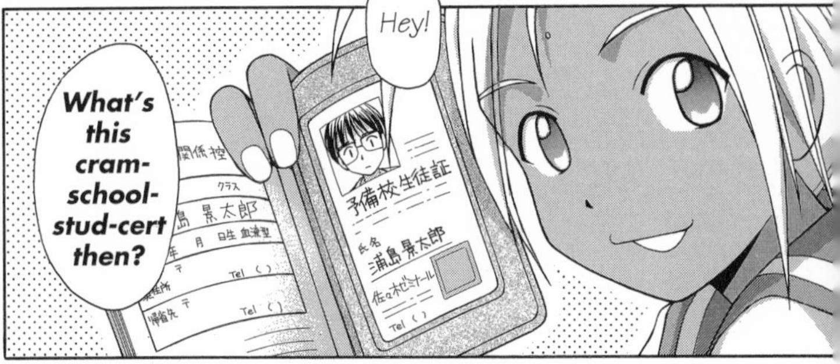
Hey!
What's this cram-school-stud-cert then?
予備校生徒証
浦島景太郎

(cram school student ID)

え？

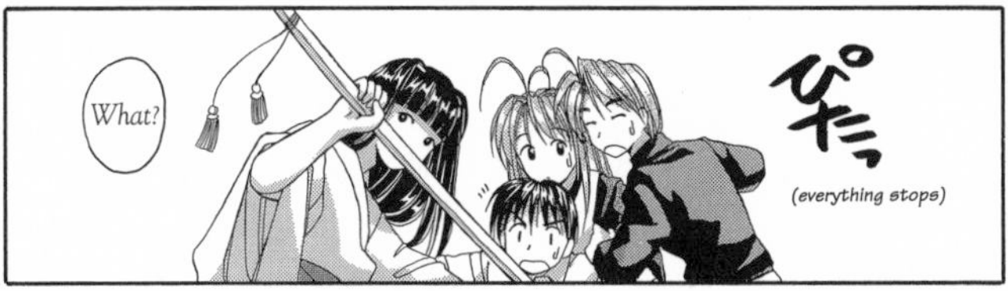
ぴたっ
(everything stops)
What?

あっ

そ‥‥
それは!!

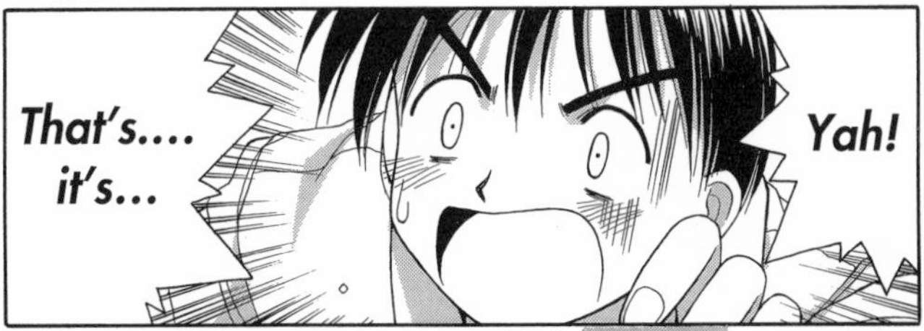
Yah!
That's.... it's...

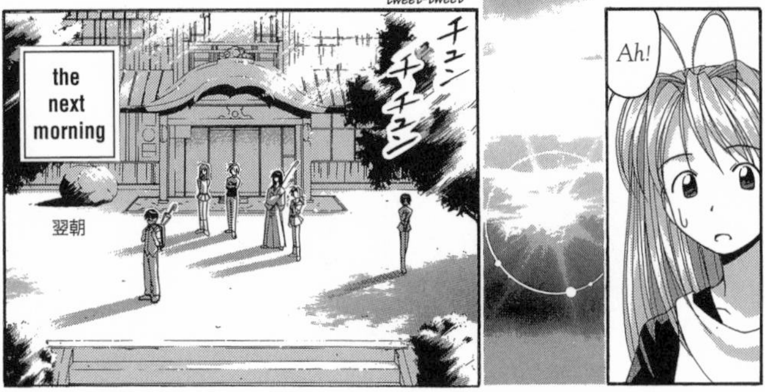
Ah!
tweet-tweet
チュン チチュン
the next morning
翌朝

あ‥‥

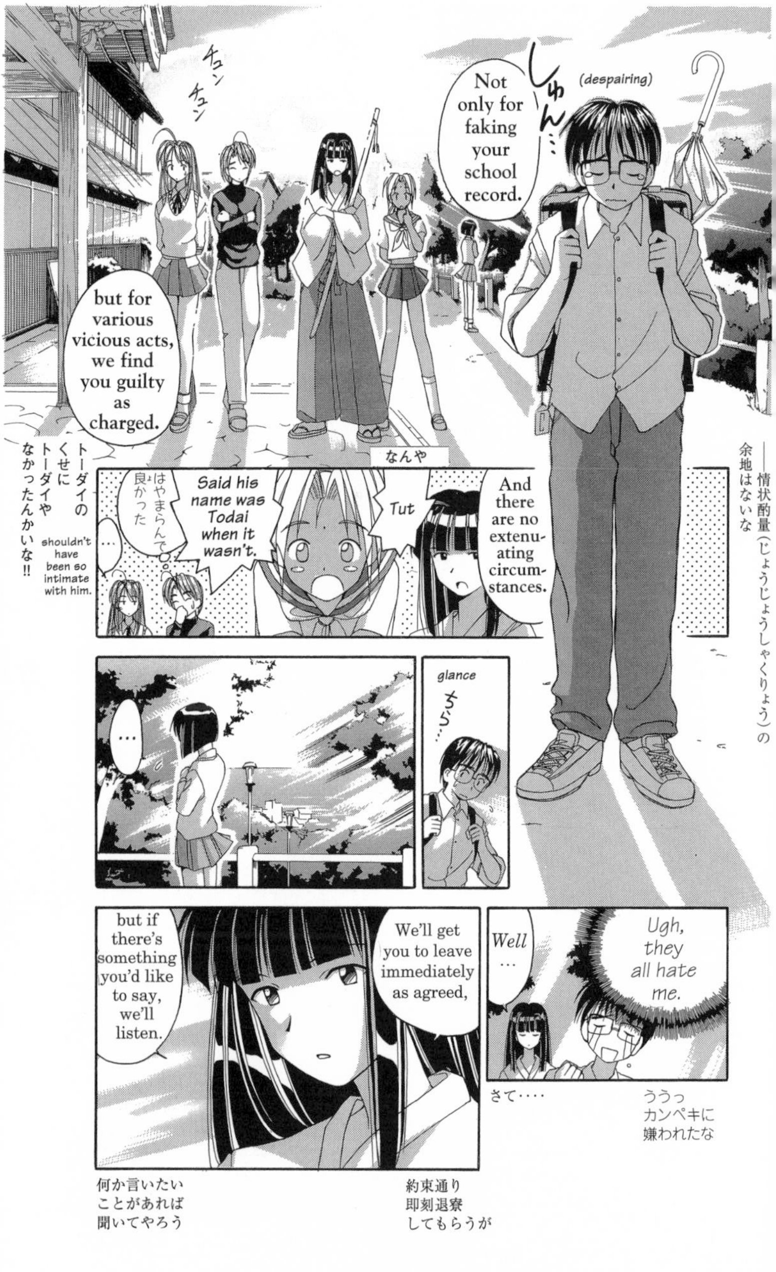
悪質な学歴詐称(さしょう)及び
ふらちな行為に至った協定違反
(despairing)
しゅん…
Not only for faking your school record,
チュン チュン
but for various vicious acts, we find you guilty as charged.
——情状酌量(じょうじょうしゃくりょう)の余地はないな
And there are no extenuating circumstances.
なんや
Tut
Said his name was Todai when it wasn't.
はやまらんで良かった
…
トーダイのくせにトーダイやなかったんかいな!!
shouldn't have been so intimate with him.
glance
ちら…
…
Ugh, they all hate me.
ううっ カンペキに嫌われたな
Well …
さて・・・・
We'll get you to leave immediately as agreed,
約束通り即刻退寮してもらうが
but if there's something you'd like to say, we'll listen.
何か言いたいことがあれば聞いてやろう

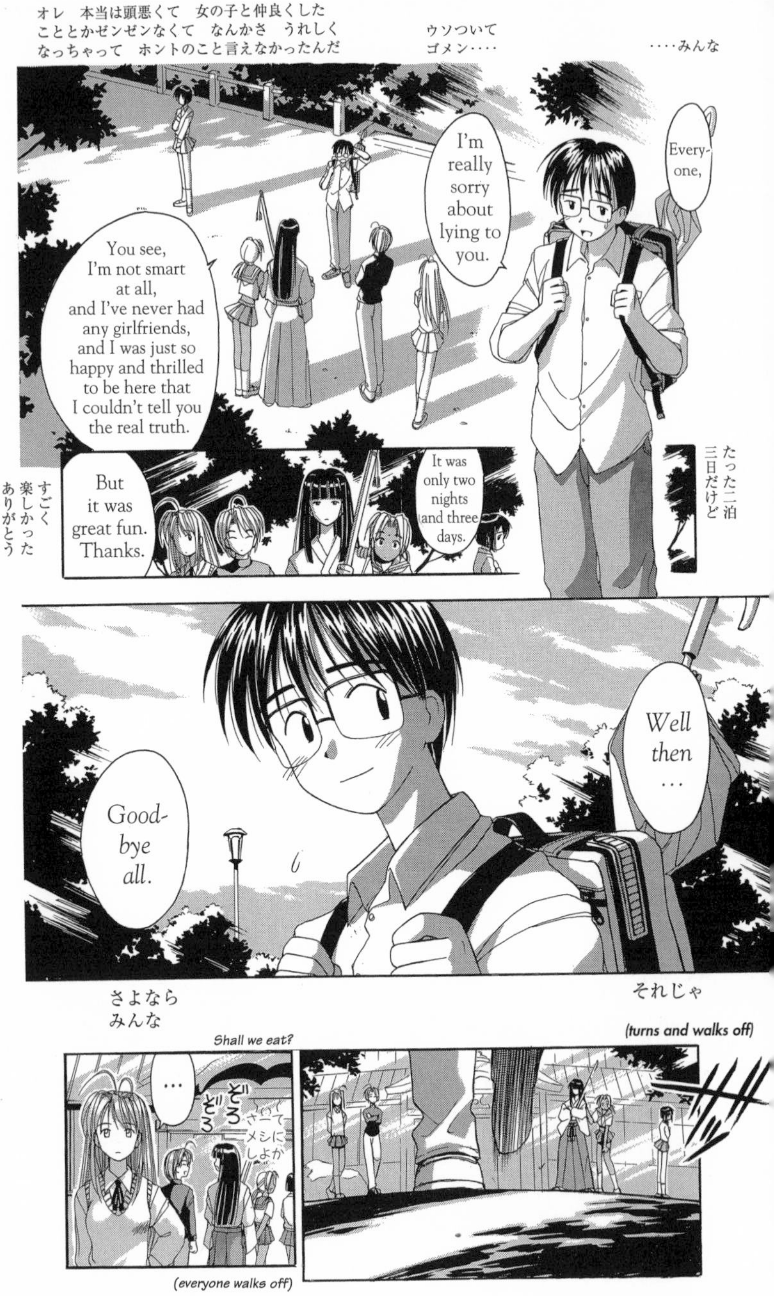

····みんな
Every-one,
ウソついて
ゴメン····
I'm really sorry about lying to you.
オレ　本当は頭悪くて　女の子と仲良くした
ことなんかゼンゼンなくて　なんかさ　うれしく
なっちゃって　ホントのこと言えなかったんだ
You see, I'm not smart at all, and I've never had any girlfriends, and I was just so happy and thrilled to be here that I couldn't tell you the real truth.
たった二泊
三日だけど
It was only two nights and three days.
すごく
楽しかった
ありがとう
But it was great fun. Thanks.
それじゃ
Well then …
さよなら
みんな
Good-bye all.
(turns and walks off)
Shall we eat?
…
どろどろ
さーて
メシに
しよか
(everyone walks off)

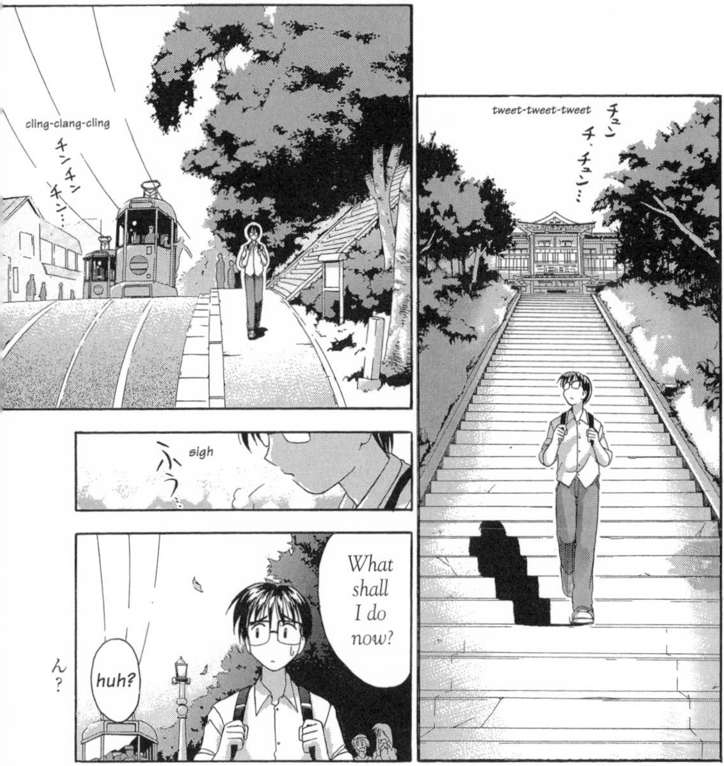
tweet-tweet-tweet
チュン
チ、チュン…
cling-clang-cling
チンチン
チン…
sigh
ふう…
What shall I do now?
huh?
ん？

さて　これから
どうしようかなあ‥‥

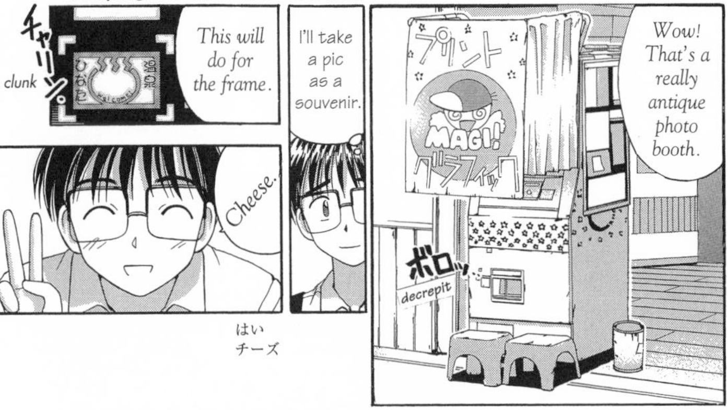
うわ ——
ボロッち ——
プリクラだな
Wow! That's a really antique photo booth.
プリント
MAGI!
グラフィック
ボロッ
decrepit
‥‥
記念に一枚
とってくか
I'll take a pic as a souvenir.
へへ
フレームは
やっぱコレかな
This will do for the frame.
Hinata Hotspring
チャリーン。
clunk
Cheese.
はい
チーズ

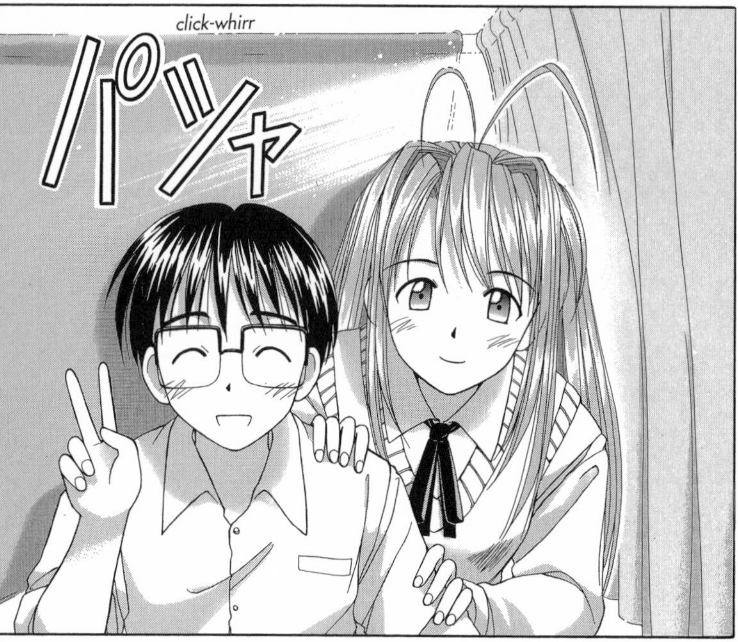
click-whirr
パシャ

あんたさ

男一人でプリクラ
とってんじゃないわよ

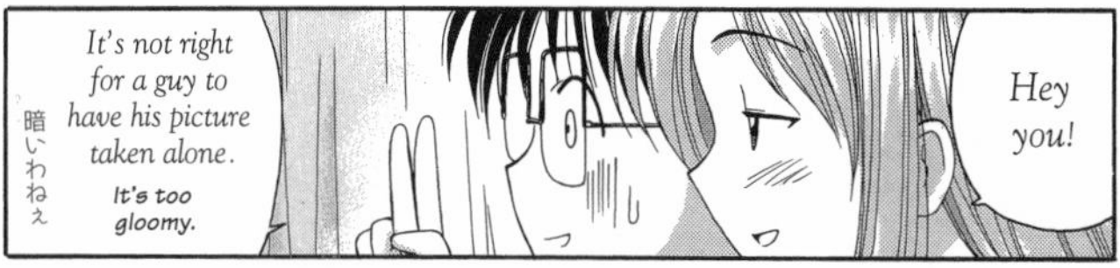
Hey you!
It's not right for a guy to have his picture taken alone.
暗いわねぇ
It's too gloomy.

うわあ〜〜　なな何(なん)だよ
俺の趣味をバカにしに
来たのかよ〜〜

なに
言ってんの？

(book falls open)

ちょっと・・・・なに
この手帳？　全部あんた
一人で写ってるじゃん？

わ――ッ
見るなあ
返せ――ッ

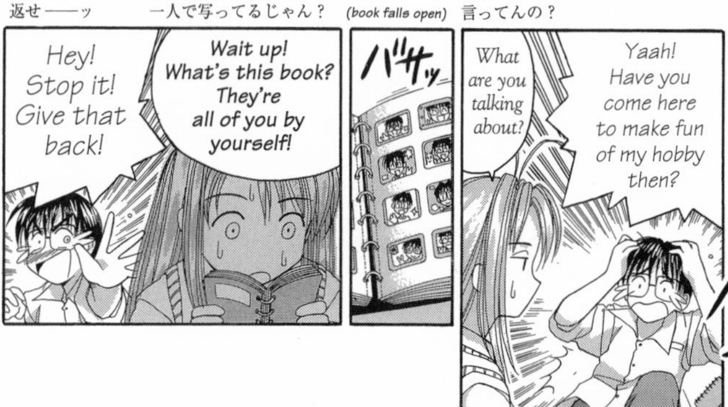
Yaah! Have you come here to make fun of my hobby then?
What are you talking about?
バサッ
Wait up! What's this book? They're all of you by yourself!
Hey! Stop it! Give that back!

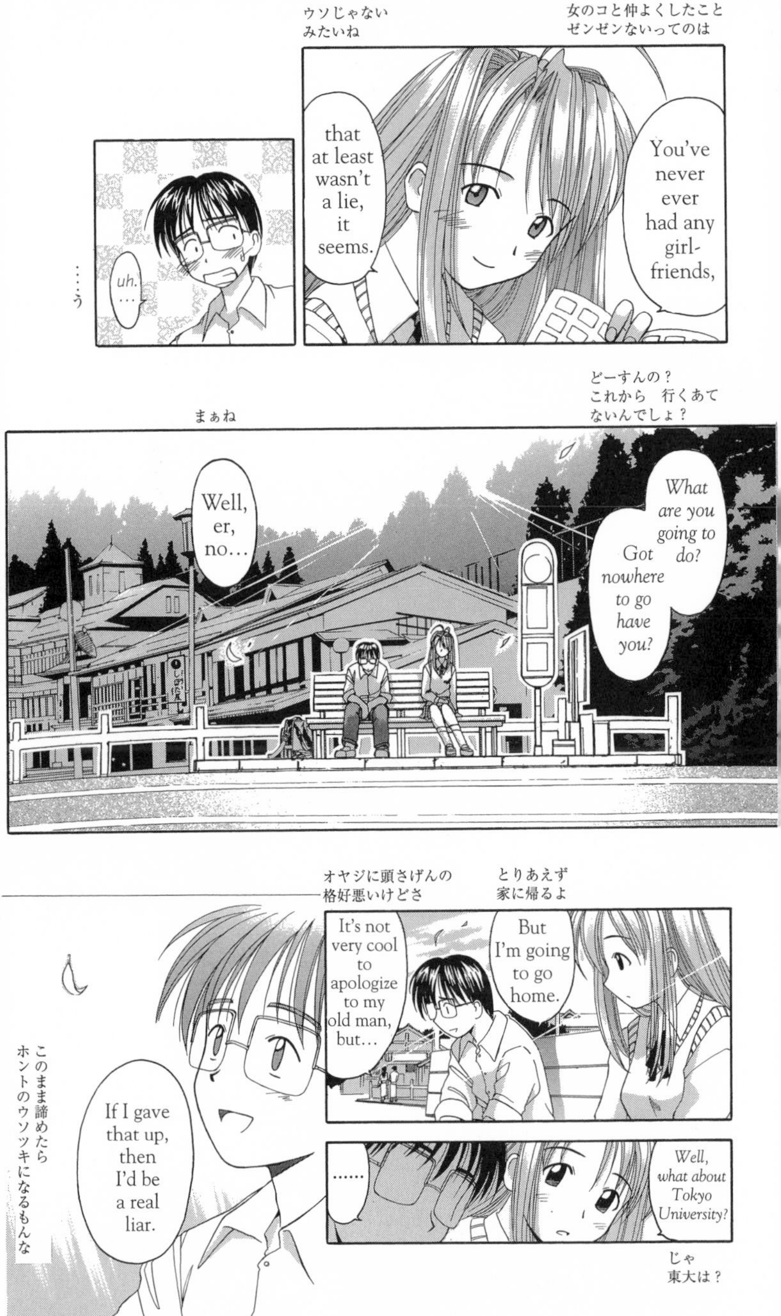
女のコと仲よくしたこと
ゼンゼンないってのは
You've never ever had any girl-friends,
ウソじゃない
みたいね
that at least wasn't a lie, it seems.
…う
uh. …
どーすんの？
これから　行くあて
ないんでしょ？
What are you going to do? Got nowhere to go have you?
まぁね
Well, er, no…
とりあえず
家に帰るよ
But I'm going to go home.
オヤジに頭さげんの
格好悪いけどさ
It's not very cool to apologize to my old man, but…
じゃ
東大は？
Well, what about Tokyo University?
……
このまま諦めたら
ホントのウソツキになるもんな
If I gave that up, then I'd be a real liar.

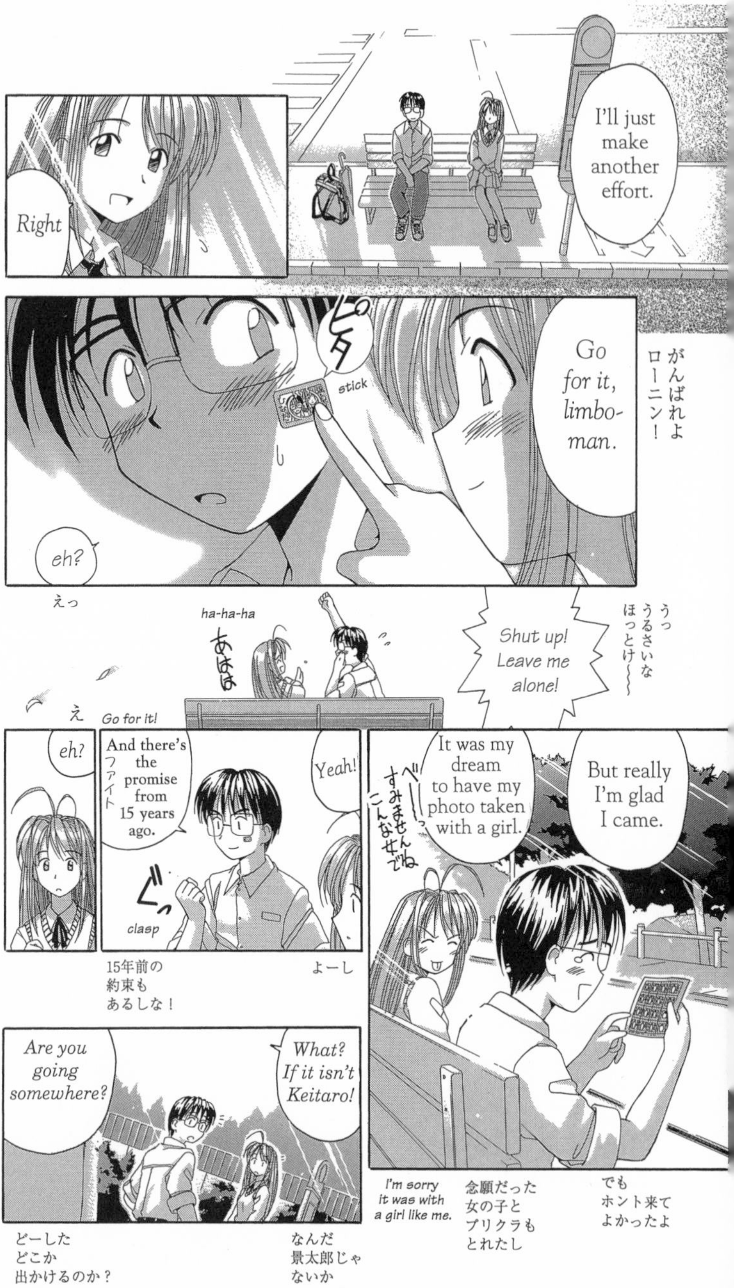
I'll just make another effort.
もうちょっとガンバってみるよ
Right
そっか
Go for it, limbo-man.
がんばれよローニン！
ピタ
stick
eh?
えっ
Shut up! Leave me alone!
うっうるさいなほっとけ〜〜
ha-ha-ha
あはは
Go for it!
ファイト
え
eh?
And there's the promise from 15 years ago.
15年前の約束もあるしな！
Yeah!
よーし
ぐっ
clasp
But really I'm glad I came.
でもホント来てよかったよ
It was my dream to have my photo taken with a girl.
念願だった女の子とプリクラもとれたし
べーっ
I'm sorry it was with a girl like me.
すみませんねこんな女で
What? If it isn't Keitaro!
なんだ景太郎じゃないか
Are you going somewhere?
どーしたどこか出かけるのか？

ふ──ん　成瀬川とも
ずいぶん仲よくなったんだな

ち
ちがいますよ
寮長!!

オバさん　実は俺さ
実家帰ることにしたんだ

だからさ
婆ちゃんに
よろしく
いっといてよ

そうか　じゃあ
それはナシだ　婆ちゃんから
ＦＡＸが届いた
大変なことになったぞ

え？

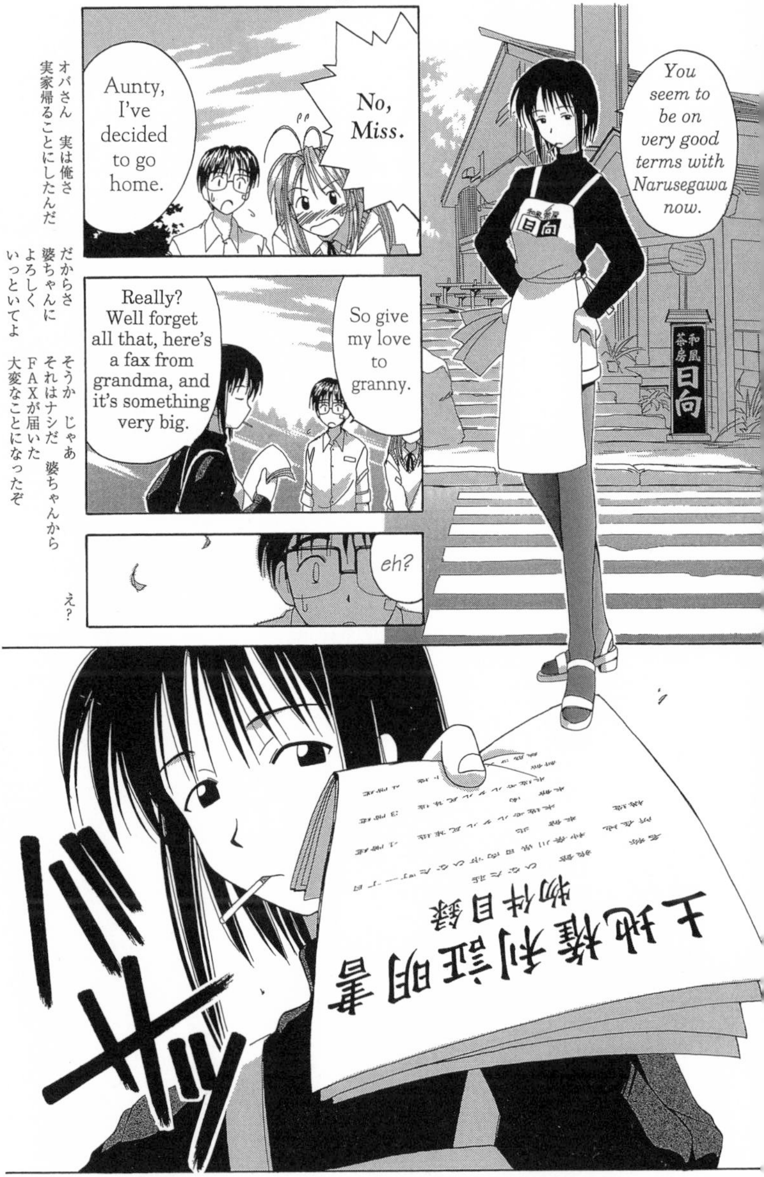

You seem to be on very good terms with Narusegawa now.
No, Miss.
Aunty, I've decided to go home.
So give my love to granny.
Really? Well forget all that, here's a fax from grandma, and it's something very big.
eh?
和風茶房
日向
土地権利証明書
物件目録

(dramatic flourish)

Deed of Land Transfer

List of Properties

土地‥‥権利
証明書？

正式な
書類だ

婆さんが
あんたに全部
あげるってさ

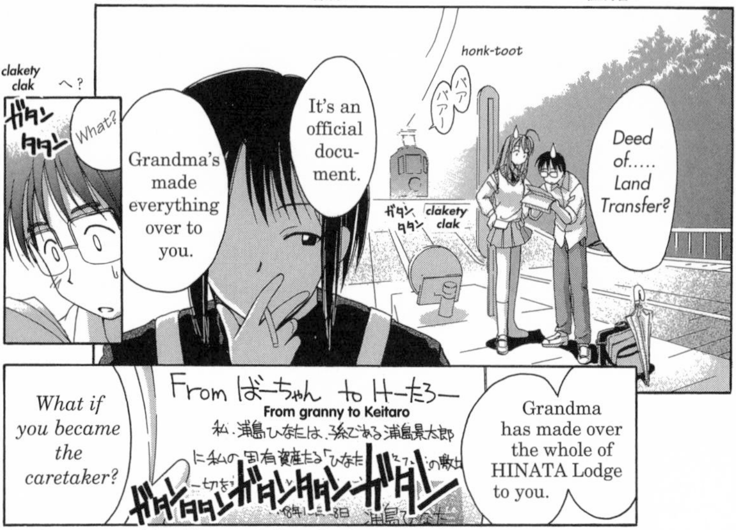

Deed of….. Land Transfer?
パア パアー
honk-toot
It's an official docu-ment.
ガタン タタン
clakety clak
Grandma's made everything over to you.
ガタン タタン
clakety clak
What?
へ？
Grandma has made over the whole of HINATA Lodge to you.
From ばーちゃん to けーたろー
From granny to Keitaro
私、浦島ひなたは、孫である浦島景太郎
に私の固有資産たる「ひなた
ガタン タタン ガタン タタン ガタン
clakety-clak-clakety-clak
What if you became the caretaker?

婆さんが　ひなた荘を全部
あんたにあげるんだって

I, Hinata Urashima, do make over HINATA Lodge, which I own, to my grandson, Keitaro Urashima…

管理人になれば

は!?

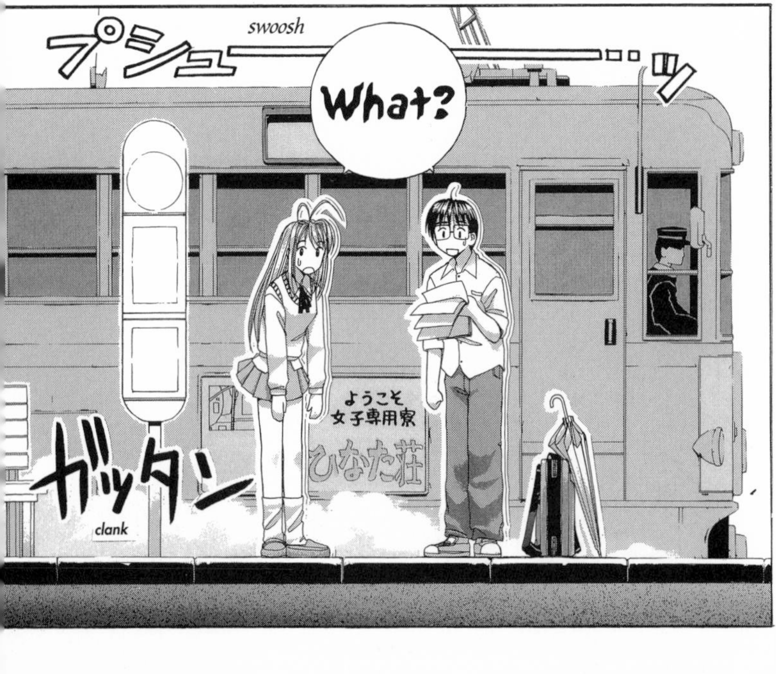

プシューーーーッ
swoosh
What?
ようこそ
女子専用寮
ひなた荘
ガッタン
clank

——というわけで
この女子寮の
管理人になりました

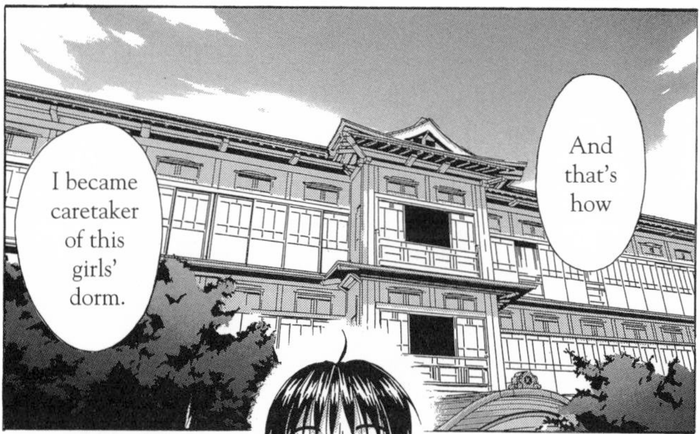
And that's how
I became caretaker of this girls' dorm.

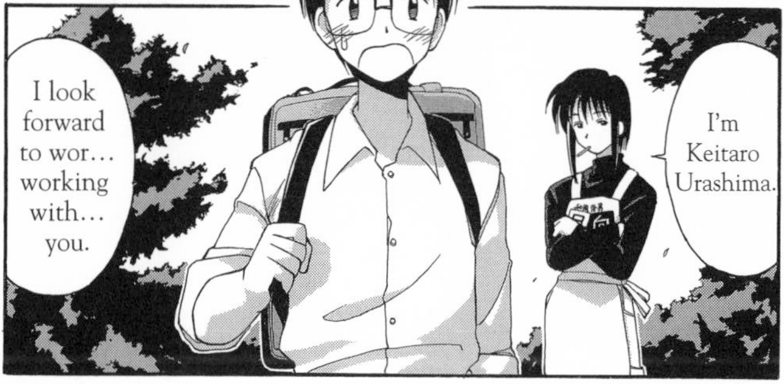
I'm Keitaro Urashima.
I look forward to wor… working with… you.

う　浦島
景太郎です

よろしくお願い
いた‥‥いた‥た

み〜〜　み

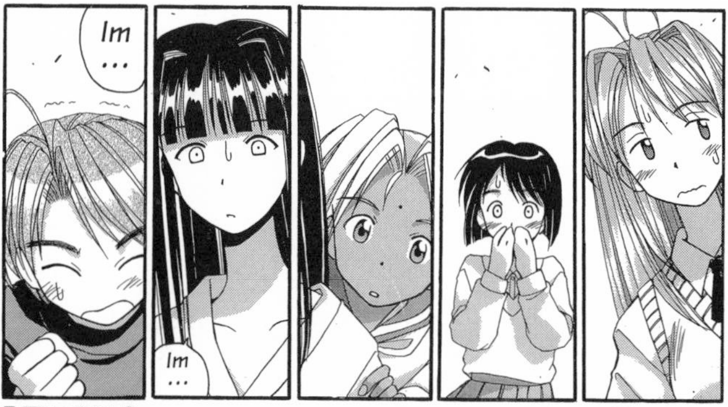
Im …
Im …

「ラブひな」　Love♡Hina

みとめなあ——い

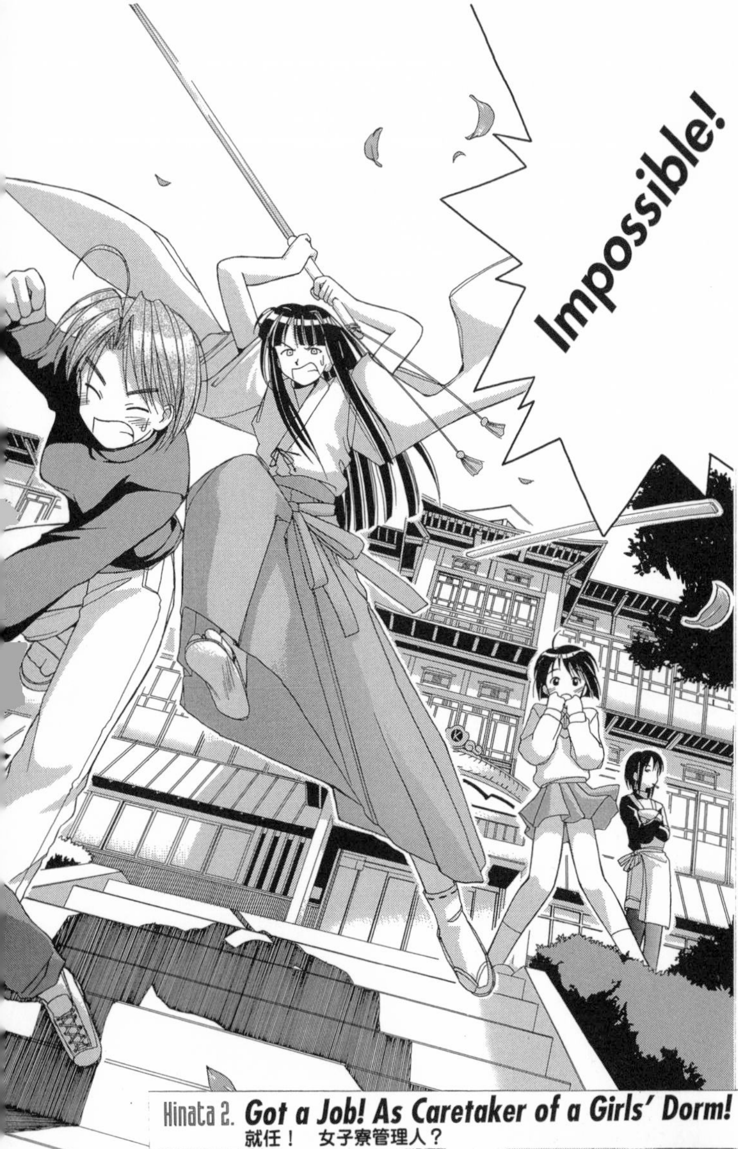
Impossible!

Hinata 2. Got a Job! As Caretaker of a Girls' Dorm!
就任！　女子寮管理人？

いえーい

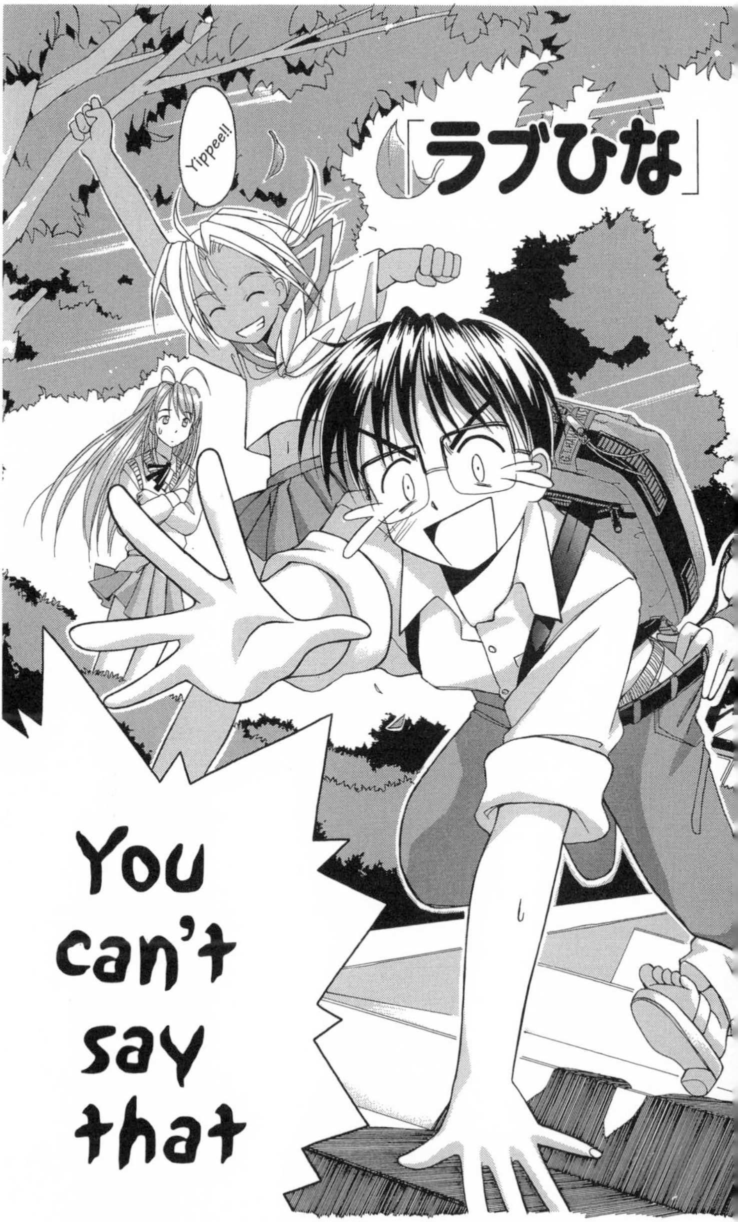
Yippee!!
「ラブひな」
You can't say that

そんなこと
言ったって〜〜〜〜

大体　なんで
男が女子寮の管理人に
なるんや⁉

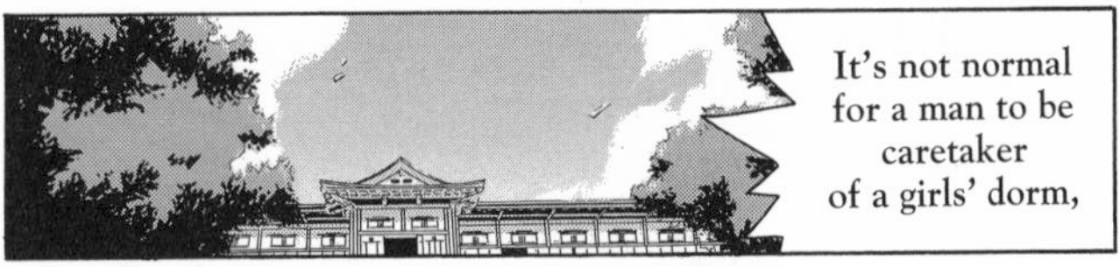
It's not normal for a man to be caretaker of a girls' dorm,

さんざん
「**東大生**」とか
大ボラ吹いて

Gulp

うっ・・

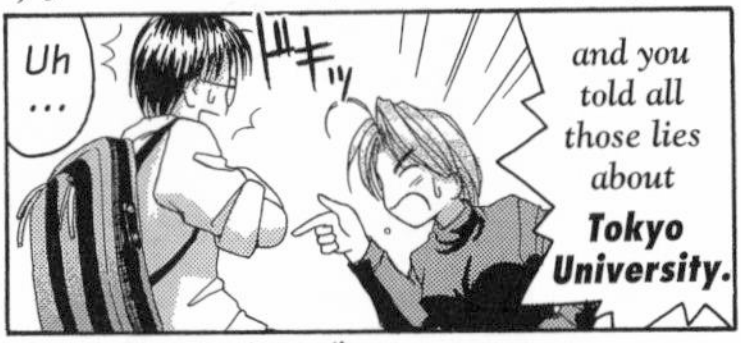
and you told all those lies about **Tokyo University.**
ドキッ
Uh …

(emotional wound)

さらにノゾキ魔
下着ドロの変質者！

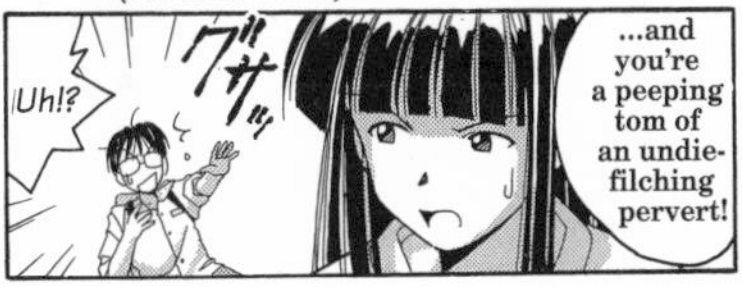
...and you're a peeping tom of an undie-filching pervert!
グザッ
Uh!?

うぅ⁉

私は裸見られて
胸もまれたわね
そーいえば

おまけに
ロリコンや！

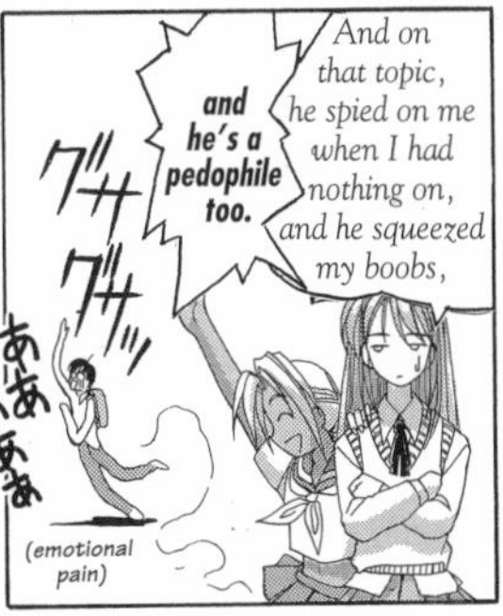
And on that topic, he spied on me when I had nothing on, and he squeezed my boobs,
and he's a pedophile too.
グザ
グザッ
ああ
あああ
(emotional pain)

Aaaaaaaaah

……これは
婆さんの指示なんだ

仕方ないだろ

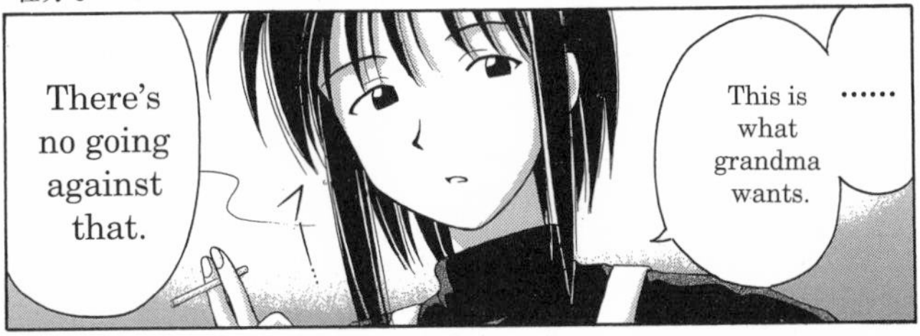
This is what grandma wants. ……
There's no going against that.

Did you hear?
The old lady, she…

We can't go against
the old lady's wishes.

ちょ　ちょっと
婆ちゃんが　なにか…？

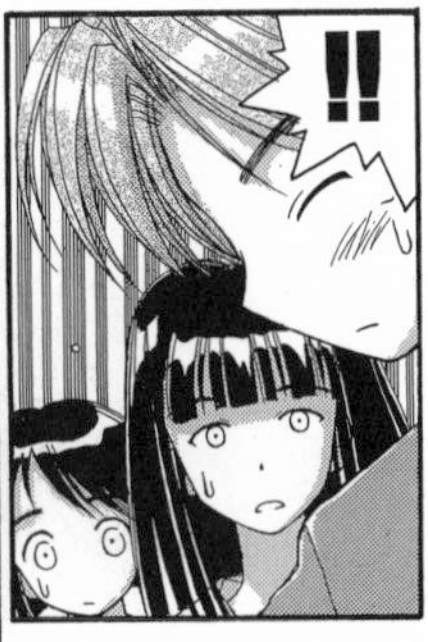
!!

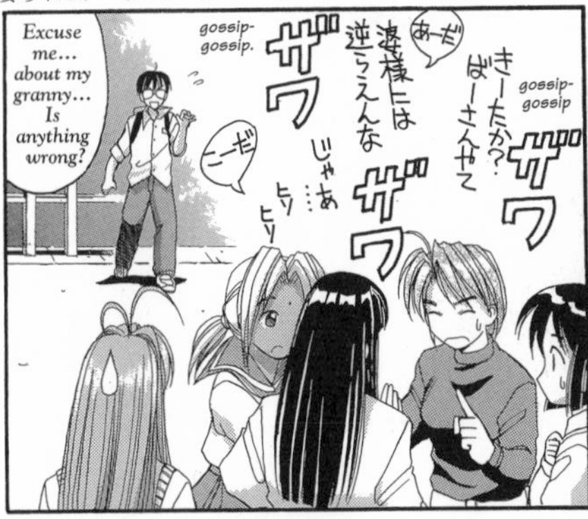
gossip-gossip
きーたか？ばーさんやて
ザワ
ザワ
あーだ
婆様には逆らえんな
gossip-gossip.
ザワ
じゃあ…ヒソヒソ
こーだ
Excuse me… about my granny… Is anything wrong?

whisper-whisper-
whisper-whisper

····分かった

あんたを当女子寮の
「管理人見習い」として
受け入れるわ

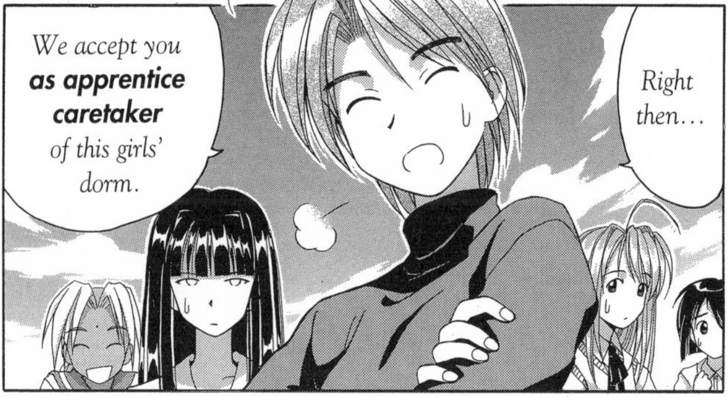
Right then…
We accept you **as apprentice caretaker** of this girls' dorm.

え····

The old lady…
Well…
Nothing we can do then.

な　何で
急に····!?

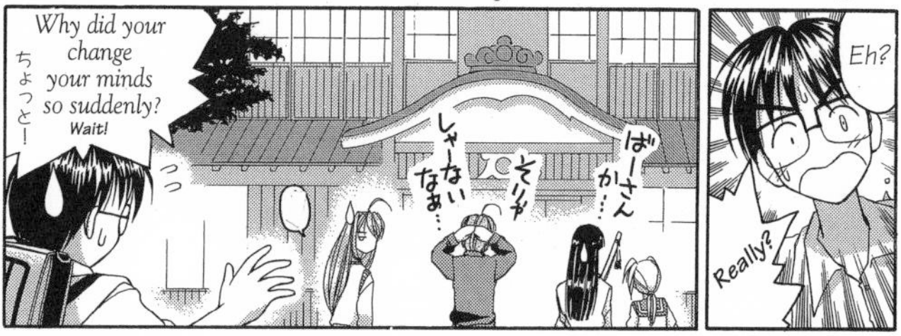
Eh?
Really?
ばーさんか…
そりゃ
しゃーないなぁ…
Why did your change your minds so suddenly?
ちょっと－!
Wait!

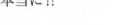

本当に!?

はっ!?

し····
しのぶちゃん

ああっ

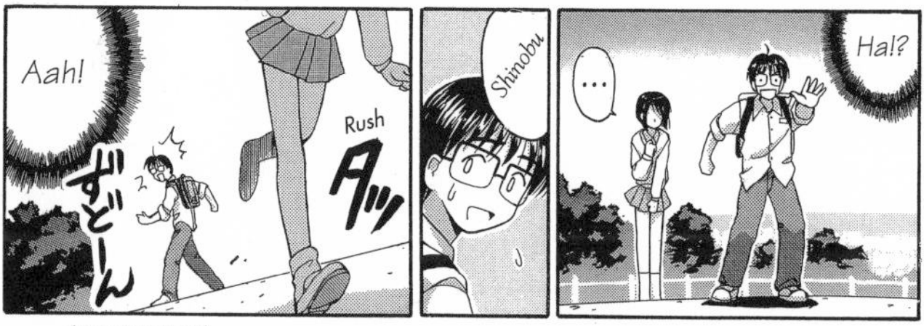
Ha!?
…
Shinobu
Aah!
Rush
タッ
ずどーん

(massive shock)

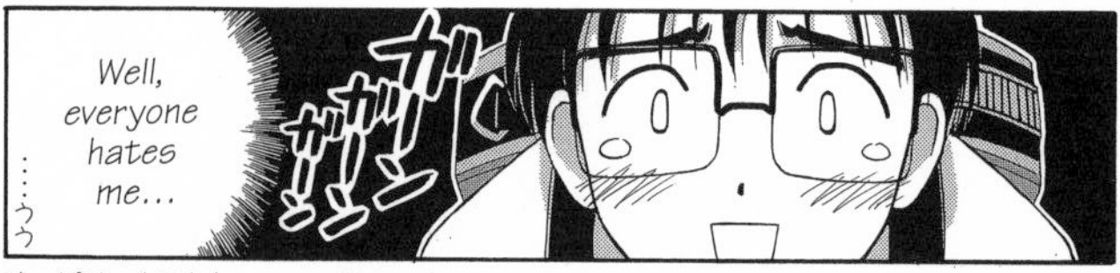
Well, everyone hates me…
…うう

やっぱり　キラわれ
ちゃったのかな

(despair)

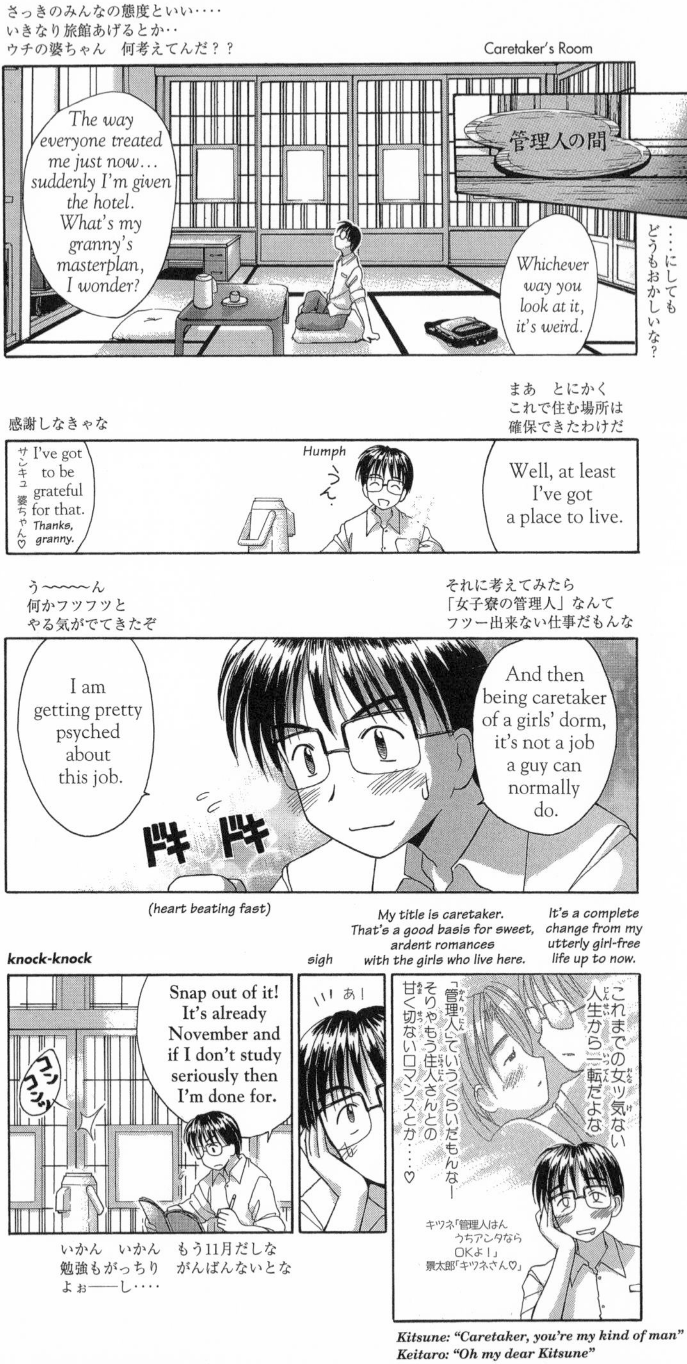
さっきのみんなの態度といい‥‥
いきなり旅館あげるとか‥
ウチの婆ちゃん　何考えてんだ？？
Caretaker's Room
管理人の間
‥‥にしても どうもおかしいな？
Whichever way you look at it, it's weird.
The way everyone treated me just now… suddenly I'm given the hotel. What's my granny's masterplan, I wonder?
まあ　とにかく これで住む場所は 確保できたわけだ
感謝しなきゃな
Well, at least I've got a place to live.
Humph
うん
I've got to be grateful for that.
サンキュ 婆ちゃん♡
Thanks, granny.
それに考えてみたら 「女子寮の管理人」なんて フツー出来ない仕事だもんな
う〜〜〜〜ん 何かフツフツと やる気がでてきたぞ
And then being caretaker of a girls' dorm, it's not a job a guy can normally do.
I am getting pretty psyched about this job.
ドキ ドキ
(heart beating fast)
これまでの女ッ気ない人生から一転だよな
「管理人」ていうくらいだもんな
そりゃもう住人さんとの甘く切ないロマンスとか‥‥♡
It's a complete change from my utterly girl-free life up to now.
My title is caretaker. That's a good basis for sweet, ardent romances with the girls who live here.
キツネ「管理人はん うちアンタなら OKよ！」
景太郎「キツネさん♡」
Kitsune: "Caretaker, you're my kind of man"
Keitaro: "Oh my dear Kitsune"
!!! あ！
sigh
Snap out of it! It's already November and if I don't study seriously then I'm done for.
コンコンッ
knock-knock
いかん　いかん　もう11月だしな
勉強もがっちり　がんばんないとな
よぉ——し‥‥

あのな　ちょっと
管理人さんに
頼みあるんや

キ・・・・
キツネさん⁉

つ
つきあうって
どこへ・・・・？

つきおうて
くれへん？

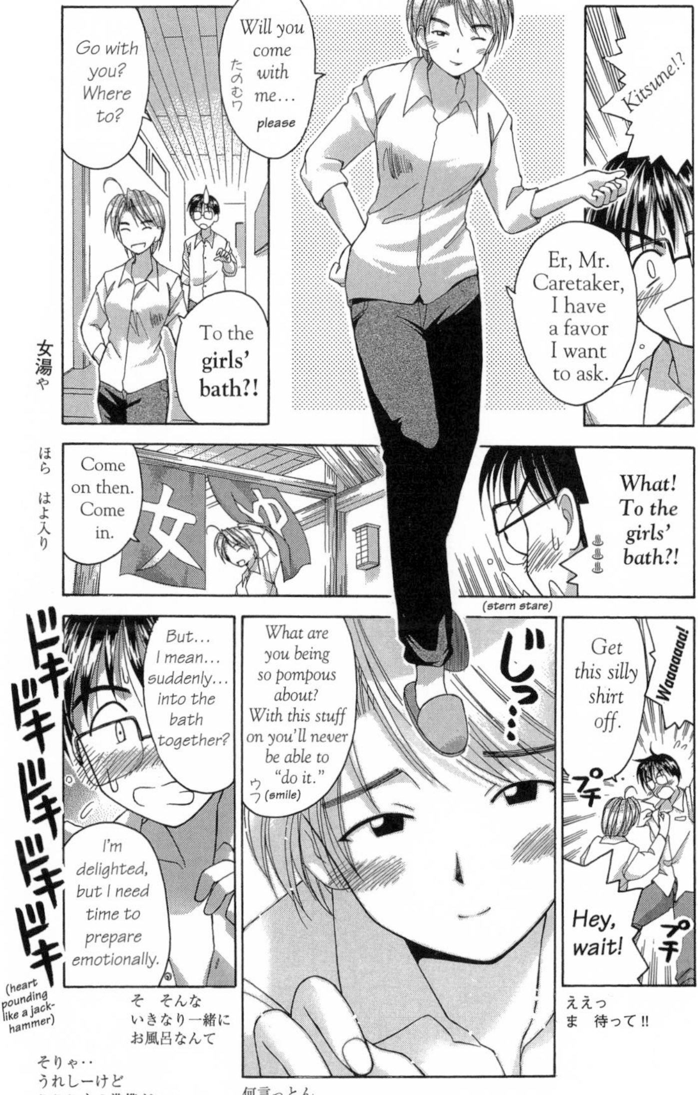
Kitsune!?
Er, Mr. Caretaker, I have a favor I want to ask.
Will you come with me…
たのむワ
please
Go with you? Where to?
To the girls' bath?!
What! To the girls' bath?!
Come on then. Come in.
Get this silly shirt off.
Waaaaaaa!
わわわ
プチ
プチ
Hey, wait!
pop pop
(stern stare)
じっ…
What are you being so pompous about? With this stuff on you'll never be able to "do it."
ウフ
(smile)
But… I mean… suddenly… into the bath together?
I'm delighted, but I need time to prepare emotionally.
ドキドキドキドキ
(heart pounding like a jack-hammer)

女湯や

ええ
「女湯」――
⁉

ほら　はよ入り

こんな
Yシャツなんか　はよ脱ぎ

ええっ
ま　待って‼

何言っとん
こんなん着とったら
邪魔くさくてできへんやろ？

そ　そんな
いきなり一緒に
お風呂なんて

そりゃ・・
うれしーけど
こここ心の準備が・・・・

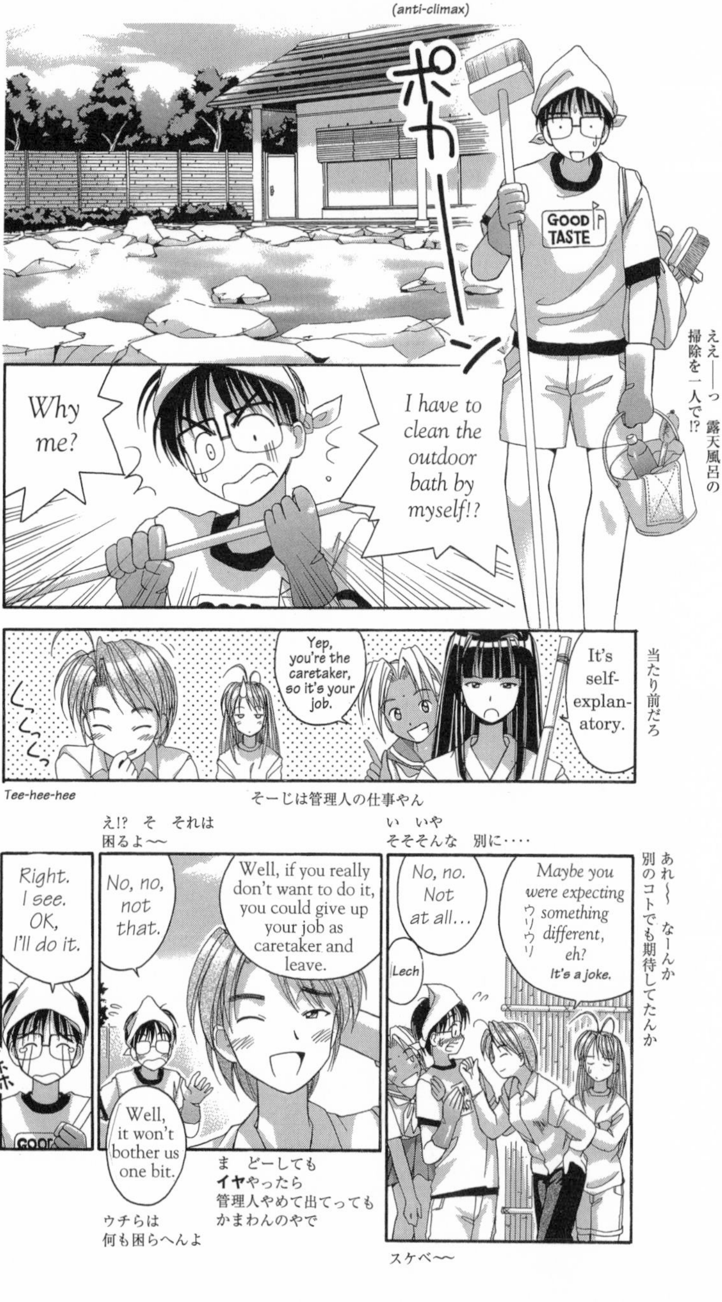
(anti-climax)
ポカーン
ええ——っ 露天風呂の掃除を一人で!?
I have to clean the outdoor bath by myself!?
なんで俺が!?
Why me?
当たり前だろ
It's self-explanatory.
そーじは管理人の仕事やん
Yep, you're the caretaker, so it's your job.
くっくっくっ
Tee-hee-hee
あれ〜 なーんか別のコトでも期待してたんか
Maybe you were expecting something different, eh?
ウリウリ
It's a joke.
い いや そそそんな 別に····
No, no. Not at all…
Lech
スケベ〜〜
ま どーしても イヤやったら 管理人やめて出てってもかまわんのやで
Well, if you really don't want to do it, you could give up your job as caretaker and leave.
ウチらは何も困らへんよ
Well, it won't bother us one bit.
え!? そ それは困るよ〜〜
No, no, not that.
…わ 分かったよ やるよ やりますよ
Right. I see. OK, I'll do it.
トホホ

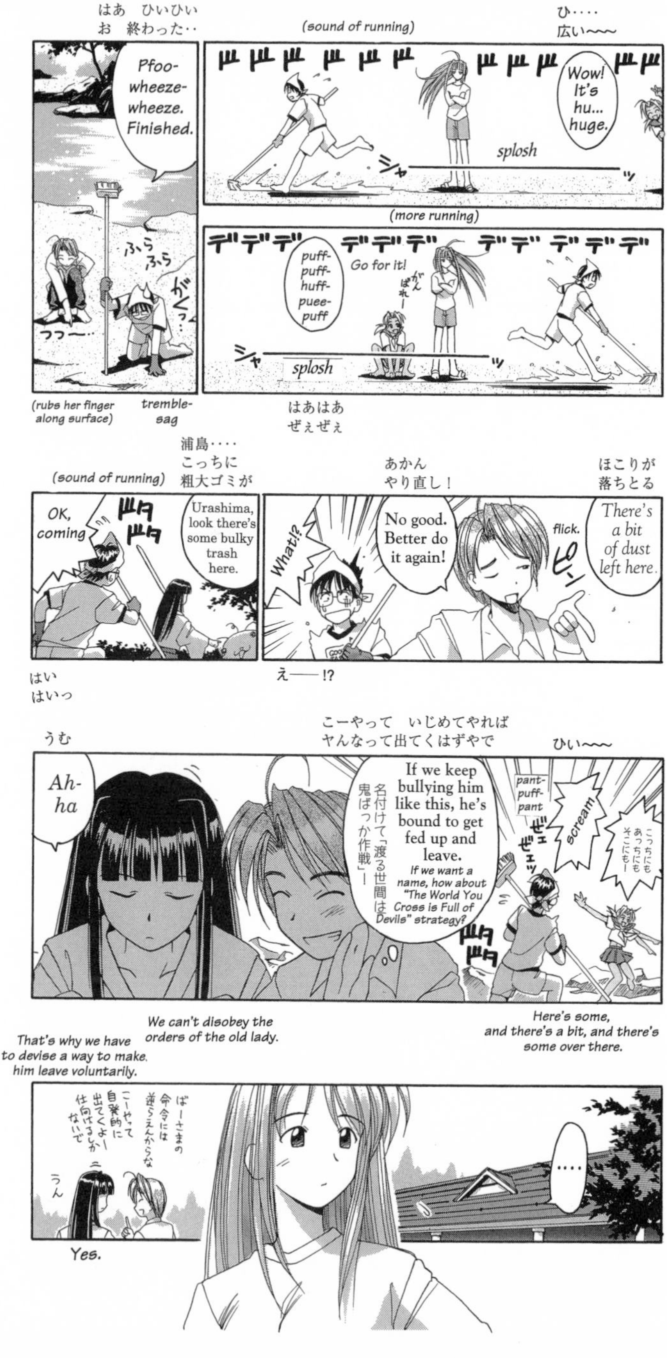
ひ····
広い~~~
Wow! It's hu... huge.
(sound of running)
splosh
シャ ッ
はあ ひいひい
お 終わった··
Pfoo-wheeze-wheeze. Finished.
ふら ふら
がくっ··
つつ~
(rubs her finger along surface)
tremble-sag
(more running)
デデデ
Go for it!
がんばれー
puff-puff-huff-puee-puff
splosh
シャ ッ
はあはあ
ぜぇぜぇ
ほこりが
落ちとる
There's a bit of dust left here.
ピン
flick.
あかん
やり直し!
No good. Better do it again!
What!?
え——!?
浦島····
こっちに
粗大ゴミが
Urashima, look there's some bulky trash here.
(sound of running)
OK, coming
はい
はいっ
ひい~~~
こっちにもあっちにもそこにもー
scream
pant-puff-pant
ゼェゼェッ
こーやって いじめてやれば
ヤんなって出てくはずやで
If we keep bullying him like this, he's bound to get fed up and leave.
名付けて「渡る世間は鬼ばっか作戦」ー
If we want a name, how about "The World You Cross is Full of Devils" strategy?
うむ
Ah-ha
Here's some, and there's a bit, and there's some over there.
We can't disobey the orders of the old lady.
That's why we have to devise a way to make him leave voluntarily.
ばーさまの命令には逆らえんからな
こーやって自発的に出てくよー仕向けるしかないで
うん
Yes.
····

露天風呂って
なんでこんな
だだっ広いんだよ

こんなの
一人でやれなんて
ムリあるよな〜〜

あたた
手が豆だらけに
なっちまったよ

コラなに
サボッてんのよ？

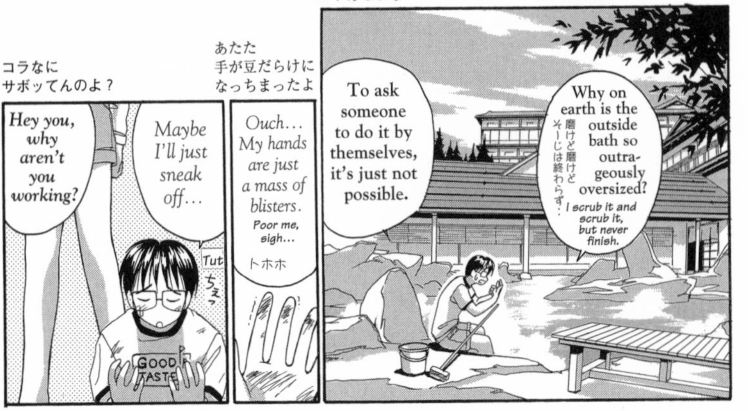
Why on earth is the outside bath so outra-geously oversized?
磨けど磨けど そーじは終わらず…
I scrub it and scrub it, but never finish.
To ask someone to do it by themselves, it's just not possible.
Ouch… My hands are just a mass of blisters.
Poor me, sigh…
トホホ
Hey you, why aren't you working?
Maybe I'll just sneak off…
Tut
ちぇっ

もう　サボッちゃ
おっかな ——

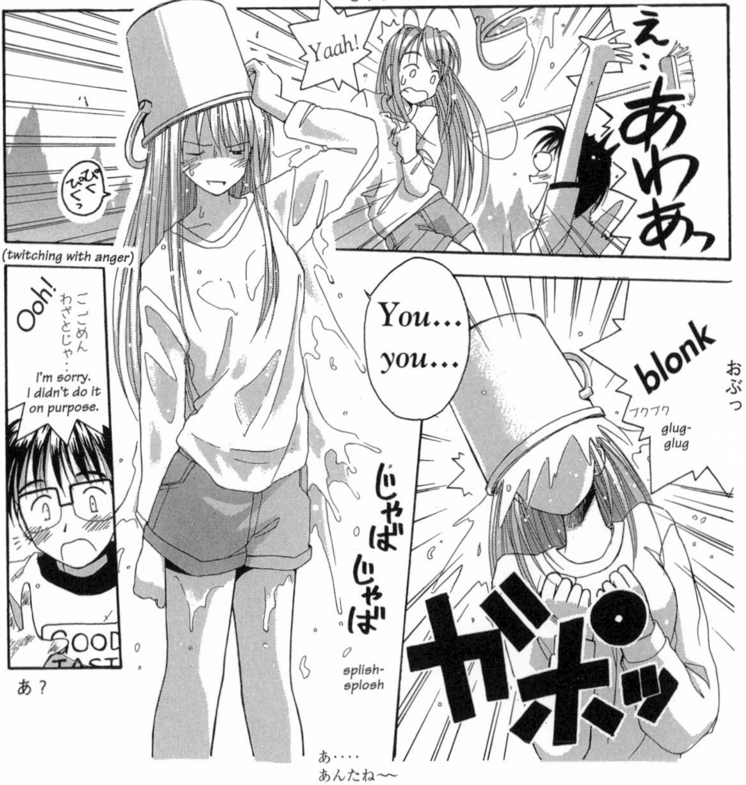
Argh!
え…あわあっ
きゃっ
Yaah!
ぴくぴくっ
(twitching with anger)
You… you…
ガポッ
blonk
おぶっ
ブクブク
glug-glug
じゃばじゃば
splish-splosh
Ooh!
ごごめん わざとじゃ…
I'm sorry. I didn't do it on purpose.

あ？

あ‥‥
あんたね〜〜

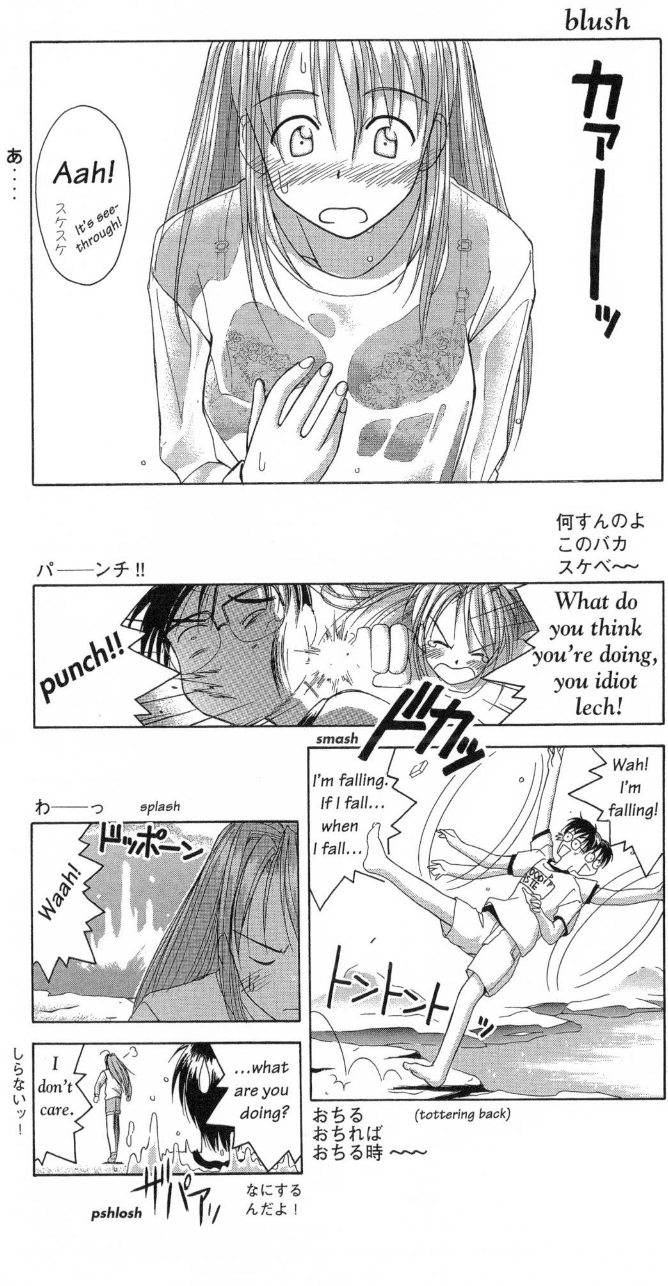
blush
カァーーッ
あ‥‥
Aah!
スケスケ
It's see-through!
何すんのよ
このバカ
スケベ〜〜
What do you think you're doing, you idiot lech!
パーーンチ!!
punch!!
ドカッ
smash
わわ‥おちる!
Wah! I'm falling!
I'm falling. If I fall… when I fall…
トントントンッ
おちる
おちれば
おちる時〜〜
(tottering back)
わーーっ
splash
ドッポーン
Waah!
…what are you doing?
なにするんだよ!
ザパァッ
pshlosh
I don't care.
しらないッ!

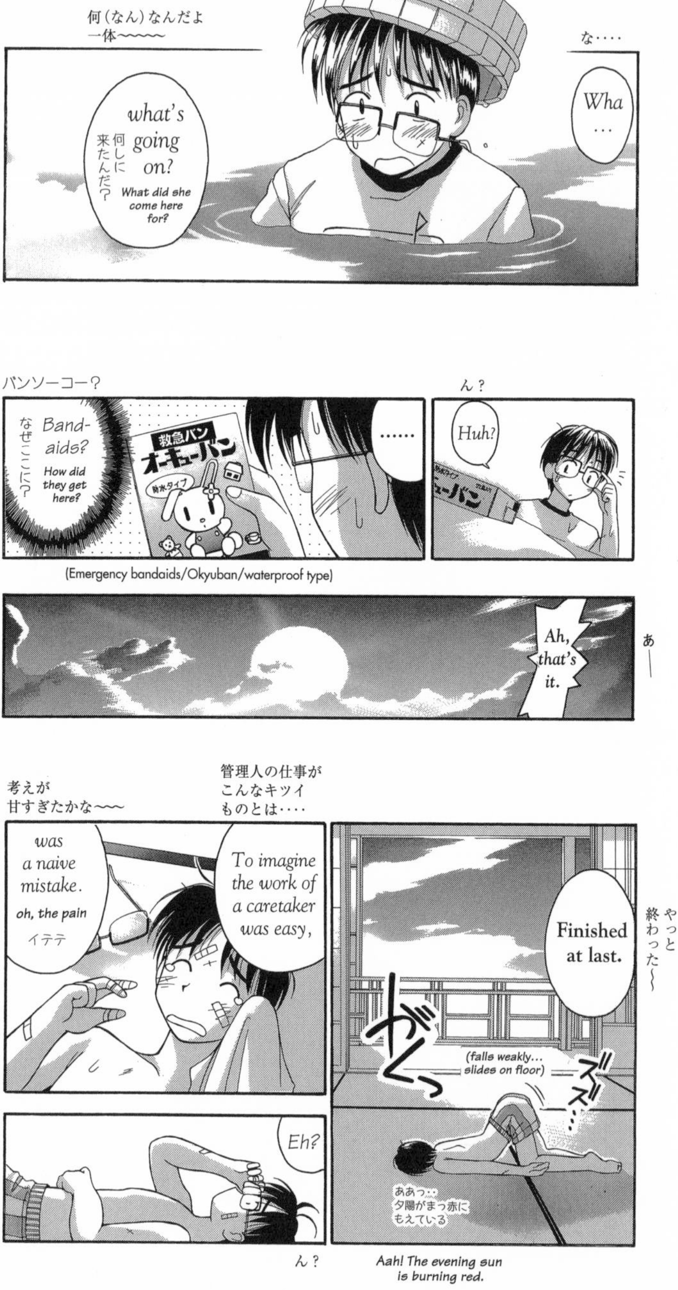
な‥‥
Wha …
何(なん)なんだよ 一体~~~~
what's going on?
何しに来たんだ?
What did she come here for?
ん?
Huh?
……
バンソーコー?
Band-aids?
なぜここに?
How did they get here?
救急バン
オーキューバン
防水タイプ
(Emergency bandaids/Okyuban/waterproof type)
あ——
Ah, that's it.
管理人の仕事が こんなキツイ ものとは‥‥
To imagine the work of a caretaker was easy,
考えが 甘すぎたかな~~~
was a naive mistake.
oh, the pain
イテテ
Eh?
ん?
やっと 終わった~
Finished at last.
がくっ
ズズズ‥
(falls weakly… slides on floor)
ああっ‥ 夕陽がまっ赤に もえている
Aah! The evening sun is burning red.

おわっ

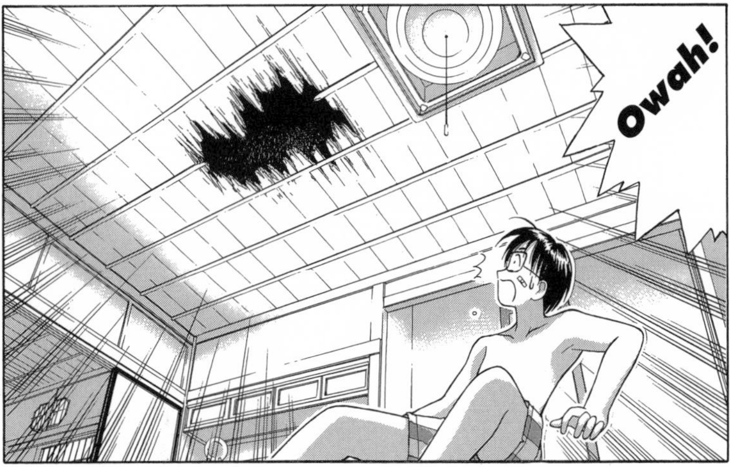
Owah!

あちゃ ——
天井に穴が
あいてるよ～

あんがい
ボロ旅館だな ——

応急処置でも
しとくか

一応
管理人だしな

・・・・アレ？
何だコレ

フタがして
あるぞ・・・・

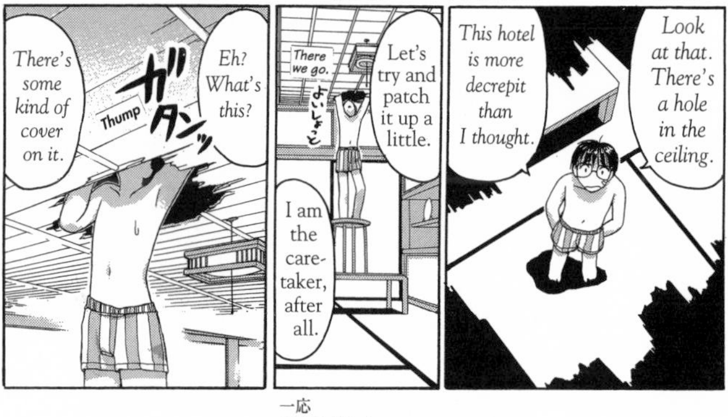
Look at that. There's a hole in the ceiling.
This hotel is more decrepit than I thought.
Let's try and patch it up a little.
There we go.
よいしょっと
I am the care-taker, after all.
Eh? What's this?
ガタンッ
Thump
There's some kind of cover on it.

wobble-bump

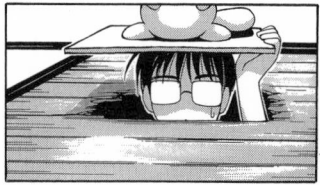

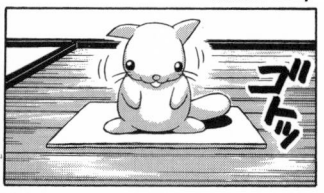

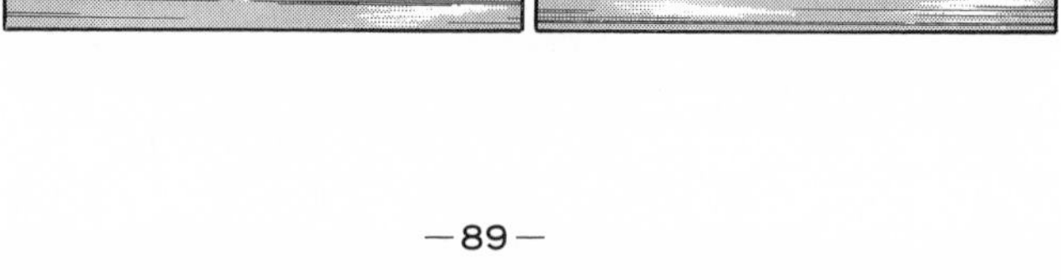
ゴトッ

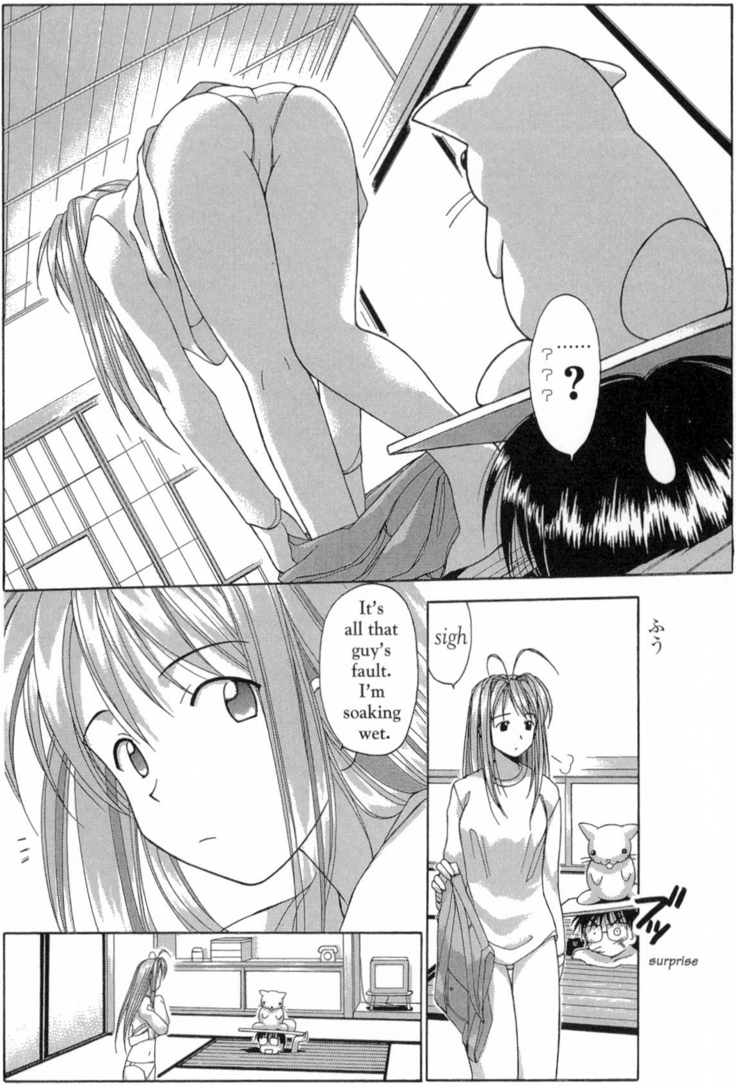
......
???
?
ふう
sigh
ブッ
surprise
It's all that guy's fault. I'm soaking wet.

全く　あいつの
せいで　びしょ
濡れじゃない‥‥

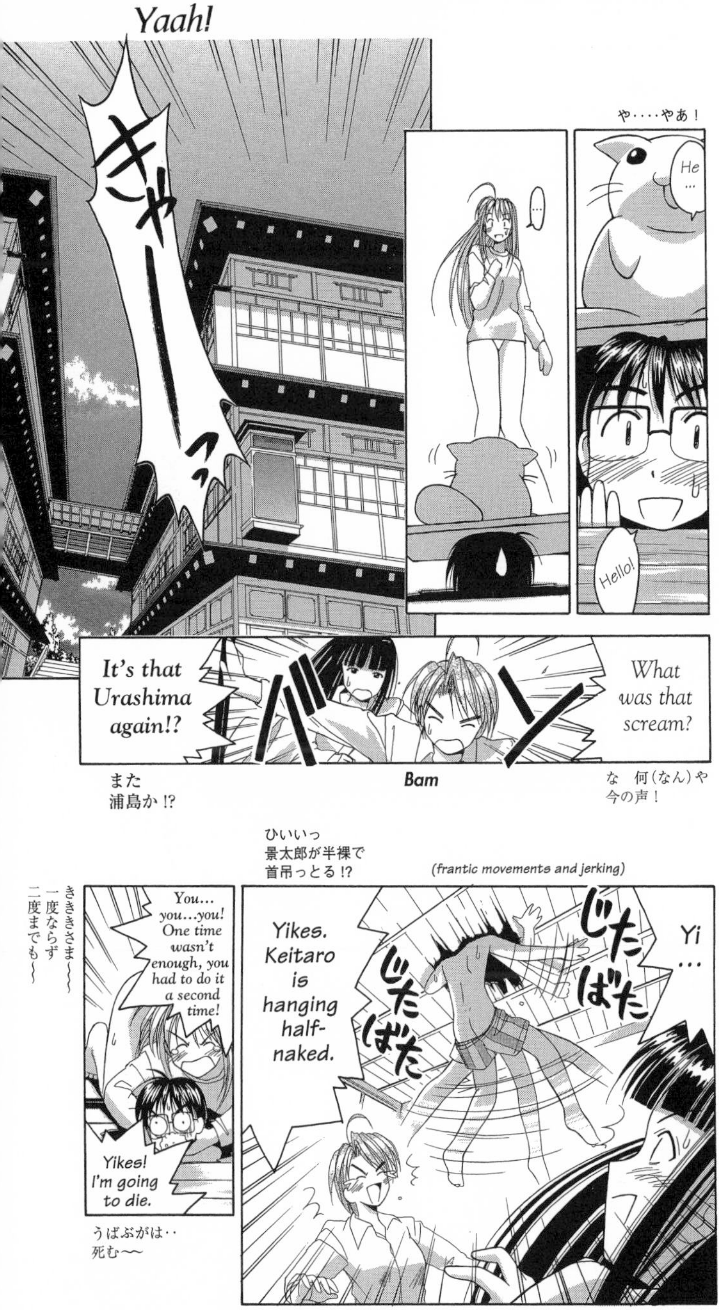
Yaah!
キャ――ッ
や・・・・やあ！
He…
…
Hello!
What was that scream?
な　何(なん)や
今の声！
It's that Urashima again!?
また
浦島か!?
Bam
ひ・・・・
Yi…
ひいいっ
景太郎が半裸で
首吊っとる!?
Yikes. Keitaro is hanging half-naked.
じたばた
じたばた
(frantic movements and jerking)
ききさま〜〜
一度ならず
二度までも〜〜
You… you…you! One time wasn't enough, you had to do it a second time!
Yikes! I'm going to die.
うばぶがは・・
死む〜〜

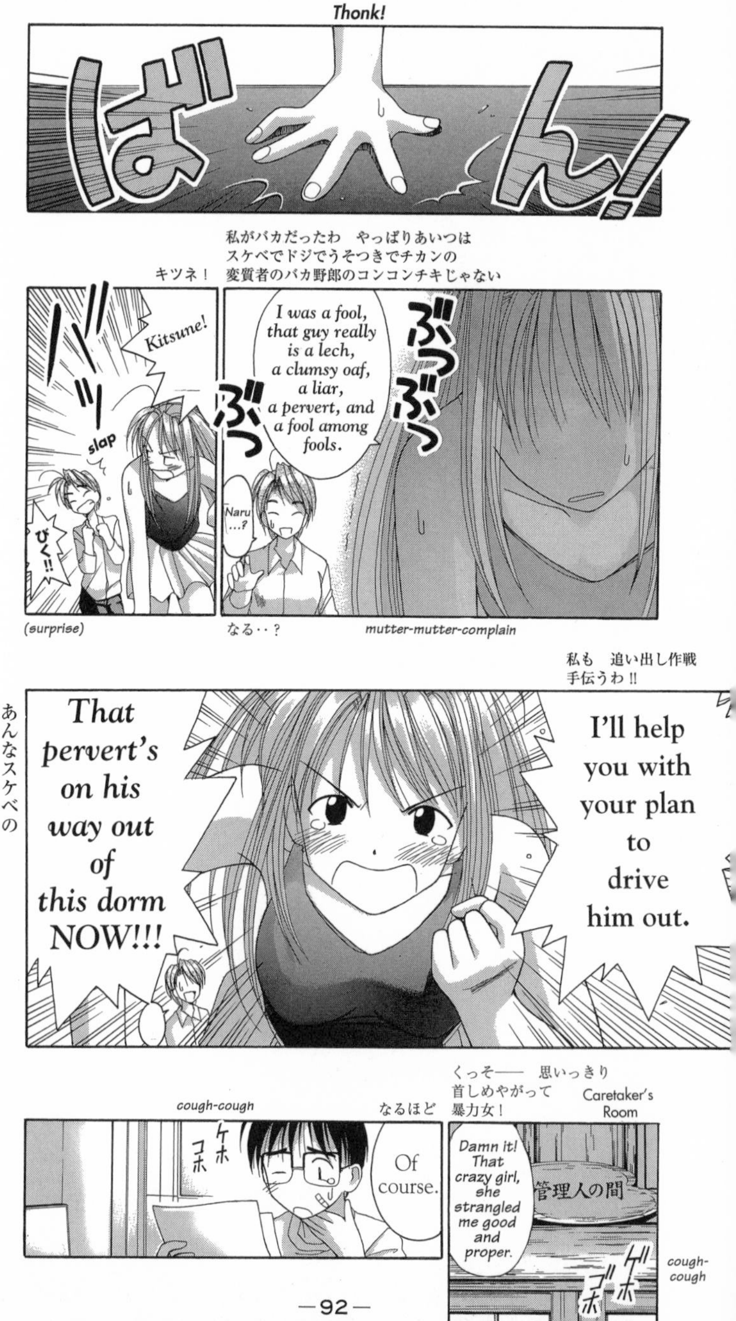
Thonk!
ばーん!
私がバカだったわ　やっぱりあいつは
スケベでドジでうそつきでチカンの
変質者のバカ野郎のコンコンチキじゃない
I was a fool, that guy really is a lech, a clumsy oaf, a liar, a pervert, and a fool among fools.
ぶつぶつぶつ
mutter-mutter-complain
Naru ...?
なる‥？
キツネ！
Kitsune!
slap
びく!!
(surprise)
私も　追い出し作戦
手伝うわ !!
I'll help you with your plan to drive him out.
あんなスケベの
バカは即刻（そっこく）退寮よっ!!!
That pervert's on his way out of this dorm NOW!!!
Caretaker's Room
管理人の間
くっそ——　思いっきり
首しめやがって
暴力女！
Damn it! That crazy girl, she strangled me good and proper.
ゲホゴホ
cough-cough
なるほど
Of course.
ケホコホ
cough-cough

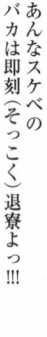

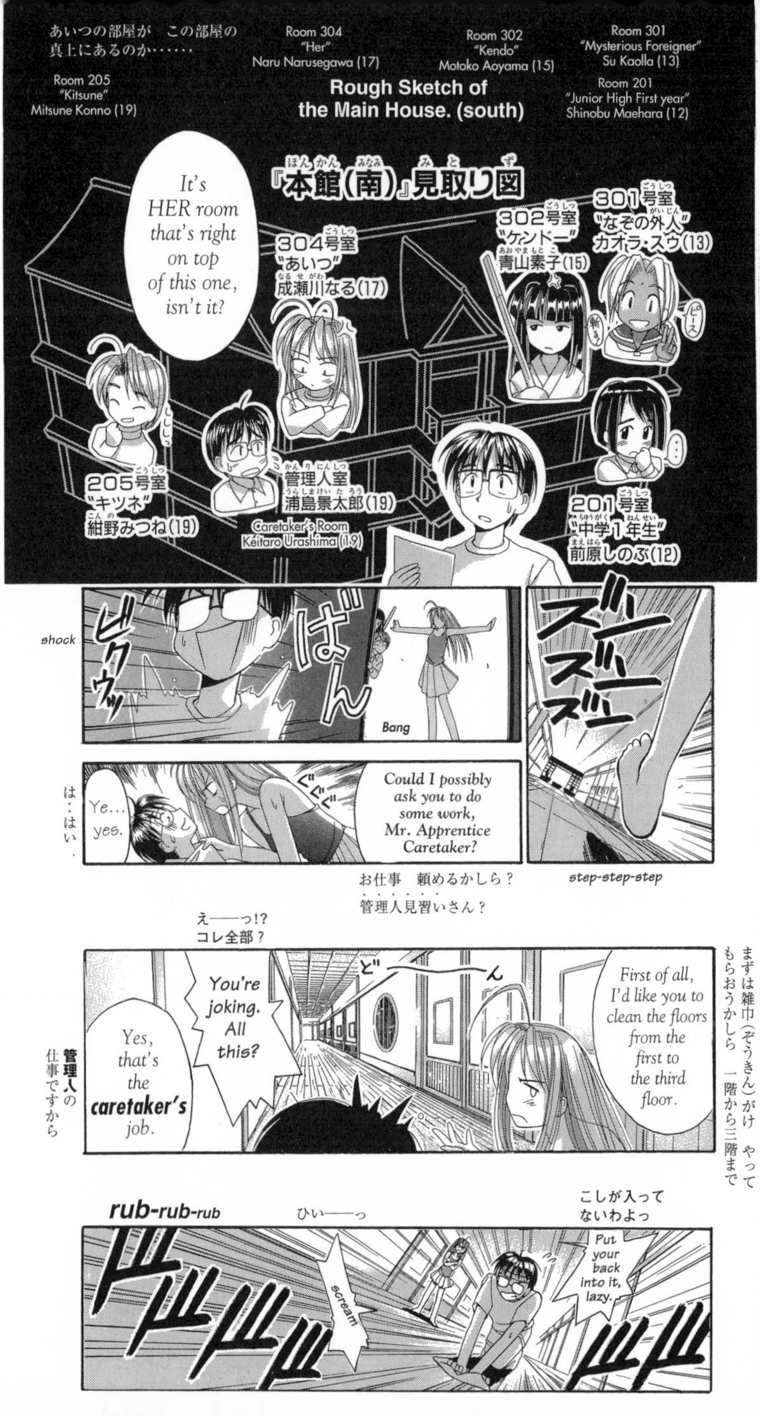

あいつの部屋が　この部屋の真上にあるのか……
Room 205
"Kitsune"
Mitsune Konno (19)
Room 304
"Her"
Naru Narusegawa (17)
Room 302
"Kendo"
Motoko Aoyama (15)
Room 301
"Mysterious Foreigner"
Su Kaolla (13)
Rough Sketch of the Main House. (south)
Room 201
"Junior High First year"
Shinobu Maehara (12)
It's HER room that's right on top of this one, isn't it?
『本館(南)』見取り図
301号室
"なぞの外人"
カオラ・スウ(13)
302号室
"ケンドー"
青山素子(15)
304号室
"あいつ"
成瀬川なる(17)
斬る
ピース
205号室
"キツネ"
紺野みつね(19)
管理人室
浦島景太郎(19)
Caretaker's Room
Keitaro Urashima (19)
201号室
"中学1年生"
前原しのぶ(12)
ズバーン
ズズズ
ばん
ビクウッ
shock
Bang
Could I possibly ask you to do some work, Mr. Apprentice Caretaker?
ぐぐぐ
Ye... yes.
は・はい・
step-step-step
お仕事　頼めるかしら？
管理人見習いさん？
First of all, I'd like you to clean the floors from the first to the third floor.
まずは雑巾(ぞうきん)がけ　やってもらおうかしら　一階から三階まで
ど―――ん
You're joking. All this?
え――っ!?
コレ全部？
Yes, that's the caretaker's job.
管理人の仕事ですから
rub-rub-rub
ひい――っ
scream
Put your back into it, lazy.
こしが入ってないわよっ

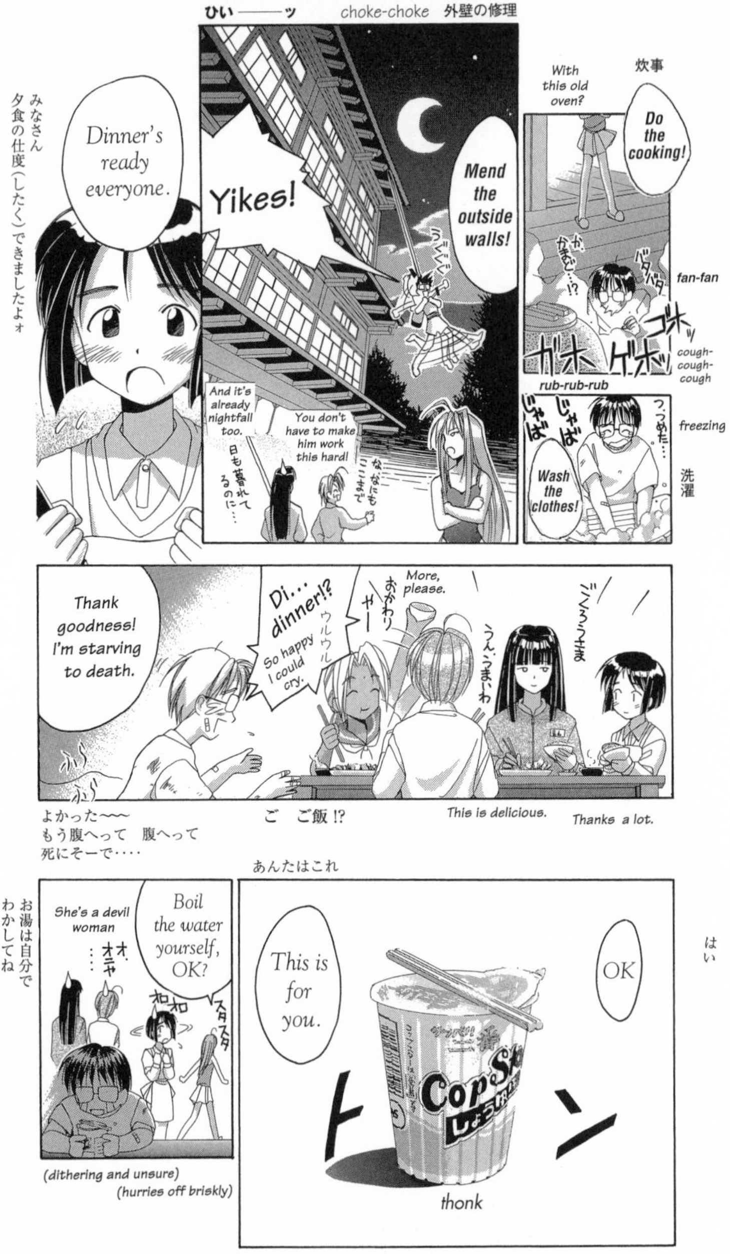

みなさん
夕食の仕度(したく)できましたよォ
Dinner's ready everyone.
ひい———ッ
Yikes!
choke-choke
うぐぐぐ
外壁の修理
Mend the outside walls!
日も暮れてるのに…
And it's already nightfall too.
ななにもここまで
You don't have to make him work this hard!
炊事
Do the cooking!
か、かまど…!?
With this old oven?
バタバタ
fan-fan
ガホ ゲボ ゴホッ
cough-cough-cough
洗濯
Wash the clothes!
じゃばじゃば
rub-rub-rub
つ、つめた…
freezing
Thank goodness! I'm starving to death.
よかった〜〜
もう腹へって　腹へって
死にそーで‥‥
Di… dinner!?
ご　ご飯 !?
ウルウル
So happy I could cry.
おかわりー
More, please.
うん、うまいわ
This is delicious.
ごくろうさま
Thanks a lot.
お湯は自分でわかしてね
Boil the water yourself, OK?
オ、オニヤ…
She's a devil woman
オロオロ
(dithering and unsure)
スタスタ
(hurries off briskly)
あんたはこれ
This is for you.
はい
OK
トン
thonk

ううっ　わびしい‥
女子寮の管理人なんて
ちょっと期待
してたけど‥‥
Cram School Boy Bath
This way (Narusegawa)
大変なばっかで
何も楽しいこと
ないじゃないか
chirp-chirp

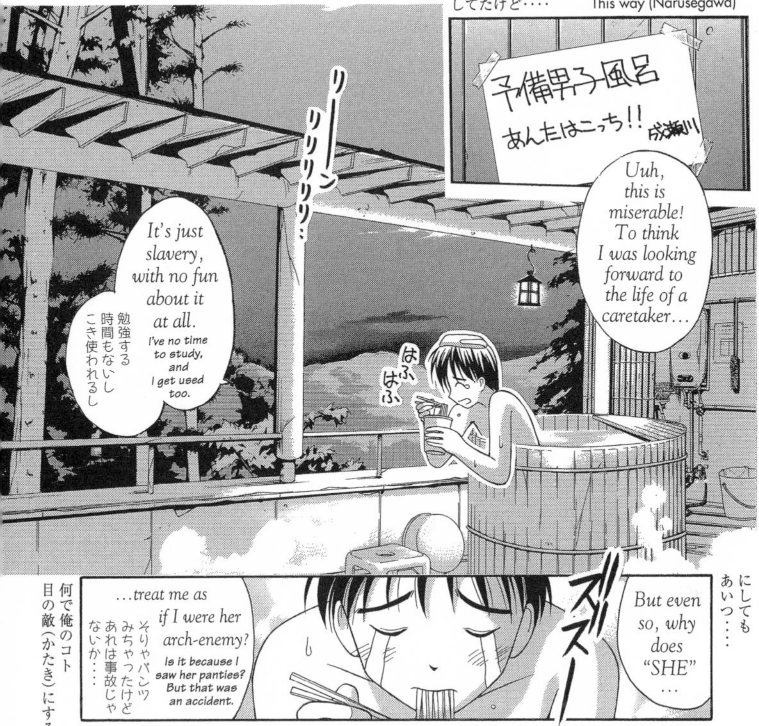
予備男子風呂
あんたはこっち!!　成瀬川
Uuh, this is miserable! To think I was looking forward to the life of a caretaker…
リーーーンリリリリリ‥
It's just slavery, with no fun about it at all.
勉強する時間もないしこき使われるし
I've no time to study, and I get used too.
はふはふ
But even so, why does "SHE"…
ズズーー
…treat me as if I were her arch-enemy?
そりゃパンツみちゃったけどあれは事故じゃないか‥‥
Is it because I saw her panties? But that was an accident.

にしてもあいつ‥‥
何で俺のコト目の敵(かたき)にするんだ?
slurp-slurp
なんだ?
話し声が
したような‥‥
chirp-chirp
plosh

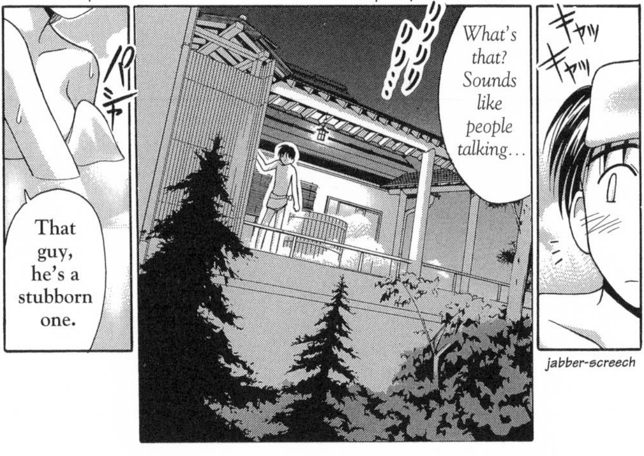
ギャッギャッ
What's that? Sounds like people talking…
リリリリリ‥‥
パシャ
That guy, he's a stubborn one.

jabber-screech
しっかし
しぶといなー　あいつ

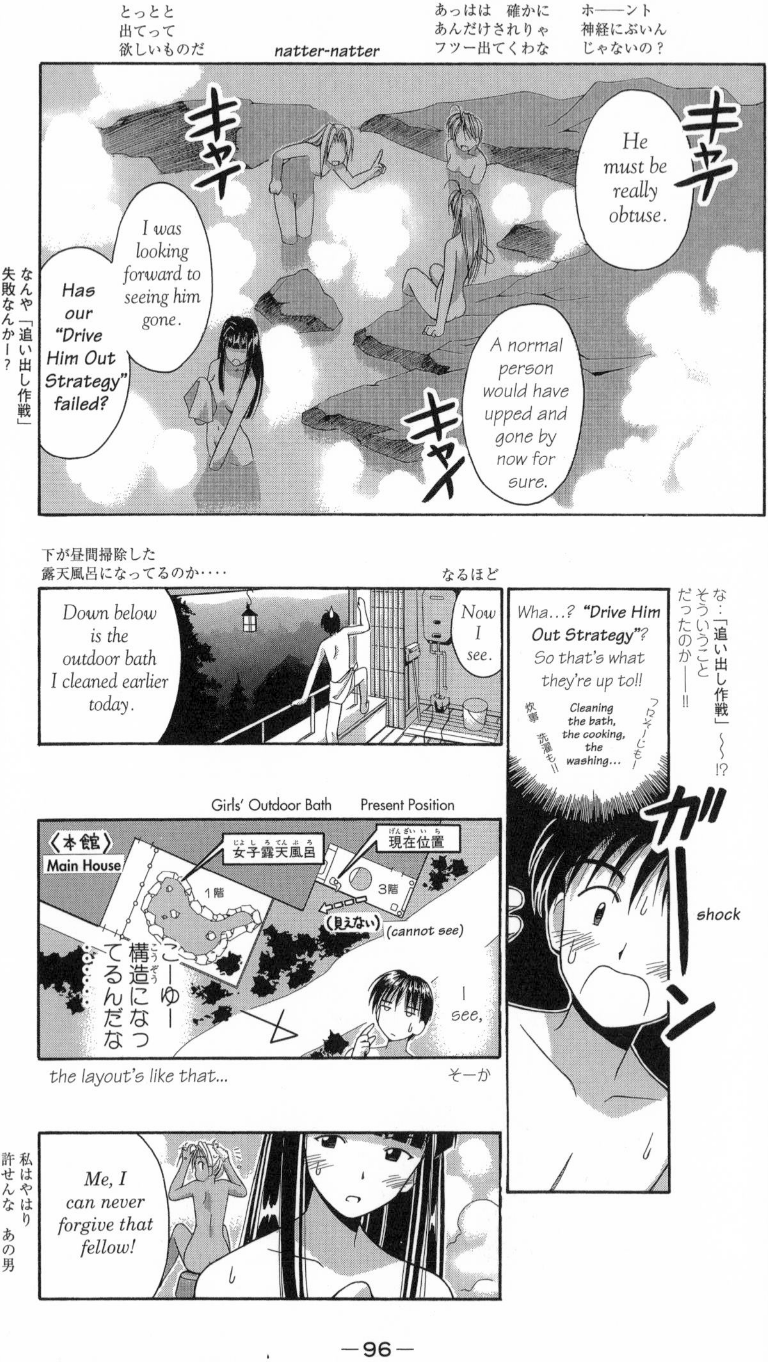
ホ――ント
神経にぶいん
じゃないの？
He must be really obtuse.
あっはは　確かに
あんだけされりゃ
フツー出てくわな
A normal person would have upped and gone by now for sure.
キャ
キャ
キャイ
natter-natter
とっとと
出てって
欲しいものだ
I was looking forward to seeing him gone.
なんや「追い出し作戦」
失敗なんかー？
Has our "Drive Him Out Strategy" failed?
なるほど
Now I see.
下が昼間掃除した
露天風呂になってるのか‥‥
Down below is the outdoor bath I cleaned earlier today.
な‥「追い出し作戦」～!?
そういうこと
だったのか――!!
Wha…? "Drive Him Out Strategy"? So that's what they're up to!!
フロそーじも‐
炊事
洗濯も!!
Cleaning the bath, the cooking, the washing…
ガ――ン
shock
Girls' Outdoor Bath
Present Position
〈本館〉
Main House
女子露天風呂
現在位置
1階
3階
(見えない)
(cannot see)
そーか
― see,
こーゆー
構造になってるんだな
the layout's like that...
私はやはり
許せんな　あの男
Me, I can never forgive that fellow!

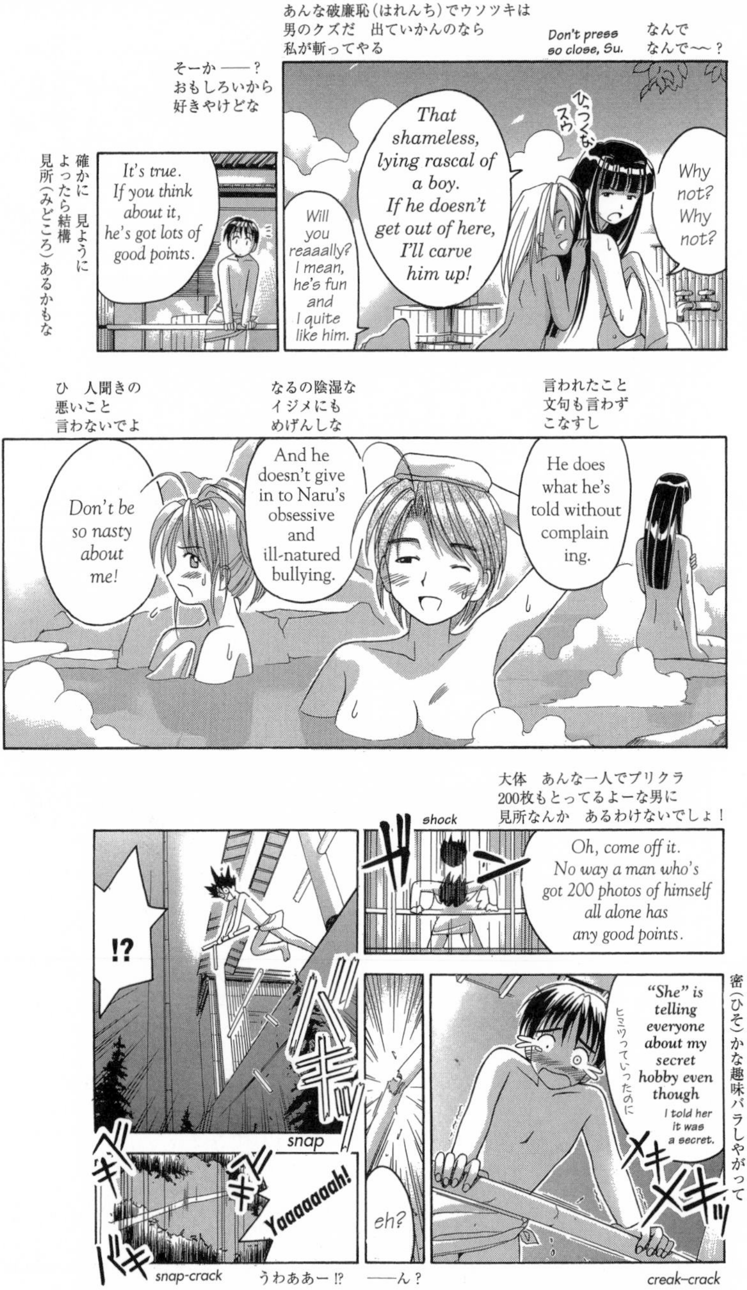
Why not? Why not?
なんで
なんで～～？
Don't press so close, Su.
ひっつくな スゥ
That shameless, lying rascal of a boy. If he doesn't get out of here, I'll carve him up!
あんな破廉恥（はれんち）でウソツキは
男のクズだ　出ていかんのなら
私が斬ってやる
Will you reaaally? I mean, he's fun and I quite like him.
そーか――？
おもしろいから
好きやけどな
It's true. If you think about it, he's got lots of good points.
確かに　見ように
よったら結構
見所（みどころ）あるかもな
He does what he's told without complain ing.
言われたこと
文句も言わず
こなすし
And he doesn't give in to Naru's obsessive and ill-natured bullying.
なるの陰湿な
イジメにも
めげんしな
Don't be so nasty about me!
ひ　人聞きの
悪いこと
言わないでよ
Oh, come off it. No way a man who's got 200 photos of himself all alone has any good points.
大体　あんな一人でプリクラ
200枚もとってるよーな男に
見所なんか　あるわけないでしょ！
shock
!?
"She" is telling everyone about my secret hobby even though I told her it was a secret.
あ　あいつ～～　俺の
密（ひそ）かな趣味バラしやがって
ヒミツっていったのに
creak-crack
eh?
――ん？
snap
Yaaaaaaah!
うわあぁー!?
snap-crack

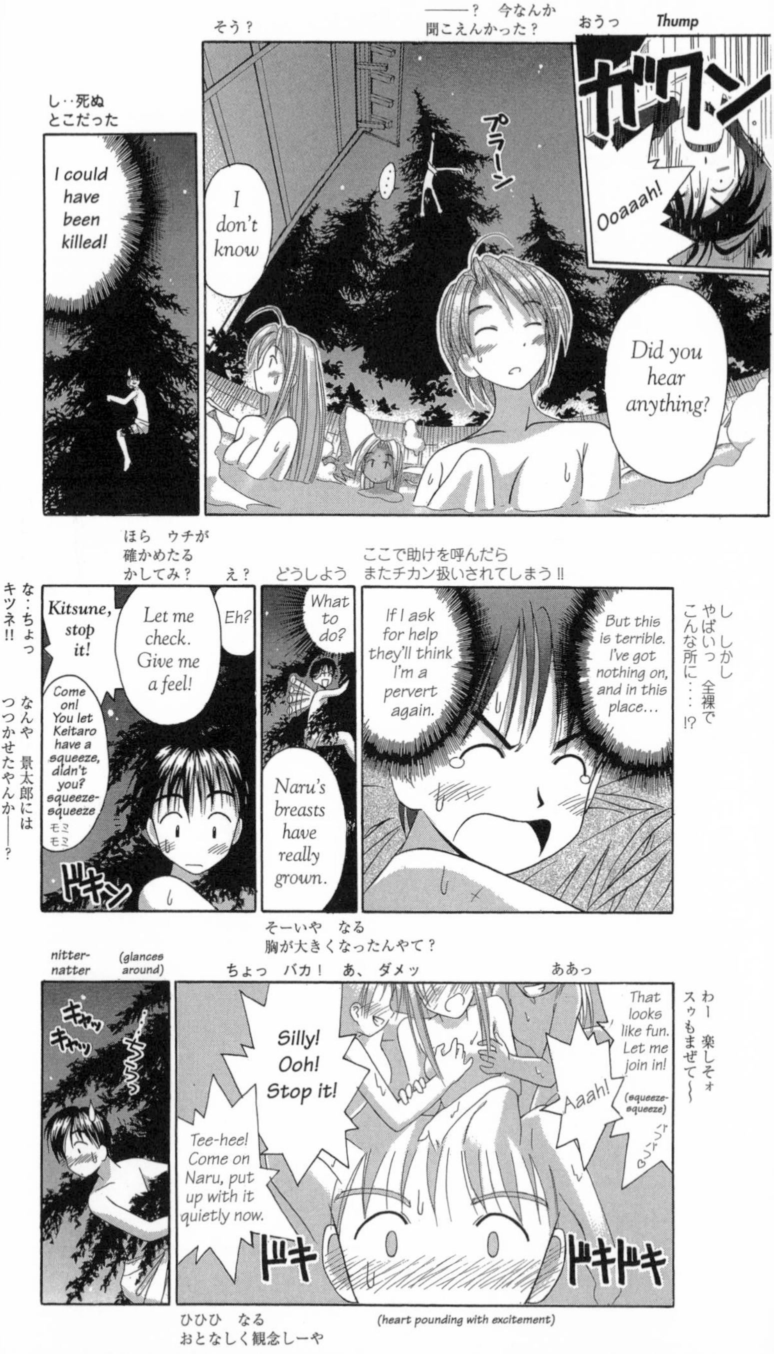
Thump
おうっ
Ooaaah!
——？ 今なんか聞こえんかった？
Did you hear anything?
そう？
I don't know
し‥死ぬとこだった
I could have been killed!
しししかし やばいっ 全裸でこんな所に‥‥!?
But this is terrible. I've got nothing on, and in this place…
ここで助けを呼んだらまたチカン扱いされてしまう!!
If I ask for help they'll think I'm a pervert again.
どうしよう
What to do?
そーいや なる 胸が大きくなったんやて？
Naru's breasts have really grown.
え？
Eh?
ほら ウチが確かめたるかしてみ？
Let me check. Give me a feel!
な‥ちょっ キツネ!!
Kitsune, stop it!
なんや 景太郎にはつつかせたやんか——？
Come on! You let Keitaro have a squeeze, didn't you? squeeze-squeeze
モミモミ
わー 楽しそォ スゥもまぜて〜
That looks like fun. Let me join in!
ああっ
Aaah!
(squeeze-squeeze)
ちょっ バカ！ あ、ダメッ
Silly! Ooh! Stop it!
ひひひ なる おとなしく観念しーや
Tee-hee! Come on Naru, put up with it quietly now.
(heart pounding with excitement)
nitter-natter
(glances around)

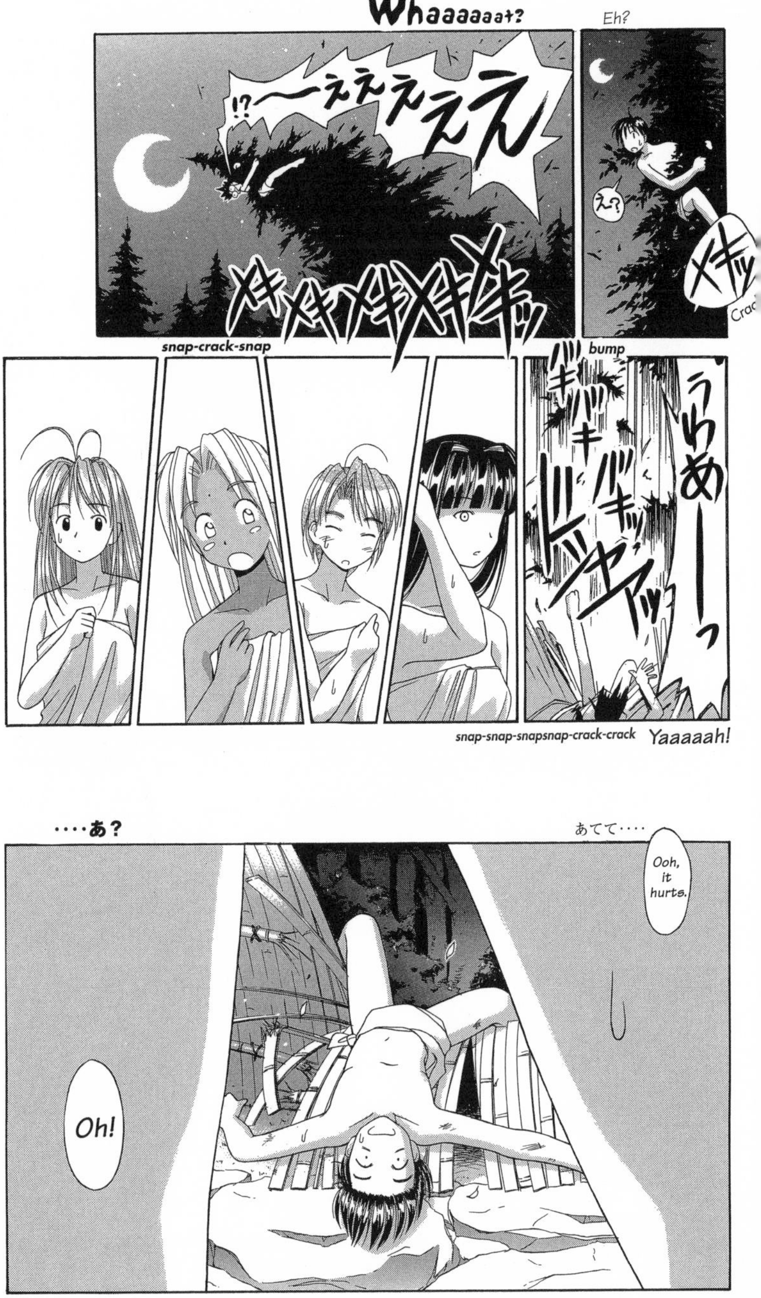

Eh?
え？
メキッ
Crack
Whaaaaaat?
!?〜ええええええ
メキメキメキメキメキッ
snap-crack-snap
bump
うわあーーっ
ギバキバキッドシャアッ
Yaaaaah!
snap-snap-snapsnap-crack-crack
あてて‥‥
Ooh, it hurts.
‥‥あ？
Oh!

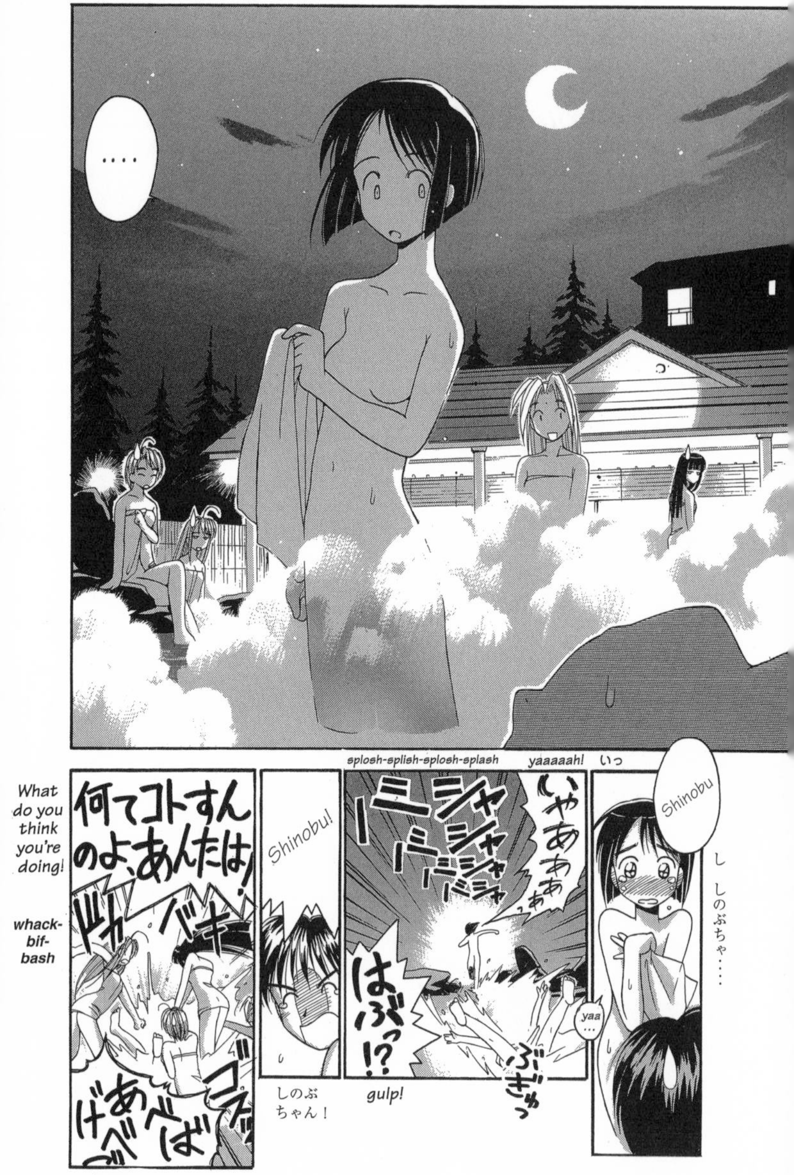
....
Shinobu
し しのぶちゃ....
いっ
yaaaaah!
いやあああぁっ
splosh-splish-splosh-splash
シャシャシャシャーー
ミ ミ ミ ミーー
yaa ...
はぶっ!?
ぶぎゅっ
gulp!
Shinobu!
しのぶちゃん!
何てコトすんのよ、あんたは!
What do you think you're doing!
バキ
whack-bif-bash
ゴズ
あげべばべ
I...er... glug...er... splodge.

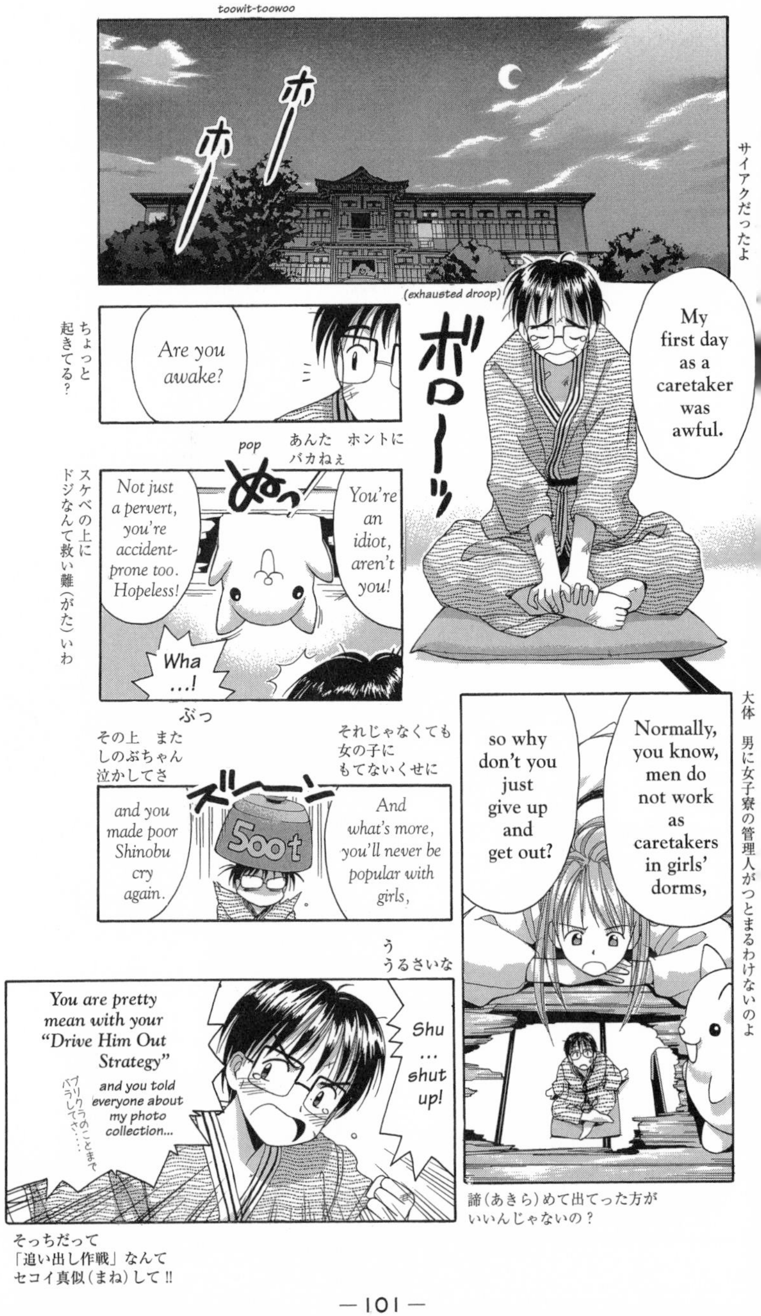
toowit-toowoo
ホー
ホー
サイアクだったよ
My first day as a caretaker was awful.
ボローーッ
(exhausted droop)
ちょっと起きてる?
Are you awake?
pop
ぬっ
あんた ホントにバカねぇ
You're an idiot, aren't you!
スケベの上にドジなんて救い難(がた)いわ
Not just a pervert, you're accident-prone too. Hopeless!
Wha ...!
ぶっ
大体 男に女子寮の管理人がつとまるわけないのよ
Normally, you know, men do not work as caretakers in girls' dorms,
諦(あきら)めて出てった方がいいんじゃないの?
so why don't you just give up and get out?
それじゃなくても女の子にもてないくせに
And what's more, you'll never be popular with girls,
その上 またしのぶちゃん泣かしてさ
and you made poor Shinobu cry again.
ズーン
500t
う うるさいな
Shu ... shut up!
そっちだって「追い出し作戦」なんてセコイ真似(まね)して!!
You are pretty mean with your "Drive Him Out Strategy"
プリクラのことまでバラしてさ……
and you told everyone about my photo collection...

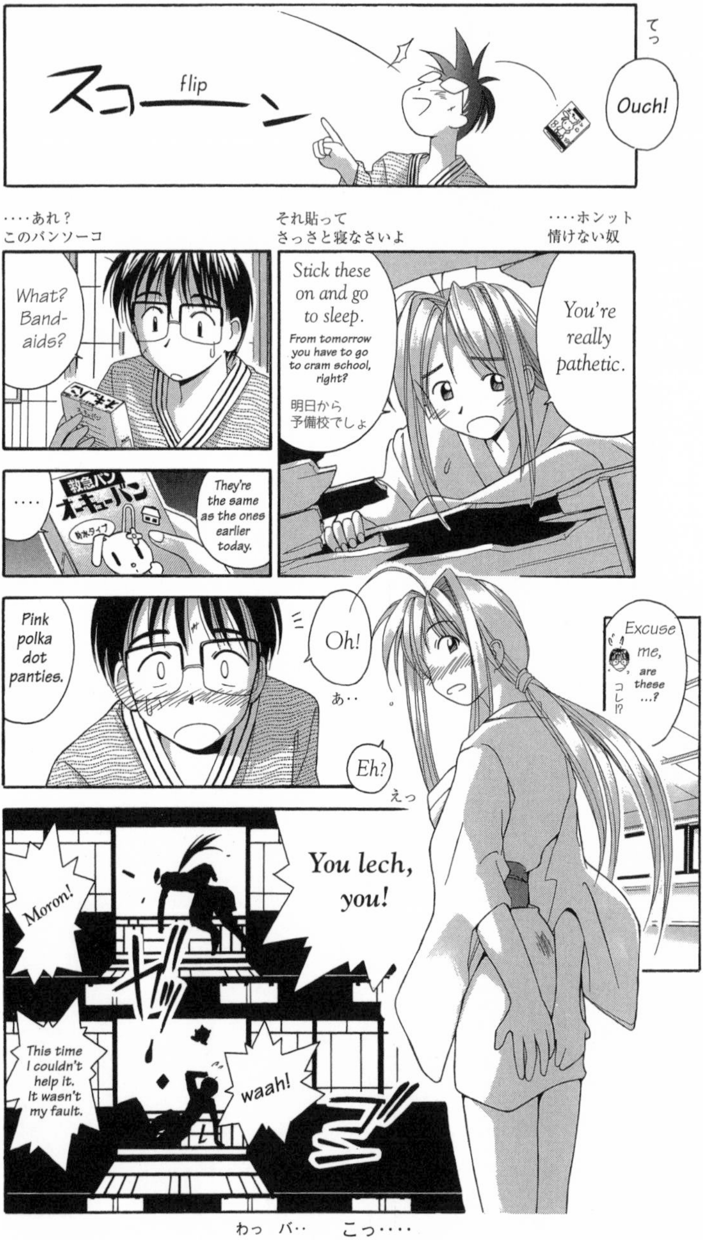
てっ
Ouch!
スコーーン
flip
・・・・ホンット 情けない奴
You're really pathetic.
それ貼って さっさと寝なさいよ
Stick these on and go to sleep.
From tomorrow you have to go to cram school, right?
明日から 予備校でしょ
・・・・あれ？ このバンソーコ
What? Band-aids?
昼間のと 同じ・・・・？
They're the same as the ones earlier today.
・・・・
救急バン
オーキューバン
防水タイプ
ちょっと！
Excuse me, are these ...?
コレ!?
Oh!
あ‥
Eh?
えっ
ピンクの水玉・・・・
Pink polka dot panties.
こっ・・・・ このスケベ！
You lech, you!
バカーーッ
Moron!
わっ バ‥
waah!
今のは不可抗・・・・ いてっ
This time I couldn't help it. It wasn't my fault.

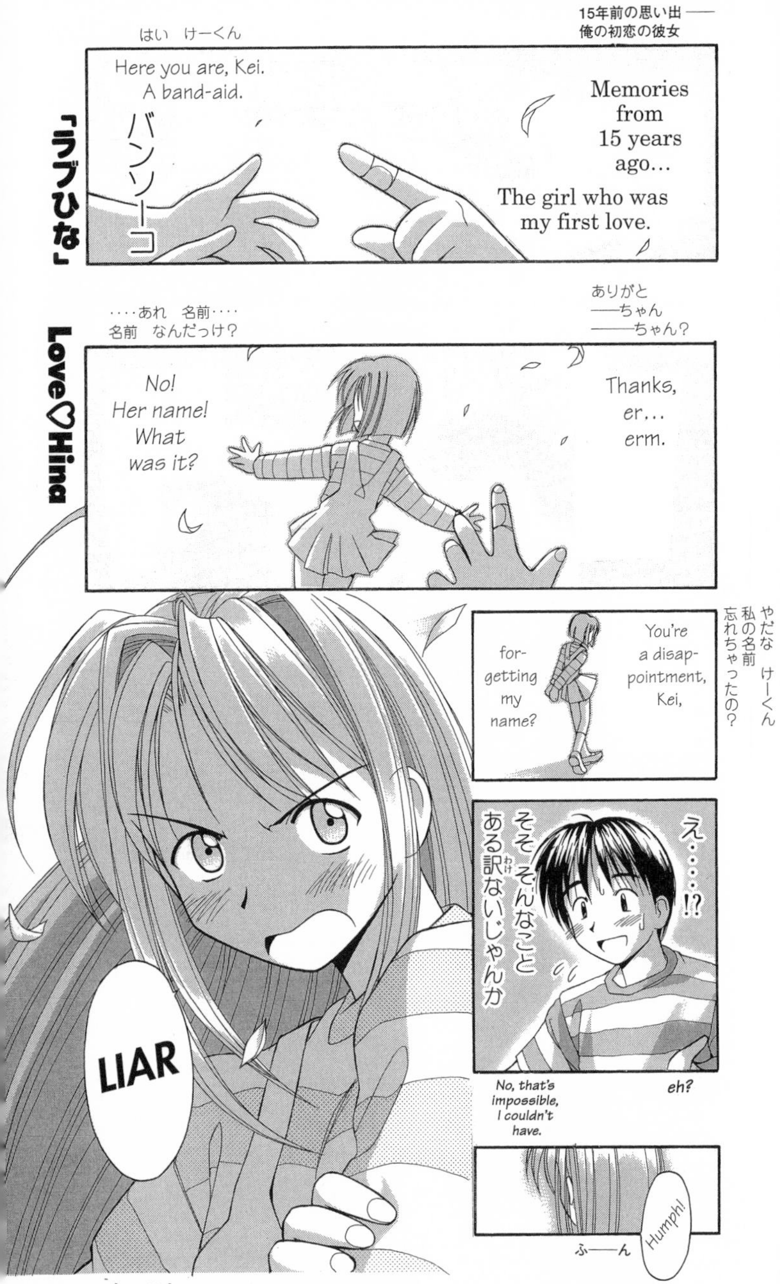
「ラブひな」
Love♡Hina
15年前の思い出——
俺の初恋の彼女
Memories from 15 years ago…
The girl who was my first love.
はい けーくん
Here you are, Kei. A band-aid.
バンソーコ
ありがと
——ちゃん
——ちゃん?
Thanks, er… erm.
····あれ 名前····
名前 なんだっけ?
No! Her name! What was it?
やだな けーくん
私の名前
忘れちゃったの?
You're a disappointment, Kei,
forgetting my name?
え····!?
eh?
そそ そんなこと
ある訳ないじゃんか
No, that's impossible, I couldn't have.
ふーん
Humph!
ウソツキ
LIAR

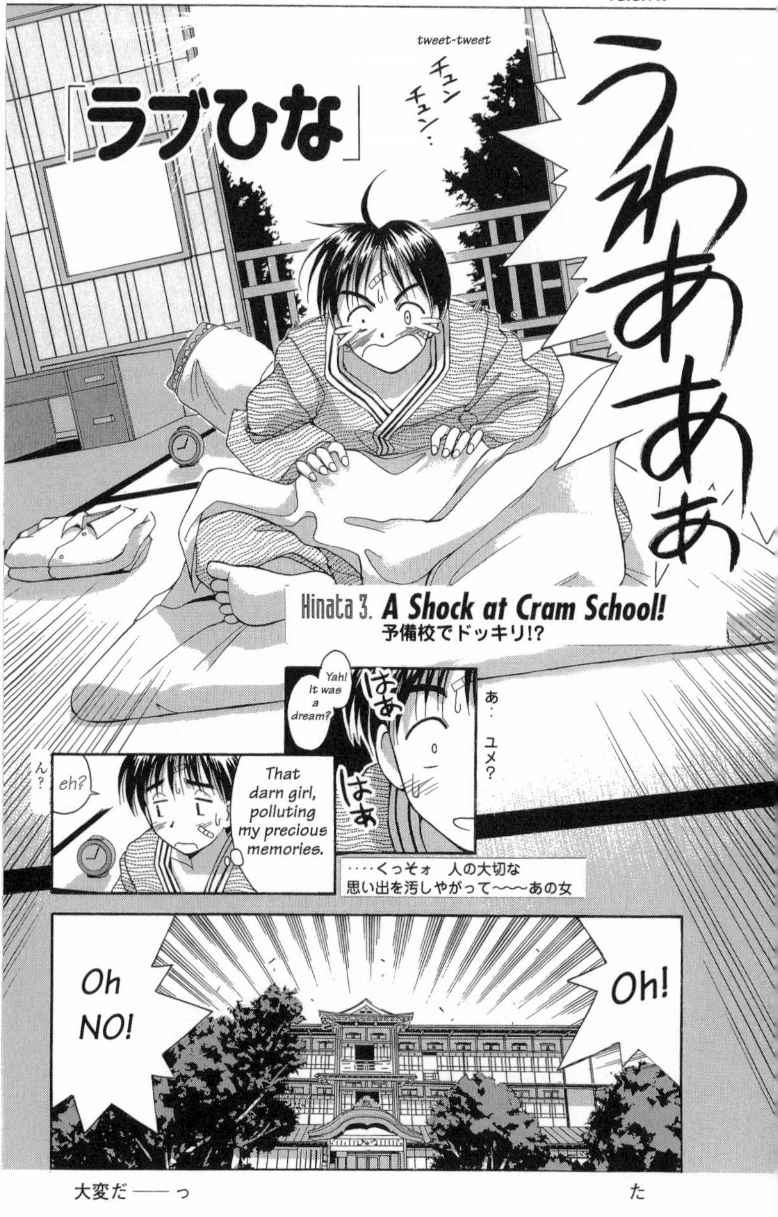
Yaah!
うわあああ
tweet-tweet
チュンチュン・・
「ラブひな」
Hinata 3. A Shock at Cram School!
予備校でドッキリ!?
Yah! It was a dream?
あ・・ユメ?
はぁ
はぁ
eh?
ん?
That darn girl, polluting my precious memories.
・・・・くっそォ　人の大切な
思い出を汚しやがって〜〜〜あの女
Oh!
Oh NO!
た
大変だ——っ

何やァ　朝から
あわただしいな

やばい――
一限遅刻だ

今日は
模試なんだよ！

なんで目覚まし
なんないんだよ？

佐々木
ゼミナール

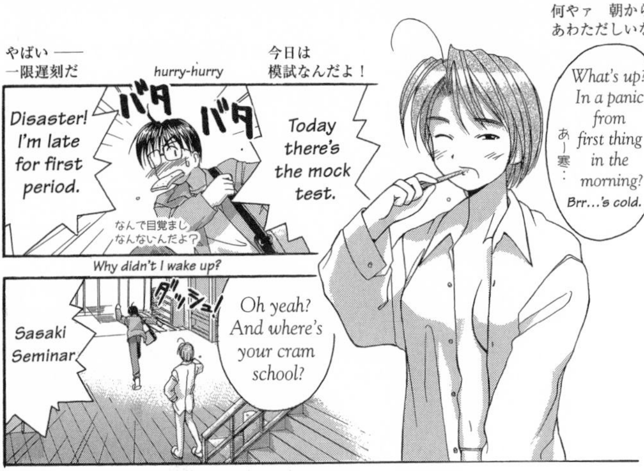
What's up? In a panic from first thing in the morning?
あー寒…
Brr…'s cold.
Disaster! I'm late for first period.
バタ　バタ
hurry-hurry
Today there's the mock test.
Why didn't I wake up?
Oh yeah? And where's your cram school?
ダッシュ!
Sasaki Seminar

そーいや
あんた予備校
どこやったけ？

ふ――ん

佐々ゼミね？

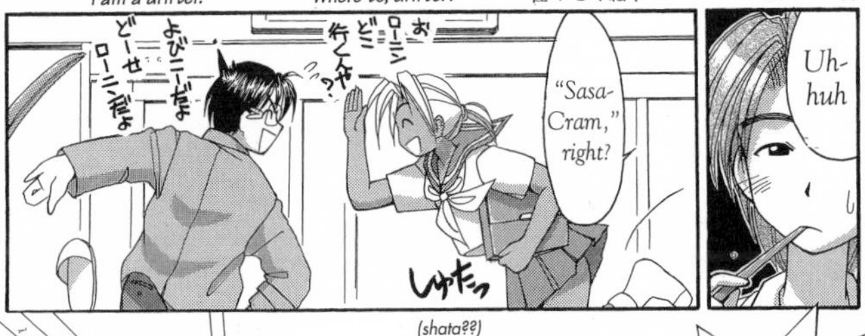
Uh-huh
"Sasa-Cram," right?
おーローニンどこ行くんや？
Where to, drifter?
よびこーだよ
どーせローニンだよ
I'm in my 2nd year at cram school, so I guess I am a drifter.
しゅたっ
(shata??)

まって――のります！
――のります

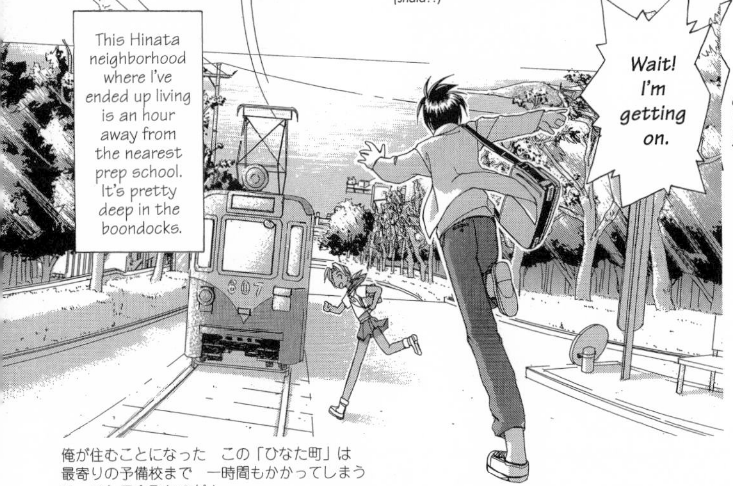
Wait! I'm getting on.
This Hinata neighborhood where I've ended up living is an hour away from the nearest prep school. It's pretty deep in the boondocks.

俺が住むことになった　この「ひなた町」は
最寄りの予備校まで　一時間もかかってしまう
けっこう田舎町なのだ！

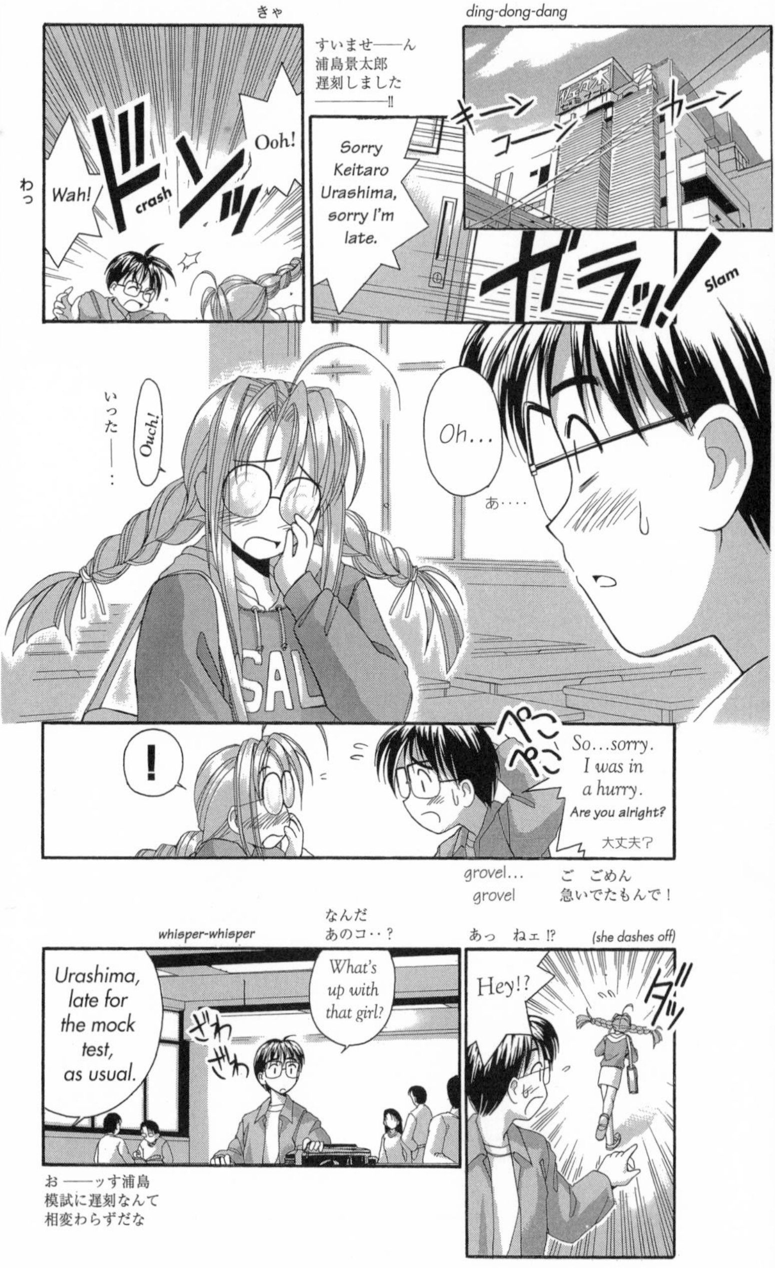
ding-dong-dang
キーン
コーン
カーン
すいませ——ん
浦島景太郎
遅刻しました
————!!
Sorry Keitaro Urashima, sorry I'm late.
ガラッ!
Slam
きゃ
Ooh!
わっ
Wah!
ドンッ
crash
Oh…
あ····
Ouch!
いった——··
!
ぺこぺこ
So…sorry. I was in a hurry.
Are you alright?
大丈夫？
grovel… grovel
ご ごめん
急いでたもんで！
あっ ねェ!?
(she dashes off)
Hey!?
ダッ
なんだ
あのコ··？
whisper-whisper
What's up with that girl?
ざわざわ
Urashima, late for the mock test, as usual.
お——ッす浦島
模試に遅刻なんて
相変わらずだな

う　うるさいなー
いろいろ
あったんだよ

一週間も休んで
自覚ある
二浪生の？

The Bespectacled Trio

このままだと
マジでヤバいよ
お前——

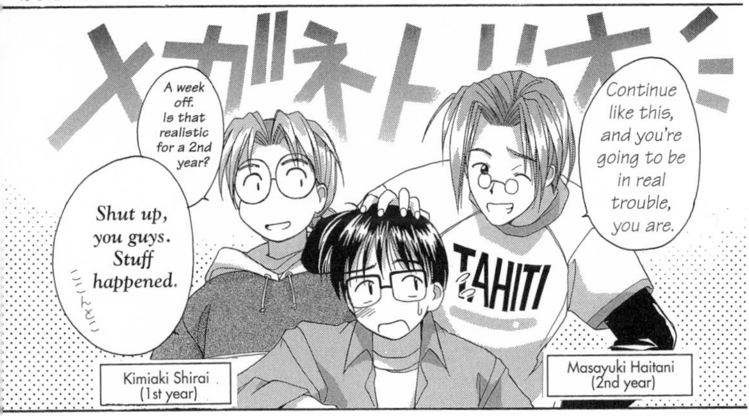

メガネトリオ
A week off. Is that realistic for a 2nd year?
Continue like this, and you're going to be in real trouble, you are.
Shut up, you guys. Stuff happened.
TAHITI
Kimiaki Shirai (1st year)
Masayuki Haitani (2nd year)

白井　功明（一浪）

灰谷　真之（二浪）

ほら前回の
模試の結果
出てるぜ

君の順位は
ここね

三浪決定
だな——

(heavy shock)

それでよく
東大目指してるよな
君は

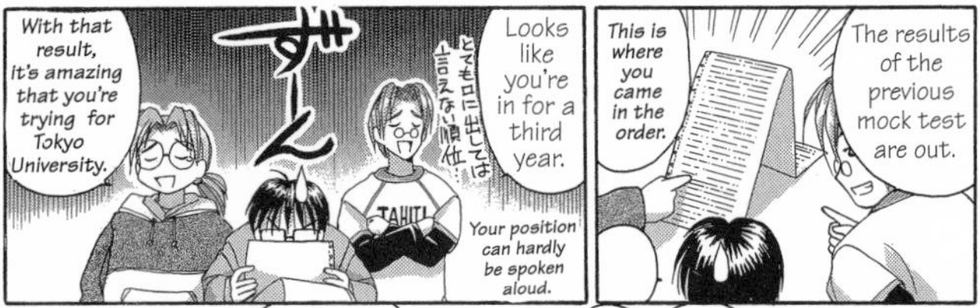

The results of the previous mock test are out.
This is where you came in the order.
Looks like you're in for a third year.
Your position can hardly be spoken aloud.
With that result, it's amazing that you're trying for Tokyo University.
TAHITI

ん？　あの女が
どうした？

い　いや…

え

あれ？

二人とも
知らないの？

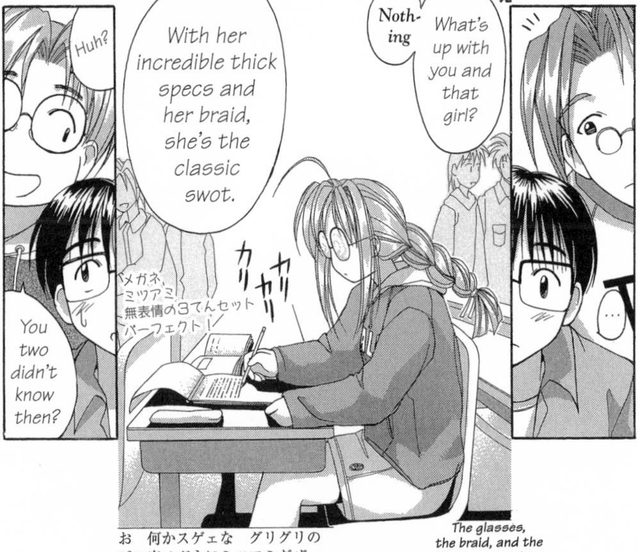

What's up with you and that girl?
Noth-ing
Huh?
With her incredible thick specs and her braid, she's the classic swot.
You two didn't know then?

お　何かスゲェな　グリグリの
ビン底メガネにミツアミだぜ
なんか絵にかいたよーな　ガリ勉少女じゃん

The glasses, the braid, and the blank expression. The whole set!

彼女この前の模試で
全国一位だったんだ

なに────っ!?
全国トップーッ!?

い　いるのかよ
そんな人間？

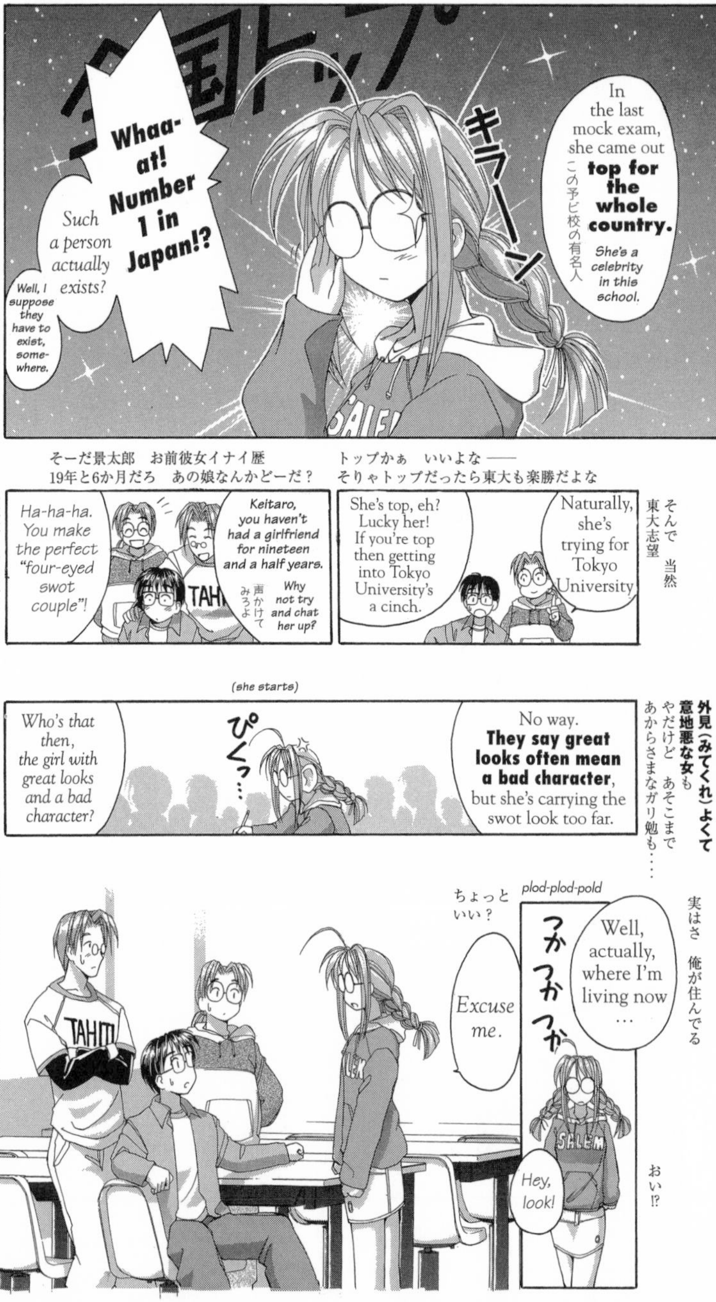
(shining with glory)
In the last mock exam, she came out **top for the whole country.**
この予ビ校の有名人
She's a celebrity in this school.
Whaa-at! Number 1 in Japan!?
Such a person actually exists?
Well, I suppose they have to exist, some-where.
Naturally, she's trying for Tokyo University
She's top, eh? Lucky her! If you're top then getting into Tokyo University's a cinch.
Keitaro, you haven't had a girlfriend for nineteen and a half years.
声かけてみろよ
Why not try and chat her up?
Ha-ha-ha. You make the perfect "four-eyed swot couple"!
(she starts)
No way. **They say great looks often mean a bad character**, but she's carrying the swot look too far.
ぴくっ…
Who's that then, the girl with great looks and a bad character?
plod-plod-pold
Well, actually, where I'm living now …
つかつかつか
Hey, look!
Excuse me.

そりゃ　どこかに
いるだろーけど

そんで　当然
東大志望

トップかぁ　いいよな ──
そりゃトップだったら東大も楽勝だよな

そーだ景太郎　お前彼女イナイ歴
19年と6か月だろ　あの娘なんかどーだ？

あはは　いーね
「ガリ勉メガネカップル」
似合うかもよ

えー　やだよ
外見(みてくれ)よくて
意地悪な女も
やだけど　あそこまで
あからさまなガリ勉も……

誰だ？　その外見よくて
意地悪な女って？

実はさ　俺が住んでる

おい!?

ちょっと
いい？

いいから
ちょっと来てよ！

え⁉
お　俺⁉

知り合いかよ
景太郎？

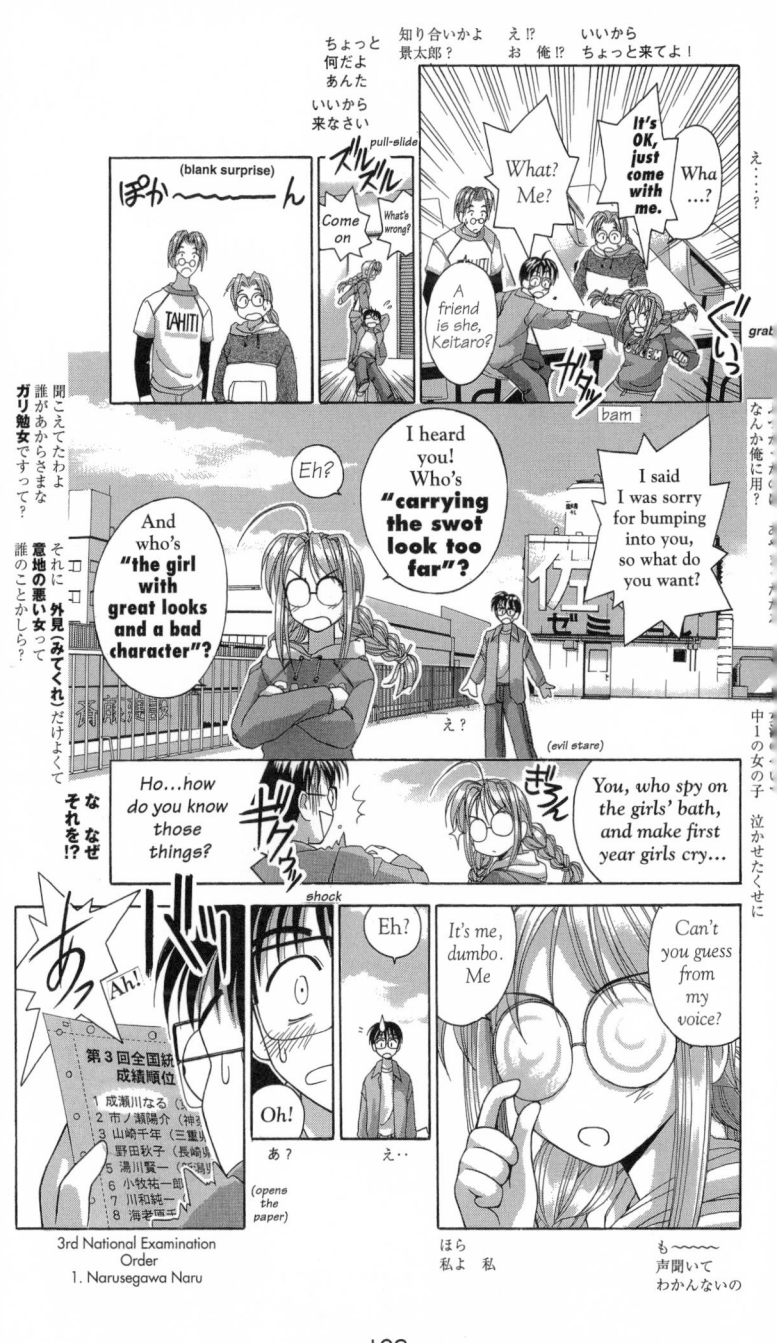

ちょっと
何だよ
あんた

いいから
来なさい

え・・・・？

なんか俺に用？

聞こえてたわよ
誰があからさまな**ガリ勉女**ですって？

それに　**外見(みてくれ)**だけよくて
意地の悪い女って
誰のことかしら？

中1の女の子　泣かせたくせに

な　なぜ
それを⁉

Wha
...?
It's OK, just come with me.
What? Me?
A friend is she, Keitaro?
grab
bam
pull-slide
What's wrong?
Come on
(blank surprise)
ぽか～～～～ん
I said I was sorry for bumping into you, so what do you want?
I heard you! Who's "carrying the swot look too far"?
Eh?
And who's "the girl with great looks and a bad character"?
(evil stare)
You, who spy on the girls' bath, and make first year girls cry...
Ho...how do you know those things?
shock
Can't you guess from my voice?
It's me, dumbo. Me
Eh?
Oh!
Ah!
あっ
第3回全国統
成績順位
1 成瀬川なる
2 市ノ瀬陽介
3 山崎千年（三重県
4 野田秋子（長崎県
5 湯川賢一
6 小牧祐一郎
7 川和純一
8 海老原

え‥

あ？

(opens the paper)

も～～～
声聞いて
わかんないの

ほら
私よ　私

3rd National Examination
Order
1. Narusegawa Naru

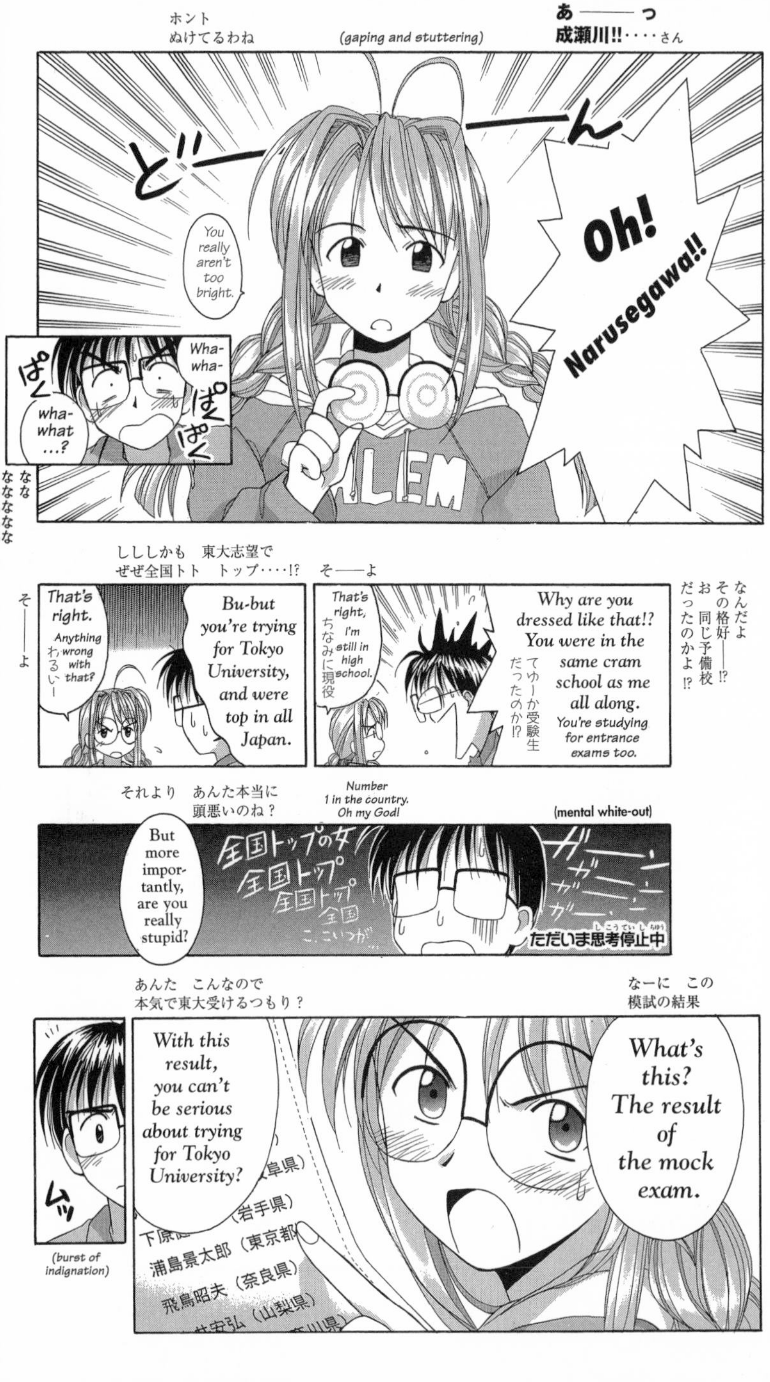
あ――っ
成瀬川!!・・・・さん
Oh! Narusegawa!!
(gaping and stuttering)
どー――ん
ホント
ぬけてるわね
You really aren't too bright.
ななななななな
Wha-wha-
wha-what ...?
ぱくぱくぱく
なんだよ
その格好――!?
お同じ予備校
だったのかよ!?
Why are you dressed like that!? You were in the same cram school as me all along.
てゆーか受験生
だったのか!?
You're studying for entrance exams too.
ちなみに現役
That's right, I'm still in high school.
しししかも　東大志望で
ぜぜ全国トト　トップ・・・・!?
Bu-but you're trying for Tokyo University, and were top in all Japan.
そ――よ
わるい――
That's right. Anything wrong with that?
それより　あんた本当に
頭悪いのね？
But more importantly, are you really stupid?
全国トップの女
全国トップ
全国トップ
全国
こ、こいつが…
Number 1 in the country. Oh my God!
ガーン
ガーン
ガーン
ただいま思考停止中
(mental white-out)
なーに　この
模試の結果
What's this? The result of the mock exam.
あんた　こんなので
本気で東大受けるつもり？
With this result, you can't be serious about trying for Tokyo University?
（岩手県）
浦島景太郎（東京都）
飛鳥昭夫（奈良県）
（山梨県）
ムッ
(burst of indignation)

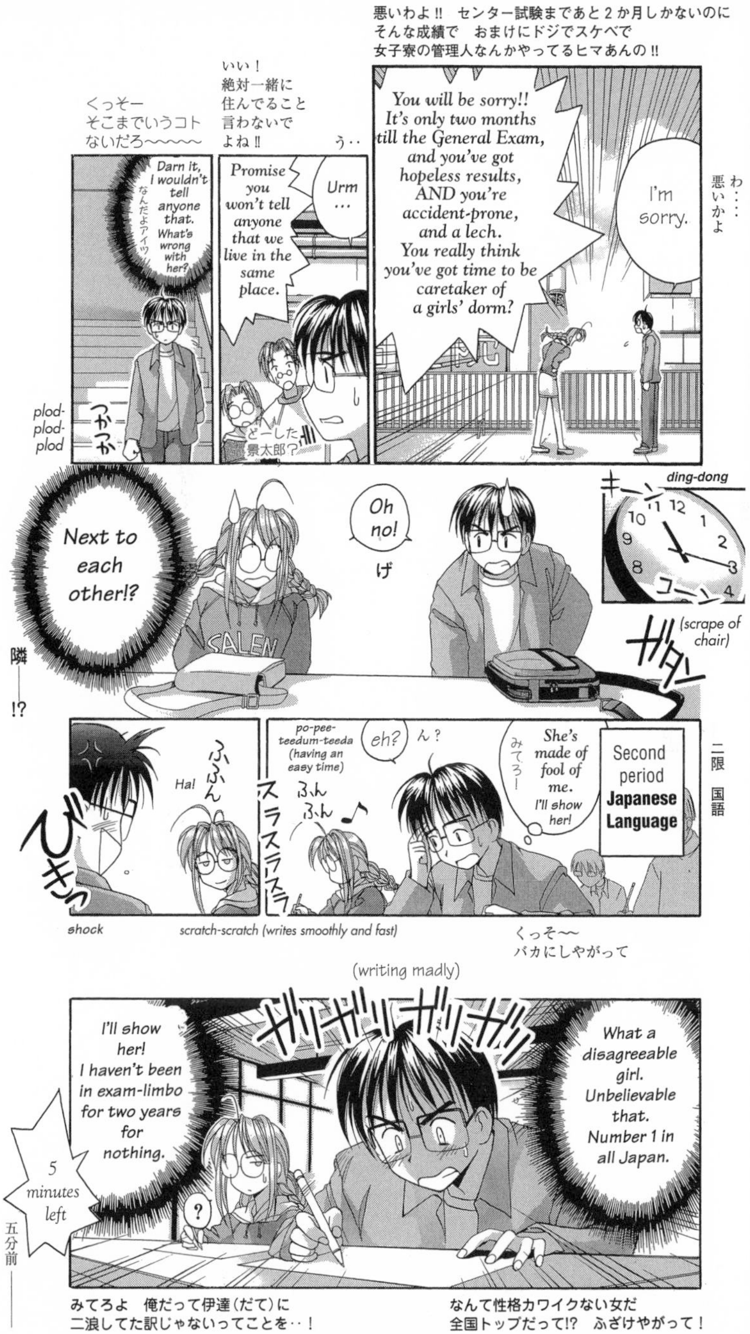
悪いわよ!! センター試験まであと2か月しかないのに
そんな成績で おまけにドジでスケベで
女子寮の管理人なんかやってるヒマあんの!!
I'm sorry.
わ‥‥悪いかよ
You will be sorry!! It's only two months till the General Exam, and you've got hopeless results, AND you're accident-prone, and a lech. You really think you've got time to be caretaker of a girls' dorm?
Urm …
う‥
Promise you won't tell anyone that we live in the same place.
いい！絶対一緒に住んでること言わないでよね!!
どーした景太郎？
Darn it, I wouldn't tell anyone that. What's wrong with her?
なんだよアイツ
くっそー そこまでいうコトないだろ〜〜〜〜〜
plod-plod-plod
つかつか
ding-dong
キーンコーン
(scrape of chair)
ガタン
Oh no!
げ
Next to each other!?
隣——!?
Second period Japanese Language
二限 国語
She's made of fool of me. I'll show her!
みてろー
くっそ〜 バカにしやがって
eh?
ん？
po-pee-teedum-teeda (having an easy time)
ふんふん♪
scratch-scratch (writes smoothly and fast)
スラスラスラ
Ha!
ふふん
shock
びきっ
(writing madly)
ガリガリガリガリ
What a disagreeable girl. Unbelievable that. Number 1 in all Japan.
なんて性格カワイクない女だ
全国トップだって!? ふざけやがって！
I'll show her! I haven't been in exam-limbo for two years for nothing.
みてろよ 俺だって伊達（だて）に
二浪してた訳じゃないってことを‥！
?
5 minutes left
五分前——

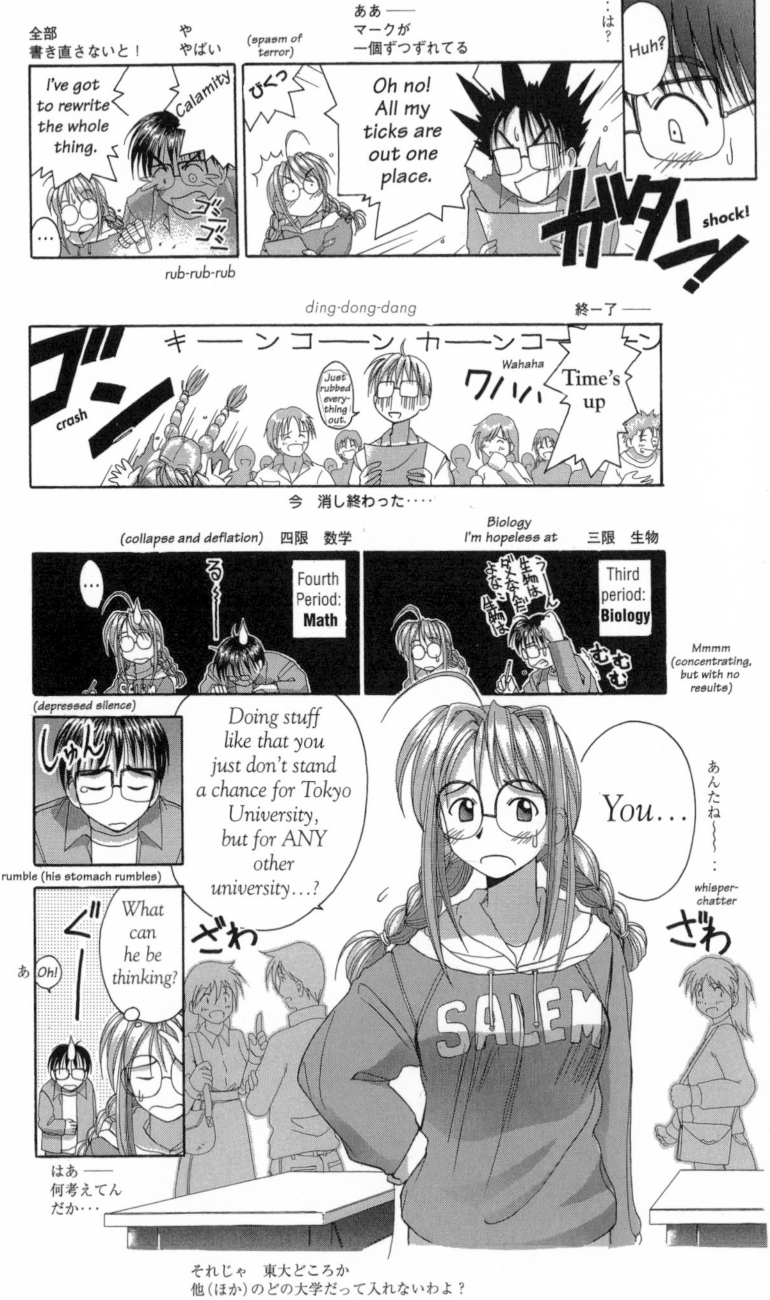
…は？
Huh?
ああ——
マークが
一個ずつずれてる
Oh no! All my ticks are out one place.
びくっ
(spasm of terror)
ガタン
shock!
や
やばい
Calamity
全部
書き直さないと！
I've got to rewrite the whole thing.
ゴシゴシ
rub-rub-rub
…
終ー了——
Time's up
キーンコーンカーンコーン
ding-dong-dang
ワハハ
Wahaha
今 消し終わった‥‥
Just rubbed everything out.
ゴン
crash
三限 生物
Third period: Biology
う〜ん 生物は ダメなんだよなぁ 生物は
Biology I'm hopeless at
むむむ
Mmmm (concentrating, but with no results)
四限 数学
Fourth Period: Math
る〜〜
(collapse and deflation)
…
あんたね〜〜：
You…
ざわ
whisper-chatter
それじゃ 東大どころか
他(ほか)のどの大学だって入れないわよ？
Doing stuff like that you just don't stand a chance for Tokyo University, but for ANY other university…?
しゅん
(depressed silence)
ざわ
ぐー
rumble (his stomach rumbles)
あ
Oh!
はあ——
何考えてん
だか・・・
What can he be thinking?

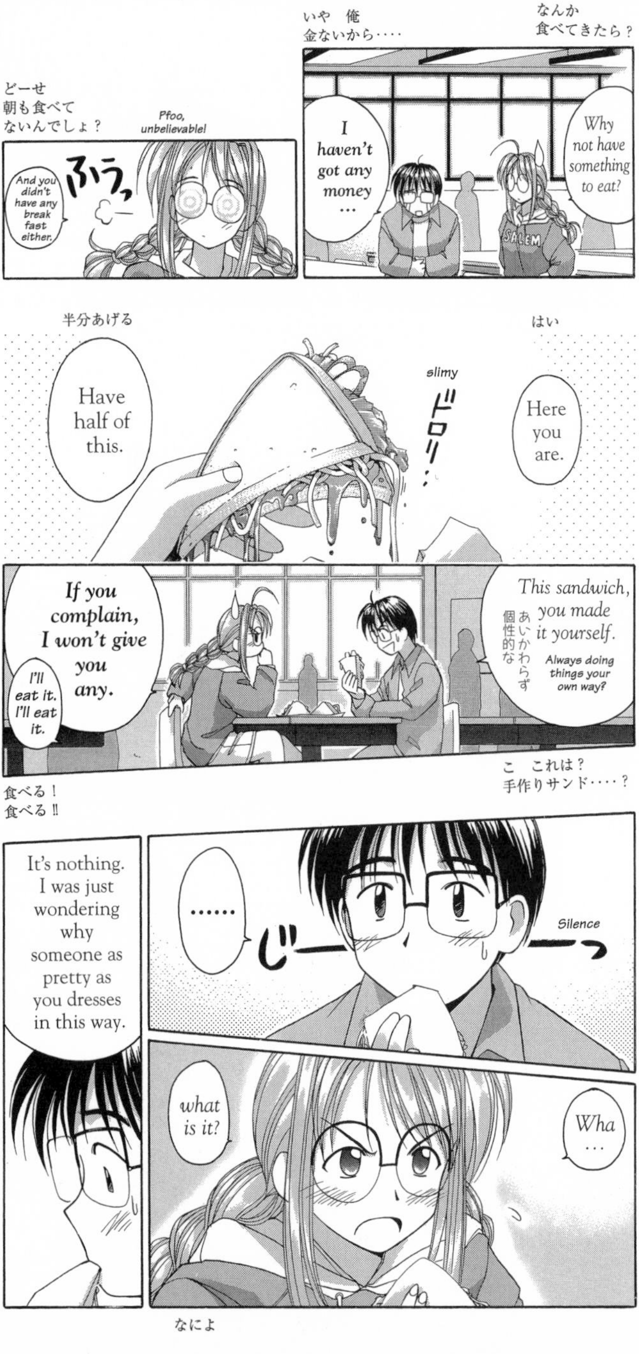
なんか
食べてきたら？
Why not have something to eat?
いや 俺
金ないから・・・・
I haven't got any money …
どーせ
朝も食べて
ないんでしょ？
Pfoo, unbelievable!
ふうっ
And you didn't have any break fast either.
はい
Here you are.
slimy
ドロリ
半分あげる
Have half of this.
こ これは？
手作りサンド・・・・？
This sandwich, you made it yourself.
あいかわらず
個性的な
Always doing things your own way?
文句言うなら
あげないわよ
If you complain, I won't give you any.
食べる！
食べる!!
I'll eat it. I'll eat it.
Silence
じーっ
……
な・・・・
Wha …
なによ
what is it?
い：いや せっかく その・・・
かわいいくせに なんでそんな格好
してるのかなって 思ってさ？
It's nothing. I was just wondering why someone as pretty as you dresses in this way.

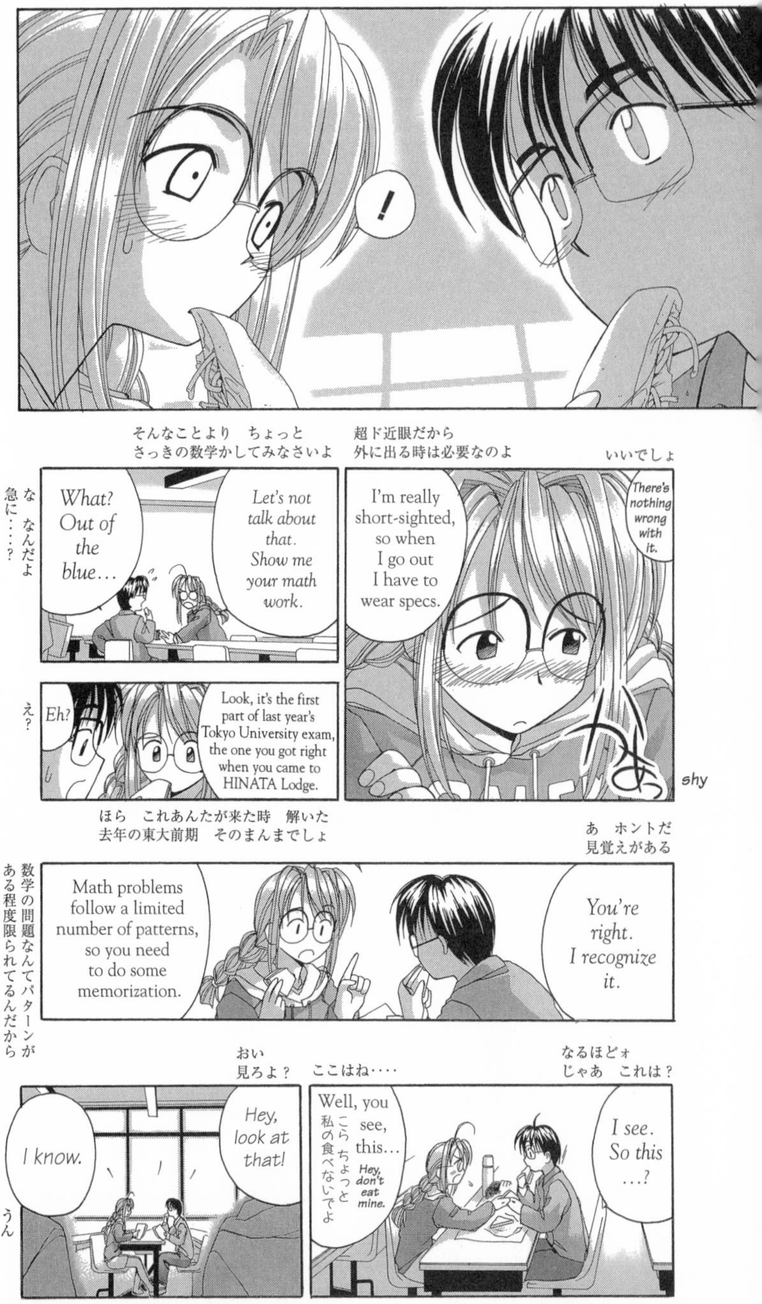
!
There's nothing wrong with it.
いいでしょ
I'm really short-sighted, so when I go out I have to wear specs.
超ド近眼だから
外に出る時は必要なのよ
shy
Let's not talk about that. Show me your math work.
そんなことより　ちょっと
さっきの数学かしてみなさいよ
What? Out of the blue…
な　なんだよ
急に・・・？
Look, it's the first part of last year's Tokyo University exam, the one you got right when you came to HINATA Lodge.
ほら　これあんたが来た時　解いた
去年の東大前期　そのまんまでしょ
Eh?
え？
You're right. I recognize it.
あ　ホントだ
見覚えがある
Math problems follow a limited number of patterns, so you need to do some memorization.
数学の問題なんてパターンが
ある程度限られてるんだから
暗記っぽいのも必要なの！
I see. So this …?
なるほどォ
じゃあ　これは？
Well, you see, this…
ここはね・・・・
こら ちょっと
私の食べないでよ
Hey, don't eat mine.
Hey, look at that!
おい
見ろよ？
I know.
うん

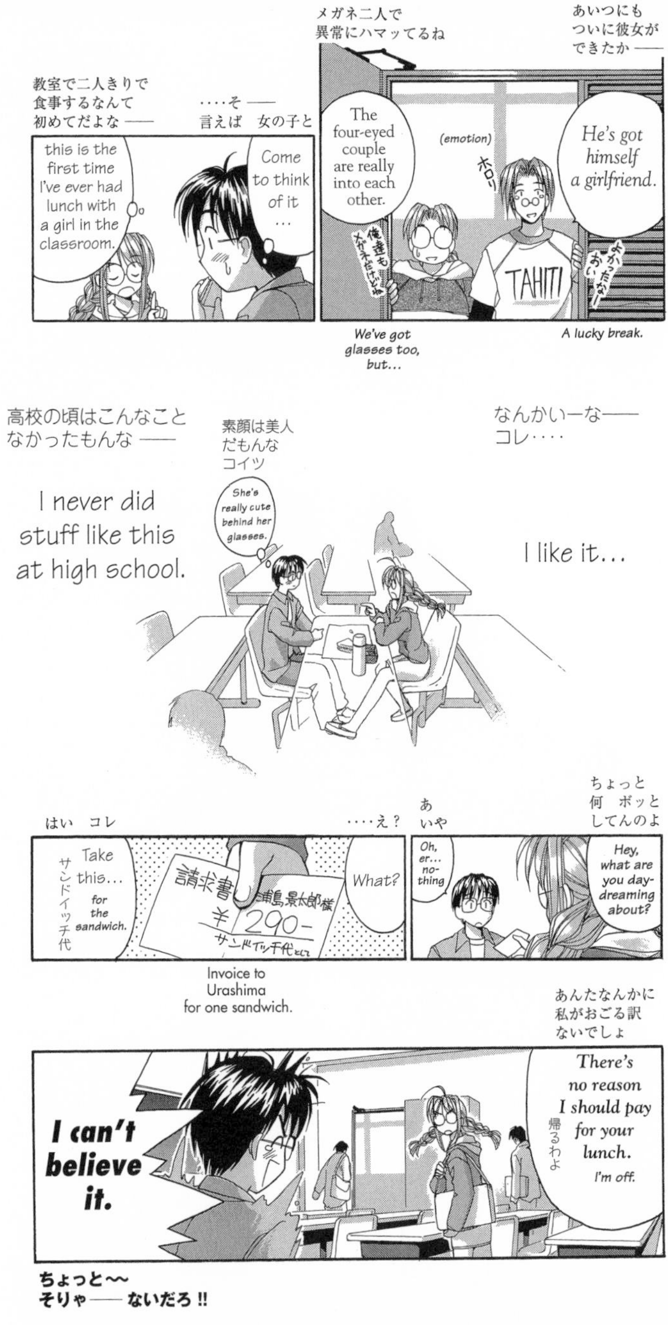

あいつにも
ついに彼女が
できたか——
He's got himself a girlfriend.
よかったなー！ おい
A lucky break.
ホロリ
(emotion)
メガネ二人で
異常にハマッてるね
The four-eyed couple are really into each other.
俺達もメガネだけどね
We've got glasses too, but…
・・・・そ——
言えば 女の子と
Come to think of it …
教室で二人きりで
食事するなんて
初めてだよな——
this is the first time I've ever had lunch with a girl in the classroom.
なんかいーな——
コレ・・・・
I like it…
素顔は美人
だもんな
コイツ
She's really cute behind her glasses.
高校の頃はこんなこと
なかったもんな——
I never did stuff like this at high school.
ちょっと
何 ボッと
してんのよ
Hey, what are you day-dreaming about?
あ
いや
Oh, er… no-thing
・・・・え？
What?
はい コレ
Take this…
サンドイッチ代
for the sandwich.
請求書 浦島景太郎様
¥290-
サンドイッチ代として
Invoice to Urashima for one sandwich.
あんたなんかに
私がおごる訳
ないでしょ
There's no reason I should pay for your lunch.
帰るわよ
I'm off.
ちょっと〜
そりゃ—— ないだろ!!
I can't believe it.

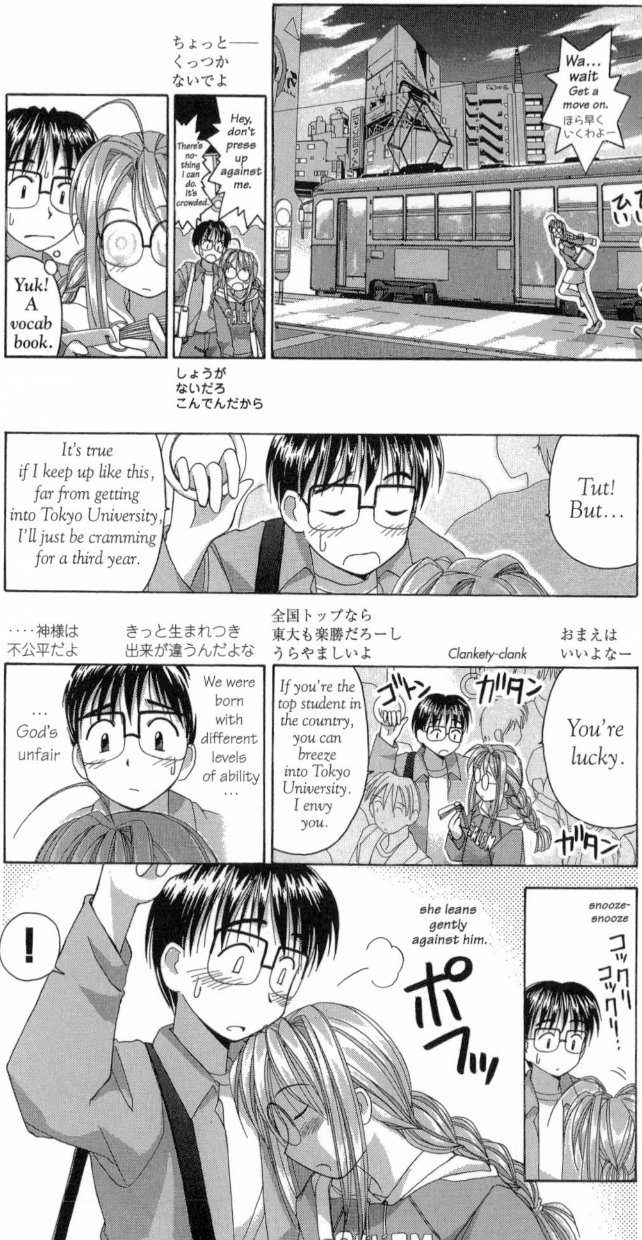
まま まって
Wa… wait
Get a move on.
ほら早く いくわよー
ひいひい
ちょっと── くっつかないでよ
Hey, don't press up against me.
There's nothing I can do. It's crowded.
しょうがないだろ こんでんだから
ゲ‥‥単語帳？
Yuk! A vocab book.
ちぇっ しかし
Tut! But…
確かに俺は このままだと 東大どころか 三浪決定だよな‥‥
It's true if I keep up like this, far from getting into Tokyo University, I'll just be cramming for a third year.
おまえは いいよなー
You're lucky.
Clankety-clank
ゴトン
ガタン
ガタン
全国トップなら 東大も楽勝だろーし うらやましいよ
If you're the top student in the country, you can breeze into Tokyo University. I envy you.
きっと生まれつき 出来が違うんだよな
We were born with different levels of ability …
‥‥神様は 不公平だよ
… God's unfair
snooze-snooze
コックリ コックリ…
she leans gently against him.
ポフッ
!

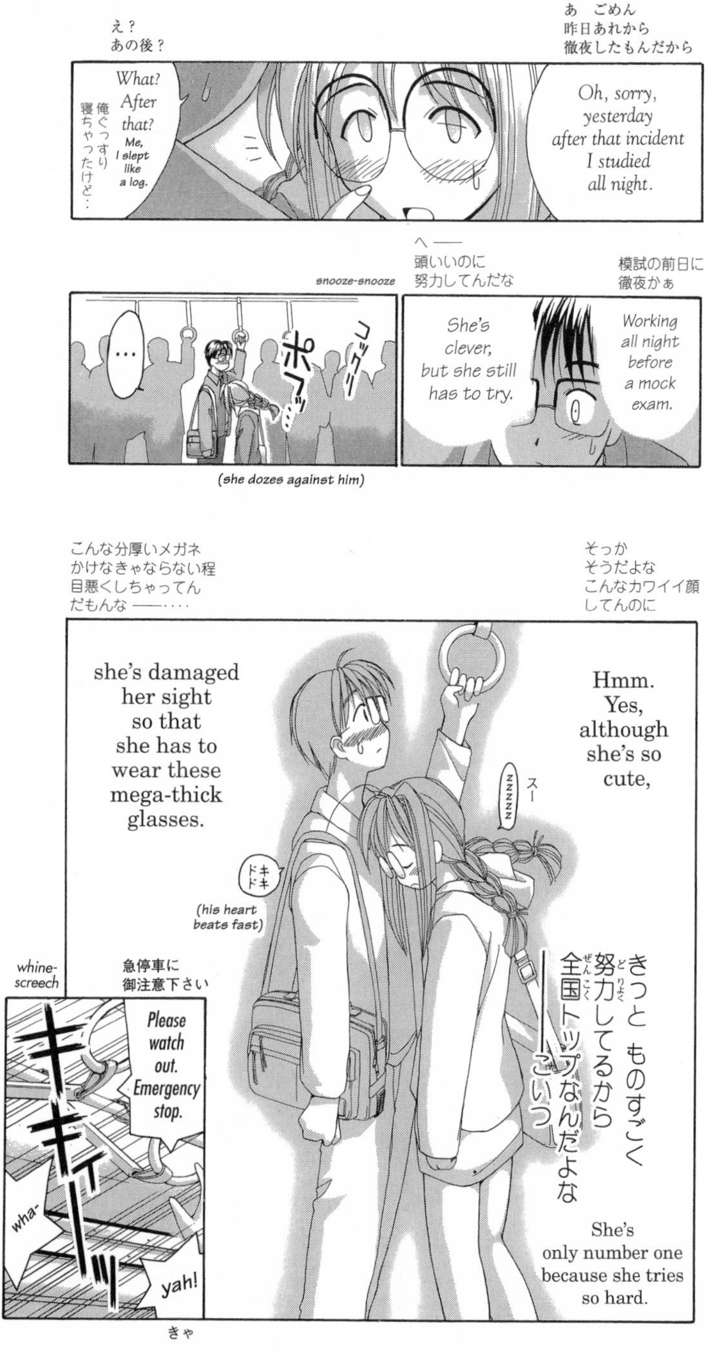
あ　ごめん
昨日あれから
徹夜したもんだから
Oh, sorry, yesterday after that incident I studied all night.
え？
あの後？
What? After that?
俺ぐっすり寝ちゃったけど‥
Me, I slept like a log.
模試の前日に
徹夜かぁ
Working all night before a mock exam.
へ——
頭いいのに
努力してんだな
She's clever, but she still has to try.
snooze-snooze
…
コックリ
ポフッ…
(she dozes against him)
そっか
そうだよな
こんなカワイイ顔
してんのに
Hmm. Yes, although she's so cute,
こんな分厚いメガネ
かけなきゃならない程
目悪くしちゃってん
だもんな——‥‥
she's damaged her sight so that she has to wear these mega-thick glasses.
スー
zzzzz
ドキドキ
(his heart beats fast)
きっと ものすごく
努力してるから
全国トップなんだよな
——こいつ
She's only number one because she tries so hard.
急停車に
御注意下さい
Please watch out. Emergency stop.
whine-screech
キキィーッ
わっ
wha-
きゃ
yah!

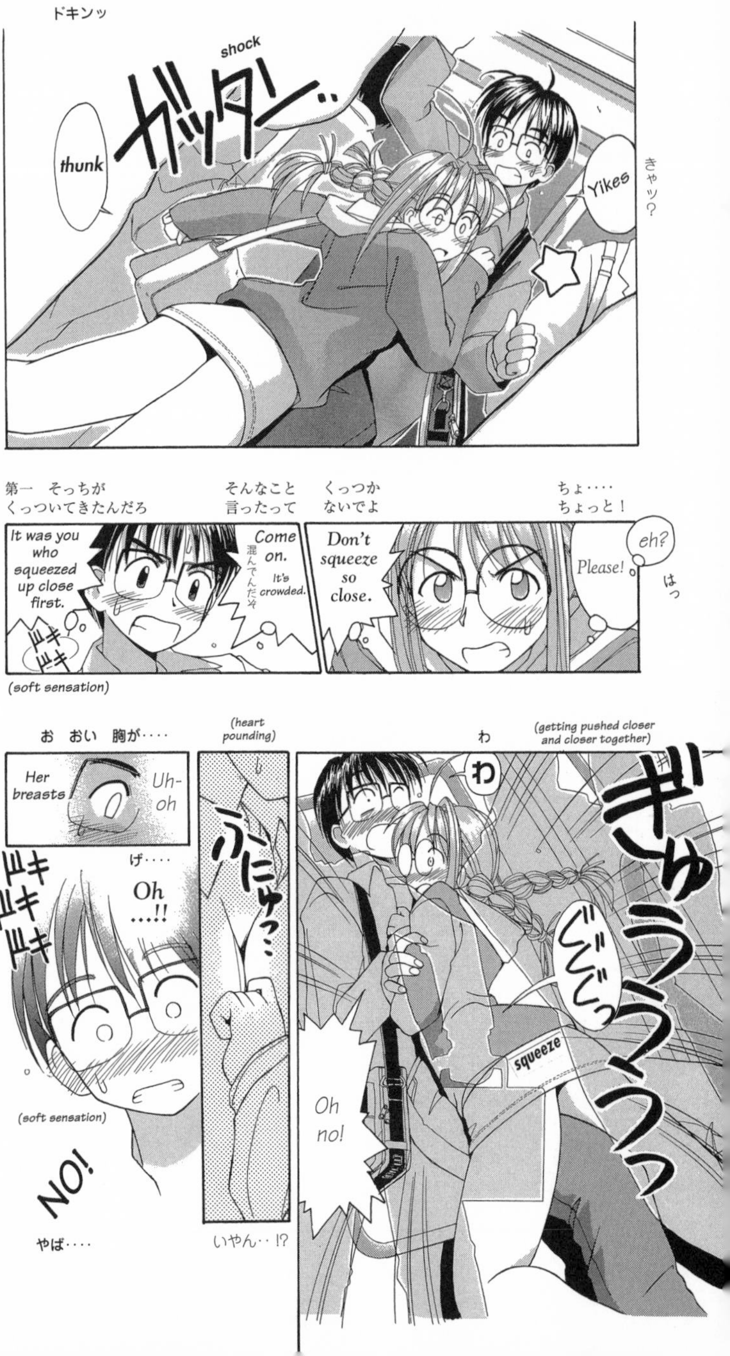
ドキンッ
shock
ガッターン
thunk
きゃッ?
Yikes
ちょ‥‥
ちょっと!
はっ
eh?
Please!
くっつか
ないでよ
Don't squeeze so close.
そんなこと
言ったって
Come on.
混んでんだぞ
It's crowded.
第一 そっちが
くっついてきたんだろ
It was you who squeezed up close first.
(soft sensation)
わ
(getting pushed closer and closer together)
ぎゅううううっ
squeeze
Oh no!
(heart pounding)
いやん‥!?
お おい 胸が‥‥
Her breasts
Uh-oh
げ‥‥
Oh ....!!
(soft sensation)
NO!
やば‥‥

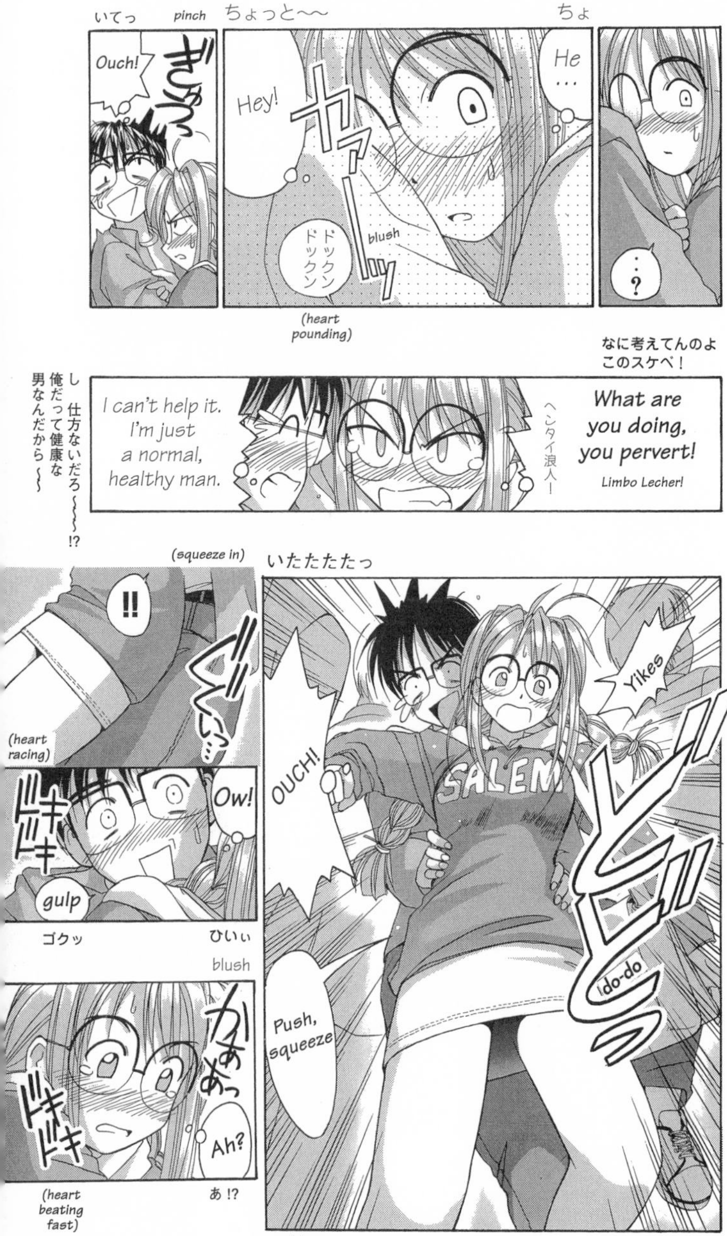
ちょ
..?
He ...
Hey!
ちょっと〜〜
ドックン ドックン
(heart pounding)
blush
Ouch!
pinch
いてっ
What are you doing, you pervert!
Limbo Lecher!
なに考えてんのよ このスケベ！
ヘンタイ浪人！
I can't help it. I'm just a normal, healthy man.
し 仕方ないだろ〜〜〜!? 俺だって健康な 男なんだから〜〜
キャア
Yikes
いたたたたっ
OUCH!
do-do
Push, squeeze
(close squeeze)
(squeeze in)
!!
(heart racing)
Ow!
gulp
ゴクッ
ひいぃ
blush
Ah?
あ!?
(heart beating fast)

あ　あれ
あれれ？

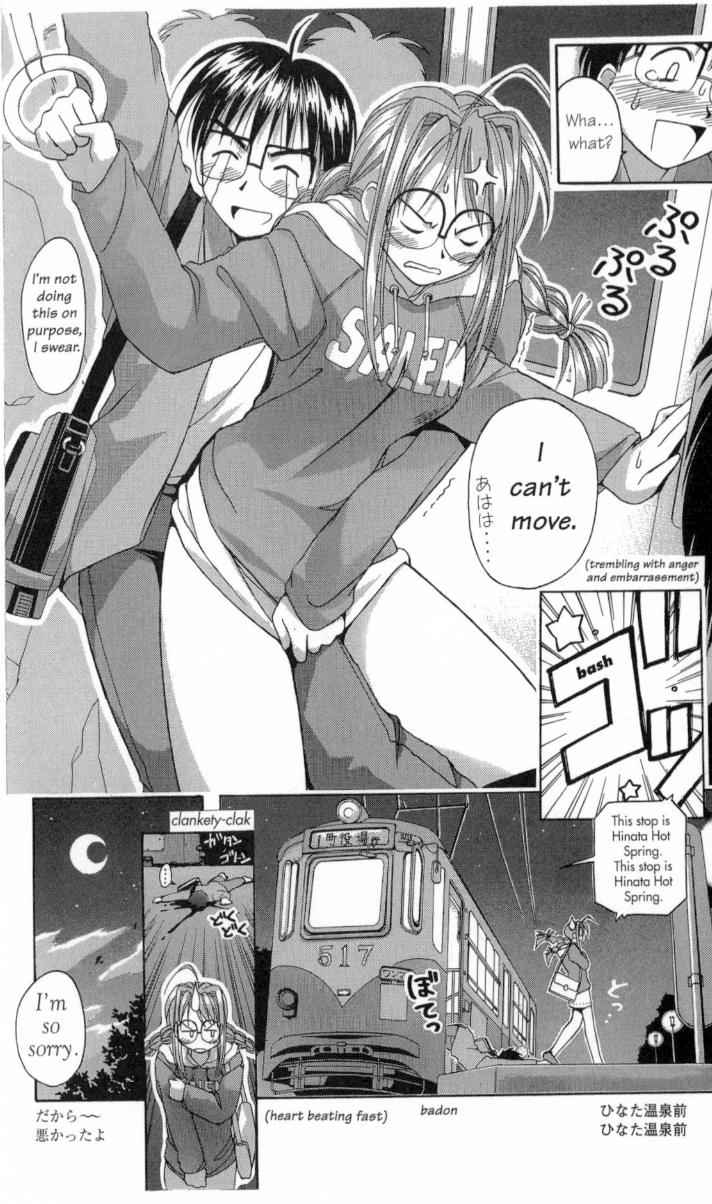
Wha... what?
ぷるぷる
I'm not doing this on purpose, I swear.
I can't move.
あはは……
(trembling with anger and embarrassment)
bash
This stop is Hinata Hot Spring. This stop is Hinata Hot Spring.
clankety-clak
...
I'm so sorry.
ぼてっ
badon
(heart beating fast)

わざとじゃない
からね　ホント……

う……動けなく
なっちゃった

だから〜
悪かったよ

ひなた温泉前
ひなた温泉前

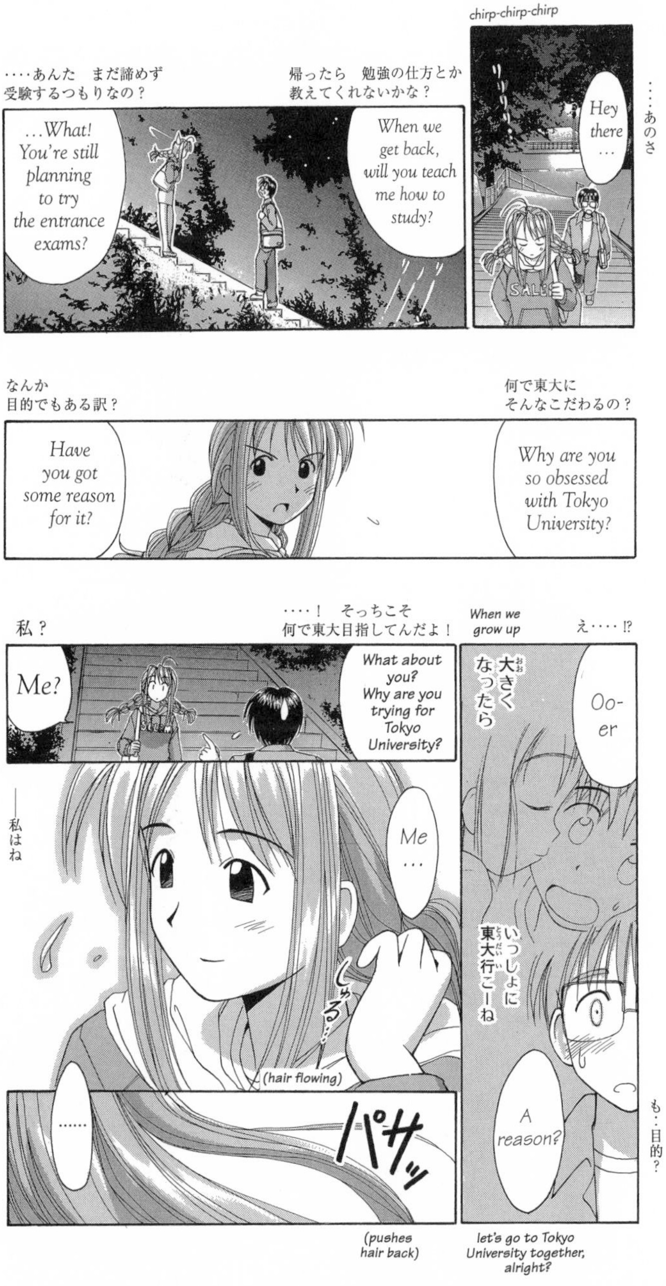
chirp-chirp-chirp
リリリリ…
Hey there …
・・・・あのさ
When we get back, will you teach me how to study?
帰ったら　勉強の仕方とか
教えてくれないかな？
…What! You're still planning to try the entrance exams?
・・・・あんた　まだ諦めず
受験するつもりなの？
Why are you so obsessed with Tokyo University?
何で東大に
そんなこだわるの？
Have you got some reason for it?
なんか
目的でもある訳？
Oo-er
え・・・・!?
A reason?
も・・目的？
What about you? Why are you trying for Tokyo University?
・・・・！　そっちこそ
何で東大目指してんだよ！
Me?
私？
大きくなったら
When we grow up
いっしょに東大行こーね
let's go to Tokyo University together, alright?
Me …
──私はね
しゅる…
(hair flowing)
パサッ
(pushes hair back)
……

I'm not
going to
tell you.

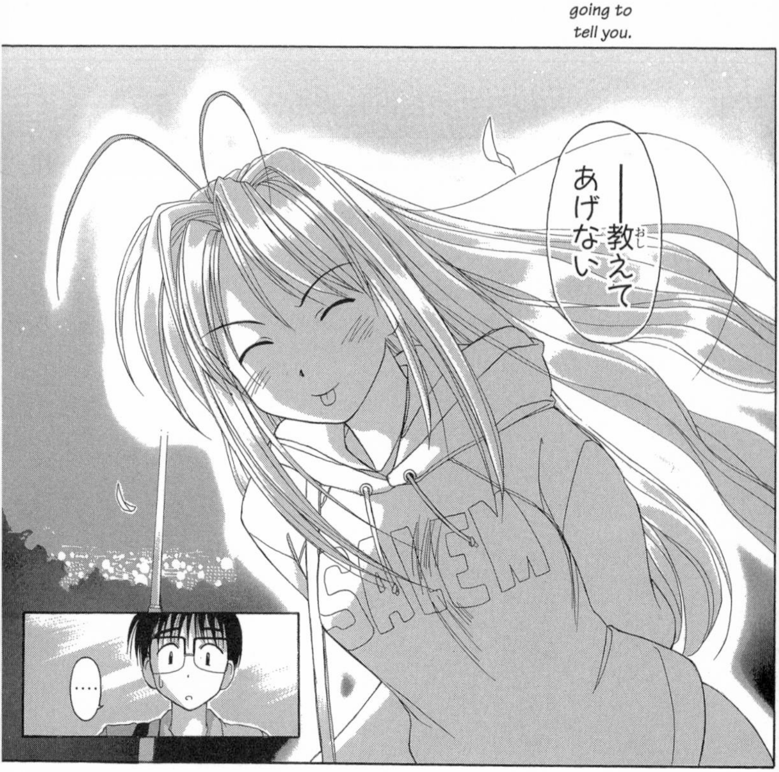

―教(おし)えて
あげない
....

ローニン！　帰ってきたなら
管理人の仕事せんか――!!

・・・・目的か

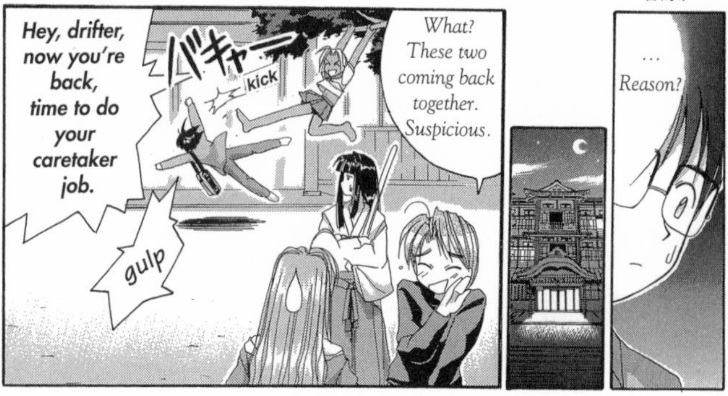

...
Reason?
What?
These two
coming back
together.
Suspicious.
Hey, drifter,
now you're
back,
time to do
your
caretaker
job.
バキャー
kick
gulp

はぐうッ

なんやなんや
二人で並んで
帰ってきて――
あやしーな？

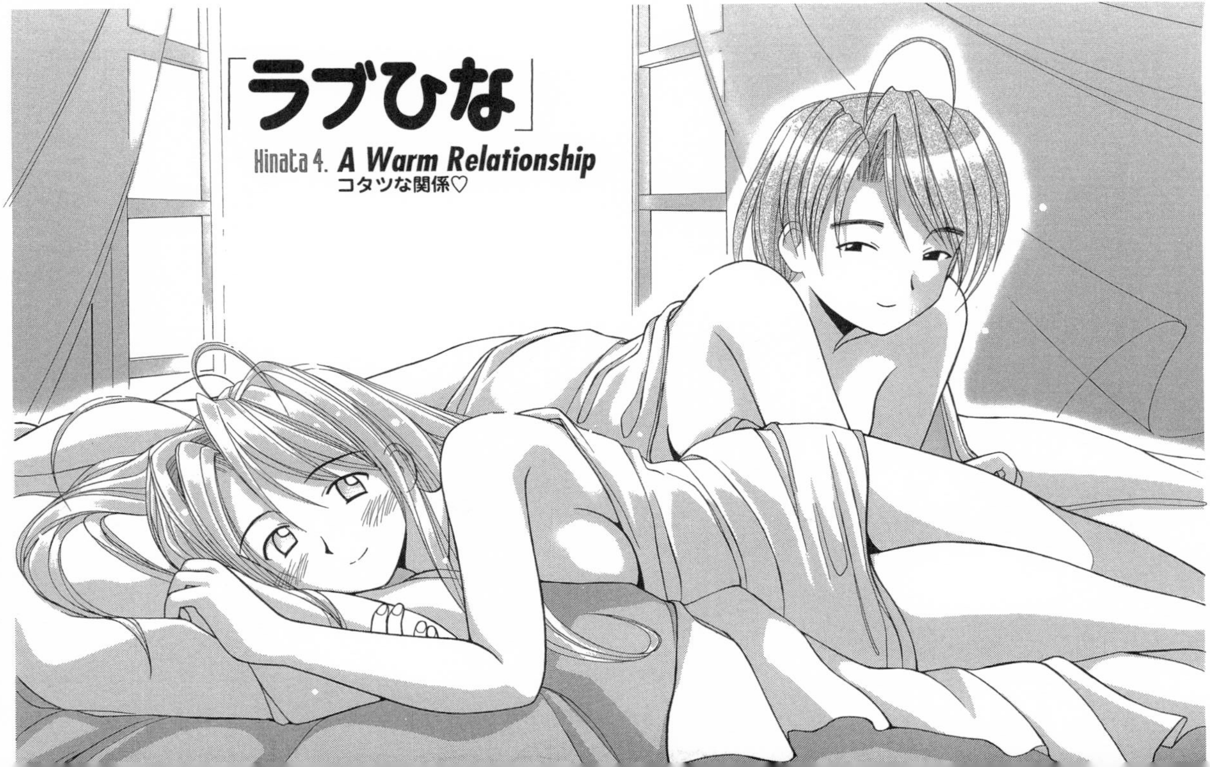
「ラブひな」
Hinata 4. A Warm Relationship
コタツな関係♡

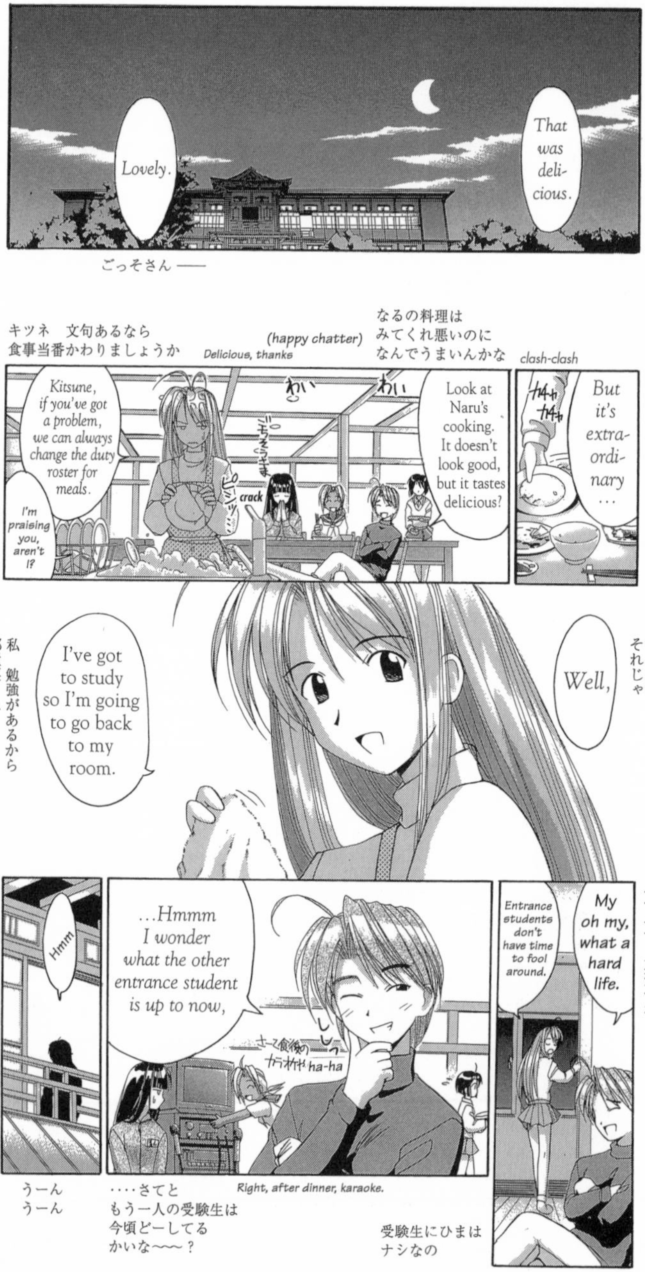
ごちそうさまー
That was deli-cious.
Lovely.
ごっそさん ——
clash-clash
But it's extra-ordi-nary …
しっかし
不思議やね——
なるの料理は
みてくれ悪いのに
なんでうまいんかな
Look at Naru's cooking. It doesn't look good, but it tastes delicious?
(happy chatter)
Delicious, thanks
わい
わい
crack
キツネ 文句あるなら
食事当番かわりましょうか
Kitsune, if you've got a problem, we can always change the duty roster for meals.
I'm praising you, aren't I?
ほめてん
やんか〜〜
Well,
それじゃ
I've got to study so I'm going to go back to my room.
私 勉強があるから
部屋戻るね
My oh my, what a hard life.
Entrance students don't have time to fool around.
おやおや 大変やねぇ
受験生にひまは
ナシなの
…Hmmm I wonder what the other entrance student is up to now,
ha-ha
Right, after dinner, karaoke.
‥‥さてと
もう一人の受験生は
今頃どーしてる
かいな〜〜？
Hmm
うーん
うーん

全っ然
わから———ん！

crash

ダメだあー

うぐぐ･･！

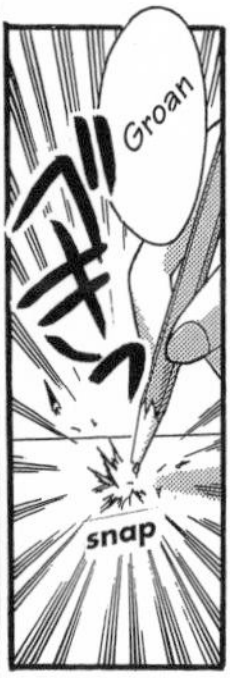
Groan
ベキッ
snap

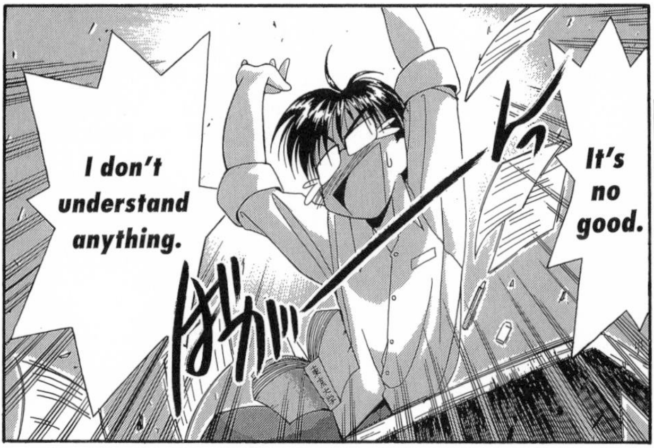
It's no good.
I don't understand anything.
ばかー

確かに成瀬川の言う通り
センター試験を２か月後にひかえて
この状態では　99%絶望的だ！
だめか———!?　だめなのか　俺は———!?

い･･いや　ここで諦めて　どうする!!
しのぶちゃんを泣かし　嘘つきと
思われたままで　いいのか!?
立て！　立つんだ　景太郎~~~~~~~~!!

It's right what Narusegawa says, with the General Exam in only two months time, the state I'm in it's 99% hopeless. It's a waste of time. I'm no good…

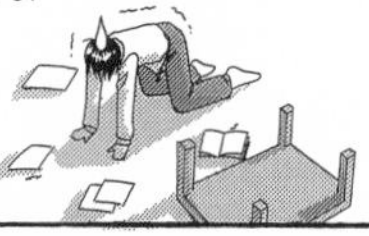

No, no. I mustn't just give in. I don't want to be thought of just as the guy who made Shinobu cry and who's a liar. Get up, Keitaro, stand up!

はあ —— それにしても
難しいよな　この問題集

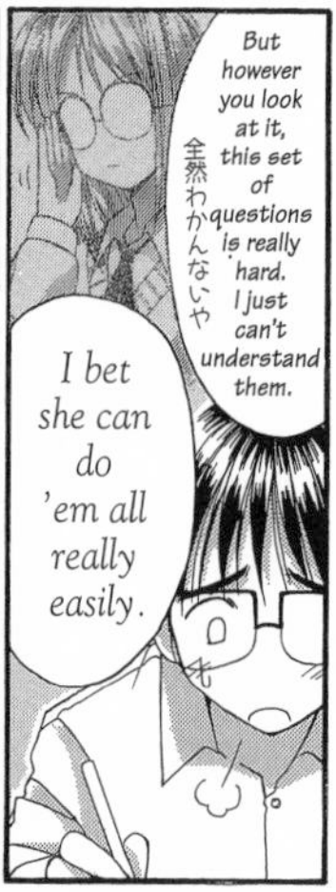
全然わかんないや
But however you look at it, this set of questions is really hard. I just can't understand them.
I bet she can do 'em all really easily.

あいつなら
こんなの楽勝で
解くんだろうなー

On the streetcar the other day.

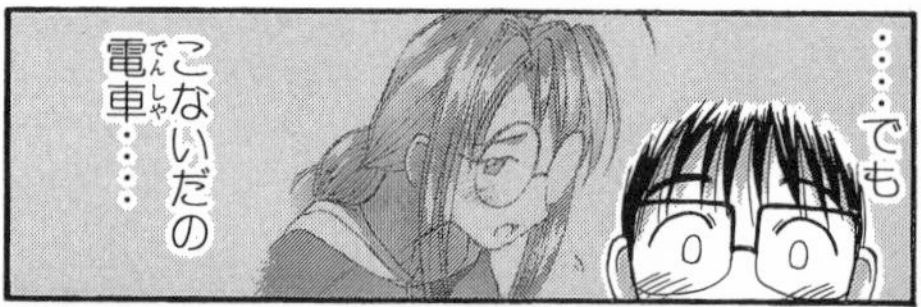
･･･でも
こないだの電車･･･

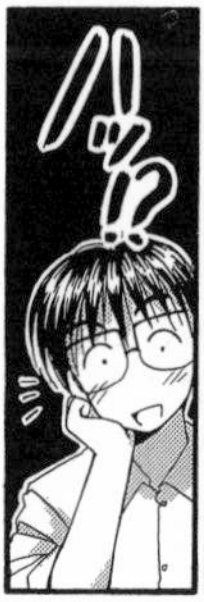
ハッ!?

Oh!

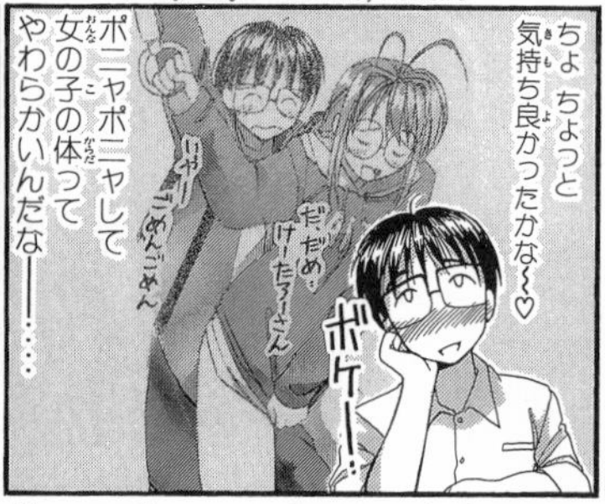
ちょ ちょっと気持ち良かったかな~♡
ボケー…
だ だめ・け－たろ－さん
いや－ごめんごめん
ポニャポニャして女の子の体ってやわらかいんだな－…

Oh, sorry, sorry.

N…no, Keitaro

It felt really nice.

(dreamy)

The pneumatic bodies of young girls are so soft…

いかんいかん！
妄想にふけってる
場合じゃない!!
集中せねば!!

(intense concentration)

しのぶちゃんの
こともあるしな!!

Ah, pretty
little
Shinobu....

Ooh,
Urashima!

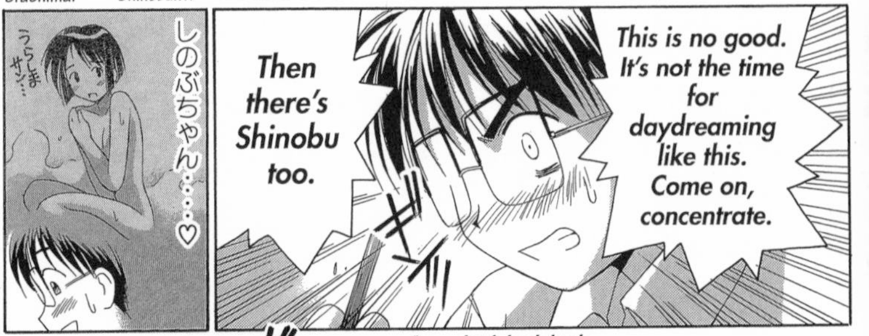
This is no good. It's not the time for daydreaming like this. Come on, concentrate.
Then there's Shinobu too.
しのぶちゃん・・・・♡
うらしまサン・・・

…って　なに回想して
赤くなってんだ　オレは〜〜!?
それで泣かしちゃったんだろ
〜〜〜〜っ!?

bash-bash-bash

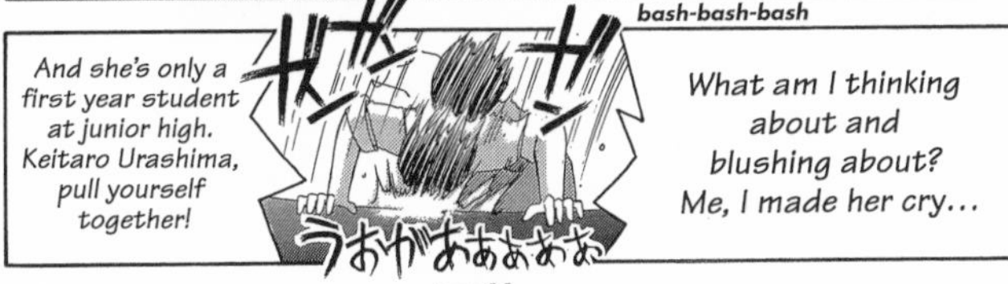
What am I thinking about and blushing about? Me, I made her cry...
And she's only a first year student at junior high. Keitaro Urashima, pull yourself together!
うおがあぁあぁあぁ

Aargh!

それに相手は中1だぞ
目を覚ませ　浦島景太郎〜〜!!

(getting nervous)

はう!?

Already 8 o'clock

このままでは
本当に ――――・・・・
3浪決定 ―― !!

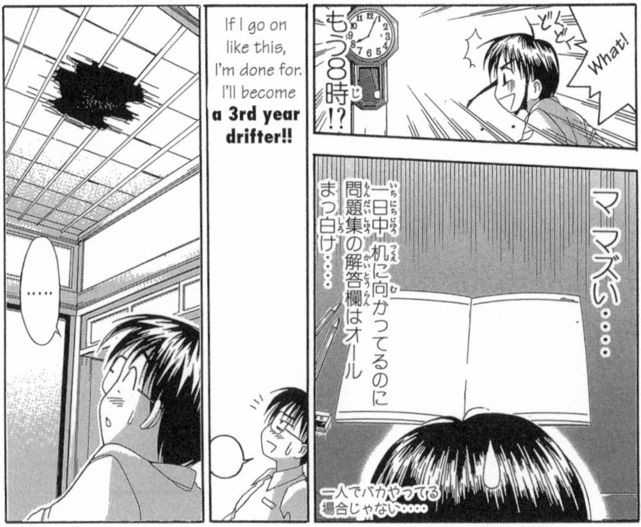
What!
もう8時!?
If I go on like this, I'm done for. I'll become **a 3rd year drifter!!**
ママズい・・・・
一日中机に向かってるのに問題集の解答欄はオールまっ白け・・・・
一人でバカやってる場合じゃない・・・・
・・・・・

That's bad.

I've been
at my desk all day,
but the answer section
is still a complete blank.

I've got to
stop behaving like
an idiot.

ん？

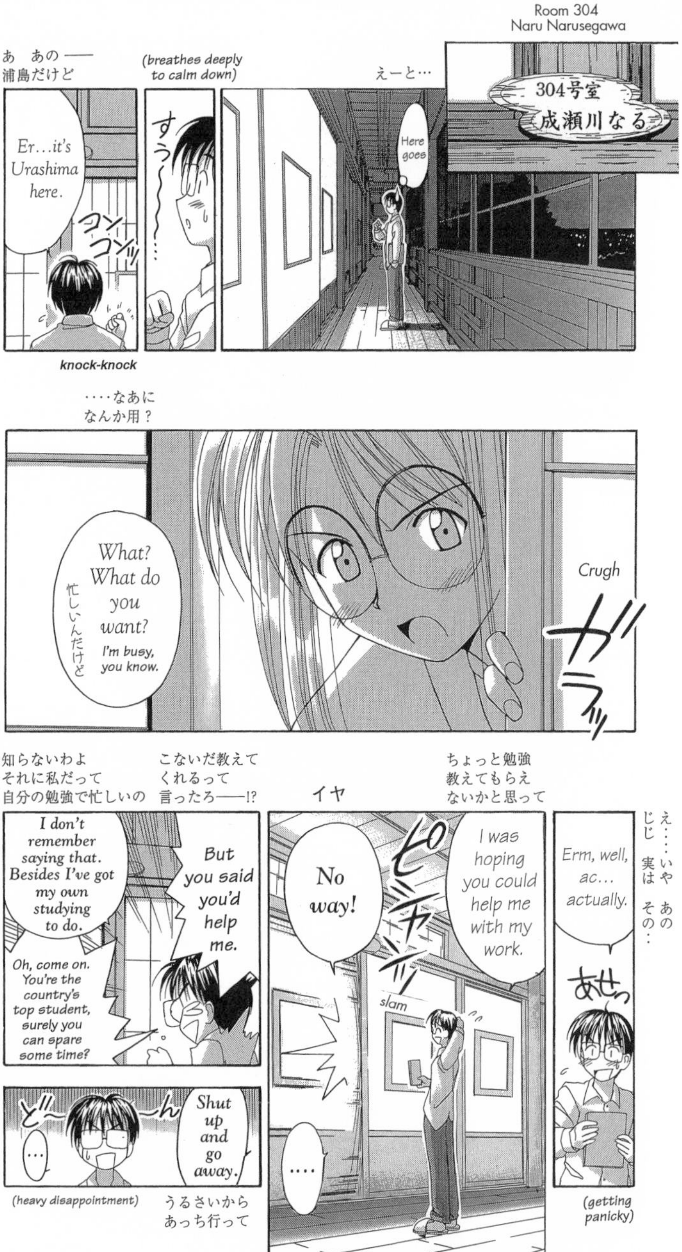
Room 304
Naru Narusegawa
304号室
成瀬川なる
えーと…
Here goes
(breathes deeply to calm down)
すう〜〜…
あ あの——
浦島だけど
Er…it's Urashima here.
コンコンッ
knock-knock
…・なあに
なんか用？
What? What do you want?
忙しいんだけど
I'm busy, you know.
ガラッ
Crugh
え…いや あの
じじ 実は その…
Erm, well, ac… actually.
あせっ
(getting panicky)
ちょっと勉強
教えてもらえ
ないかと思って
I was hoping you could help me with my work.
イヤ
No way!
ピシャッ
slam
….
こないだ教えて
くれるって
言ったろ——!?
But you said you'd help me.
知らないわよ
それに私だって
自分の勉強で忙しいの
I don't remember saying that. Besides I've got my own studying to do.
全国トップなんだから
ちょっとぐらい
いーじゃん!!
Oh, come on. You're the country's top student, surely you can spare some time?
うるさいから
あっち行って
Shut up and go away.
ど〜〜ん
…
(heavy disappointment)

う――――
さむっ！

い――か
げんに‥

あ　あったかい
ココアでもどう？

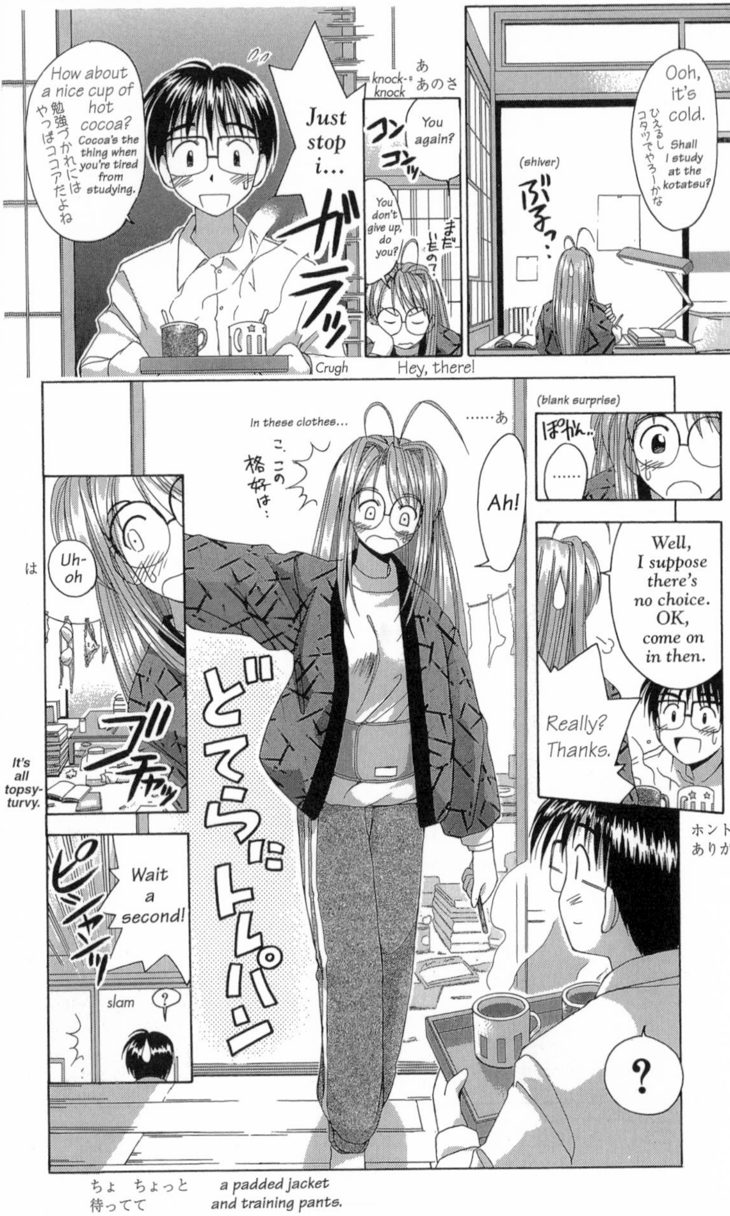
Ooh, it's cold.
ひえるし
コタツでやろーかな
Shall I study at the kotatsu?
(shiver)
ぶるっ‥
あ
あのさ
knock-knock
コン
コンッ
You again?
まだ
いたの？
You don't give up, do you?
Just stop i…
ガラッ
Crugh
Hey, there!
How about a nice cup of hot cocoa?
勉強づかれには
やっぱココアだよね
Cocoa's the thing when you're tired from studying.
(blank surprise)
ぽかん‥
……
……あ
Ah!
In these clothes…
こ、この
格好は‥
Well, I suppose there's no choice. OK, come on in then.
はぁ‥ったく
わかったわよ
しょーがないわね
さっさと入んなさいよ
Really? Thanks.
ホント⁉
ありがと！
Uh-oh
は
ゴチャッ
It's all topsy-turvy.
どてら‼ トレパン
a padded jacket and training pants.
Wait a second!
ちょ　ちょっと
待ってて
ピシャッ
slam
?
?

は　はい
どーーぞ
clean and tidy

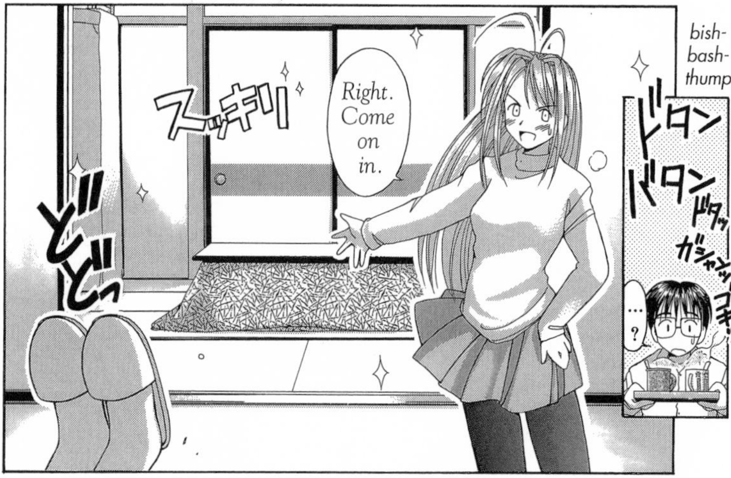
Right. Come on in.
スッキリ
どどっ
bish-bash-thump
ドタンバタンドタッガシャッゴキッ
…?

crash (he falls over from surprise)

べ　別にちょっとぐらい
散らかってても
気にしないよ!!

う….
うるさいわね ——

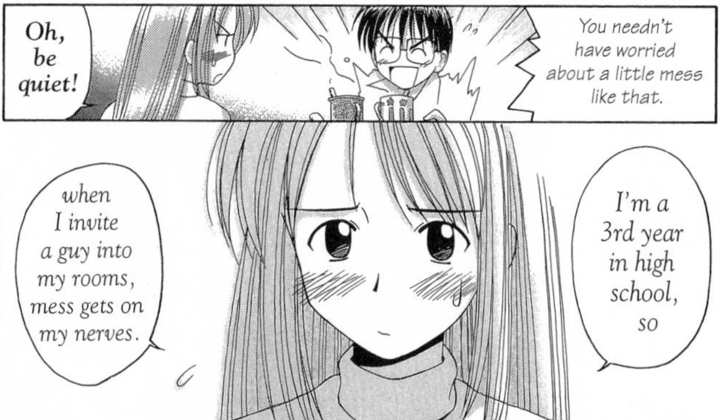
You needn't have worried about a little mess like that.
Oh, be quiet!
I'm a 3rd year in high school, so
when I invite a guy into my rooms, mess gets on my nerves.

女の子なんだからね！

男の人を部屋に入れる時は
ちょっとは気にするわよ

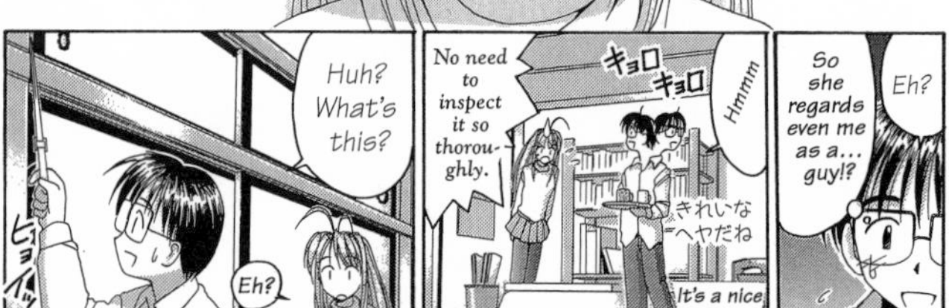
Huh? What's this?
Eh?
ヒョイッ
Hmmm
キョロキョロ
No need to inspect it so thorou-ghly.
きれいなヘヤだね
It's a nice room.
Eh?
So she regards even me as a… guy!?

え？

squeak

え　　あれ？
何これ‥

あんまり
じろじろ
見ないでよ

ふーーーん
(looking everywhere)

一応　オレも
男として
見られてるって
ことか

うわっ!!?

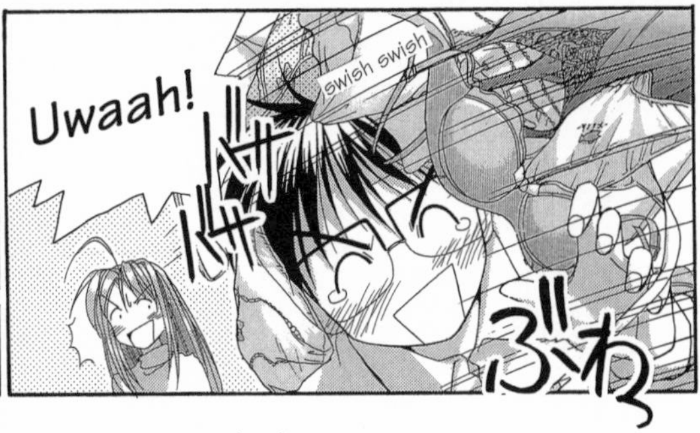
Uwaaah!
swish swish

キャー
バカ〜〜!!

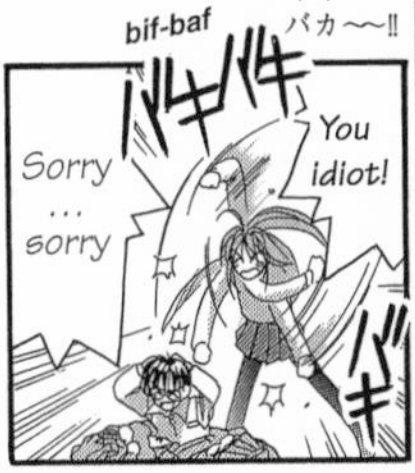
bif-baf
You idiot!
Sorry … sorry

ごめん　ごめん〜〜!!

——で

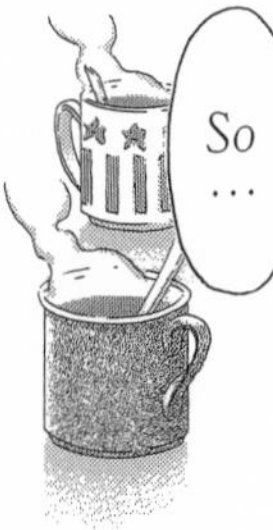
So …

どこが
わかんないのよ？

あ　ここ
なんだけど

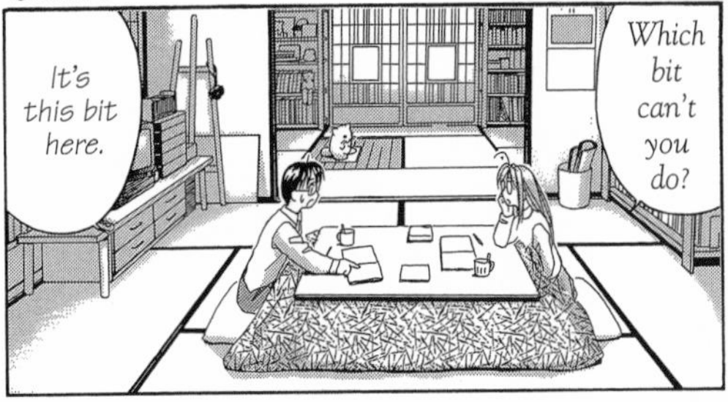
Which bit can't you do?
It's this bit here.

はあ!?

(powerful shock)

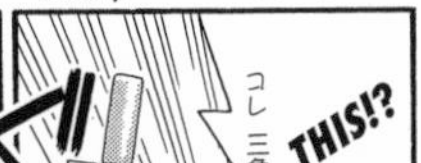
THIS!?
コレ 三角関数の初歩じゃない！
It's the first step of a trigono-metric function.
Are you genuinely stupid?

あんた　ホンキで
バカね？

し　仕方
ないだろ？

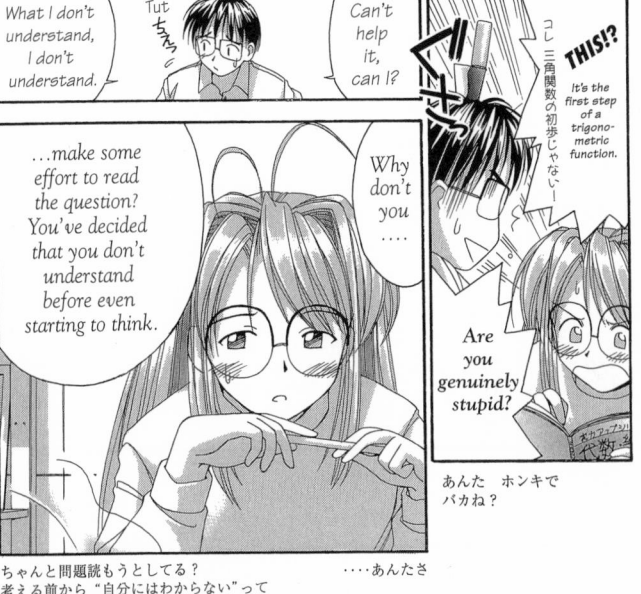

わかんないもんは
わかんないんだからさ

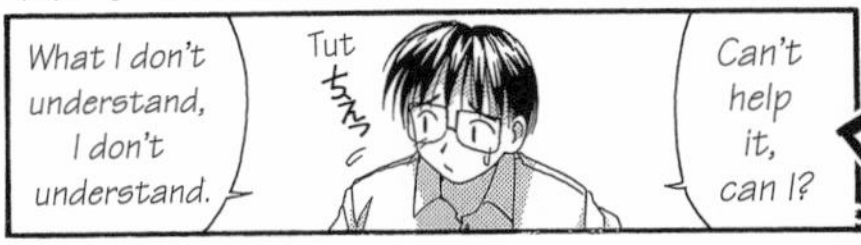
Can't help it, can I?
Tut
What I don't understand, I don't understand.

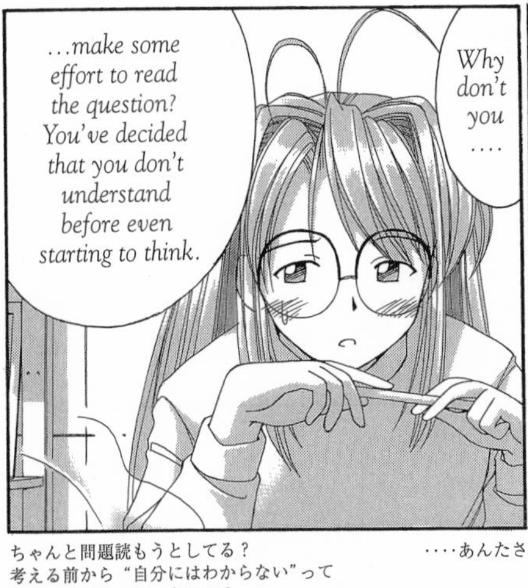
Why don't you ….
…make some effort to read the question? You've decided that you don't understand before even starting to think.

····あんたさ

ちゃんと問題読もうとしてる？
考える前から“自分にはわからない”って
決めつけてるんじゃないの？

受験勉強なんて
メンドーで
将来　役に立たない
ムダなモノだって
思ってるでしょ？

う？

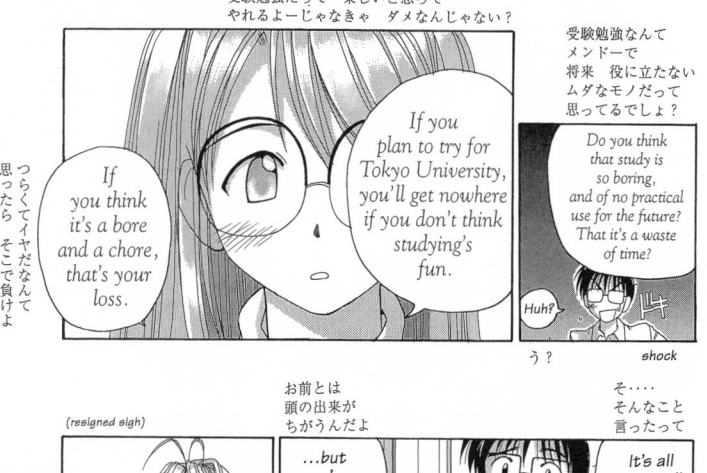

東大受けるんだったら
受験勉強だって　楽しいと思って
やれるよーじゃなきゃ　ダメなんじゃない？

つらくてイヤだなんて
思ったら　そこで負けよ

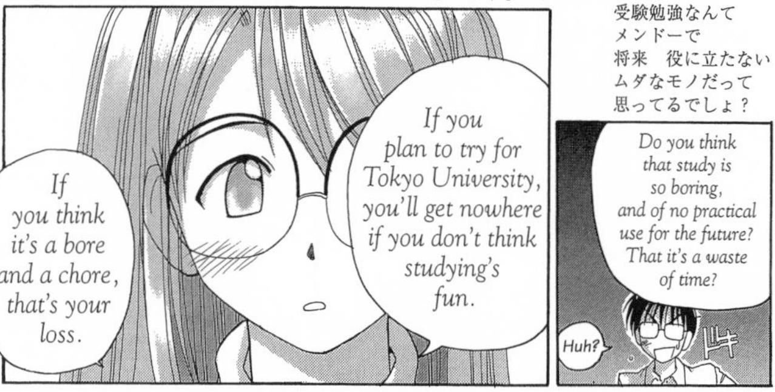
Do you think that study is so boring, and of no practical use for the future? That it's a waste of time?
Huh?
shock
If you plan to try for Tokyo University, you'll get nowhere if you don't think studying's fun.
If you think it's a bore and a chore, that's your loss.

そ····
そんなこと
言ったって

お前とは
頭の出来が
ちがうんだよ

いい　三角関数は公式をマスターして
確実に計算するのがキホンよ！

たとえば
$\tan\frac{\theta}{2}=-2$ のとき
$\tan\theta$ の値(あたい)をもとめるには？
$\tan(\alpha+\beta)=\frac{\tan\alpha+\tan\beta}{1-\tan\alpha\cdot\tan\beta}$
だから
$\tan\theta=\frac{2\tan\frac{\theta}{2}}{1-\tan^2\frac{\theta}{2}}$ となるでしょ

これに $\tan\frac{\theta}{2}=-2$ を
代入(だいにゅう)すれば
$\tan\theta=\frac{2\times(-2)}{1-(-2)^2}=\frac{4}{3}$
ってなるの！
カンタンでしょー

ヤレヤレ

わかった？

いいや
あんまり···

そっから後は
自分で解いて
みなさい

え····!?
ムリだよ

くっそ――
こんなことで解けるくらい
だったら　わざわざ
怒鳴(どな)られにこんなとこに
なんか来ないっての····

ん？

あれ？

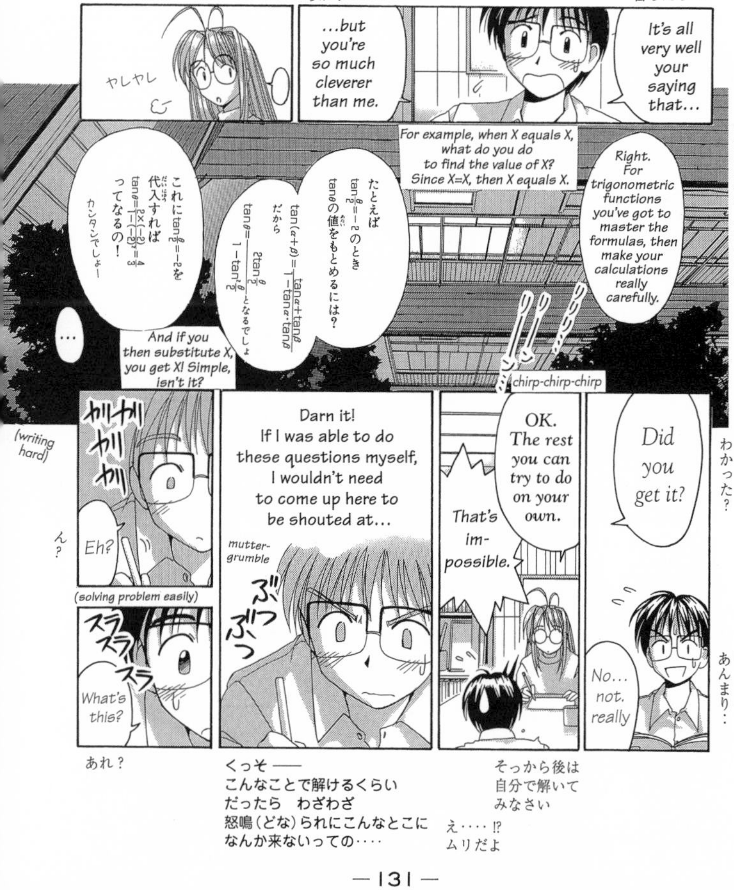
It's all very well your saying that…
…but you're so much cleverer than me.
(resigned sigh)
Right. For trigonometric functions you've got to master the formulas, then make your calculations really carefully.
For example, when X equals X, what do you do to find the value of X? Since X=X, then X equals X.
And if you then substitute X, you get X! Simple, isn't it?
…
chirp-chirp-chirp
Did you get it?
No… not. really
OK. The rest you can try to do on your own.
That's im-possible.
Darn it! If I was able to do these questions myself, I wouldn't need to come up here to be shouted at…
mutter-grumble
(writing hard)
Eh?
(solving problem easily)
What's this?

と‥‥
解けたっ

やれば
できるでしょ

おまえ　教えるのうまいな——！
この２浪のオレが　こんなスラスラ
解けるなんて!!

感心してるひまがあったら
次やんなさいよ

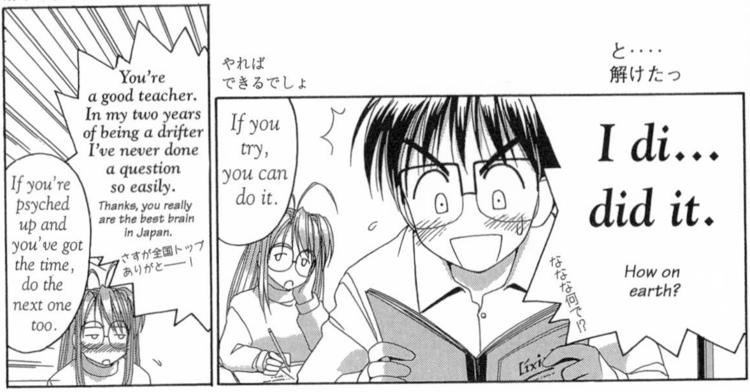
I di…
did it.
How on earth?
ななな何で!?
If you try, you can do it.
You're a good teacher. In my two years of being a drifter I've never done a question so easily.
Thanks, you really are the best brain in Japan.
さすが全国トップ
ありがと——！
If you're psyched up and you've got the time, do the next one too.

う
うん

あれ‥？
分かんない
‥‥

(deep disappointment)

やっぱ
面倒見きれ
ないわ

そ　そんなこと
言わないでー　同じ東大
めざす仲間だろ!?

いつ私が仲間に
なったのよ

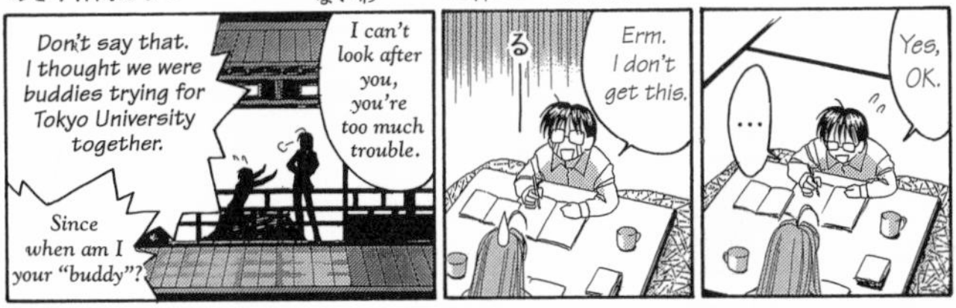
Yes, OK.
…
Erm. I don't get this.
る
I can't look after you, you're too much trouble.
Don't say that. I thought we were buddies trying for Tokyo University together.
Since when am I your "buddy"?

いや —— こんなにスラスラ
数学が解けたの
生まれて初めてだ！

おまえのおかげ
だよ〜〜〜〜っ

その程度の問題で　大ゲサねー

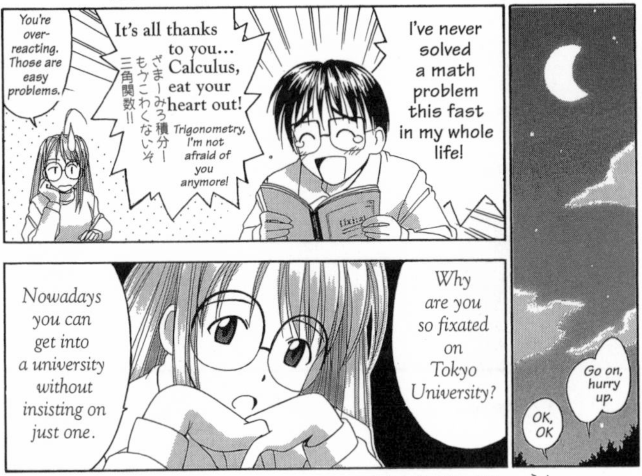
I've never solved a math problem this fast in my whole life!
It's all thanks to you… Calculus, eat your heart out!
ざまーみろ積分ー
もうこわくないぞ
三角関数!!
Trigonometry, I'm not afraid of you anymore!
You're over-reacting. Those are easy problems.
Why are you so fixated on Tokyo University?
Nowadays you can get into a university without insisting on just one.
Go on, hurry up.
OK, OK

ほら　ほら！
さっさとやる！

うん
うん

‥‥あんた何でそんなに
東大にこだわるの？

今時（いまどき）　こだわんなきゃ
大学なんて入れるじゃない

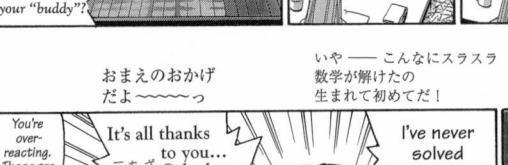

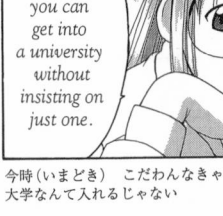

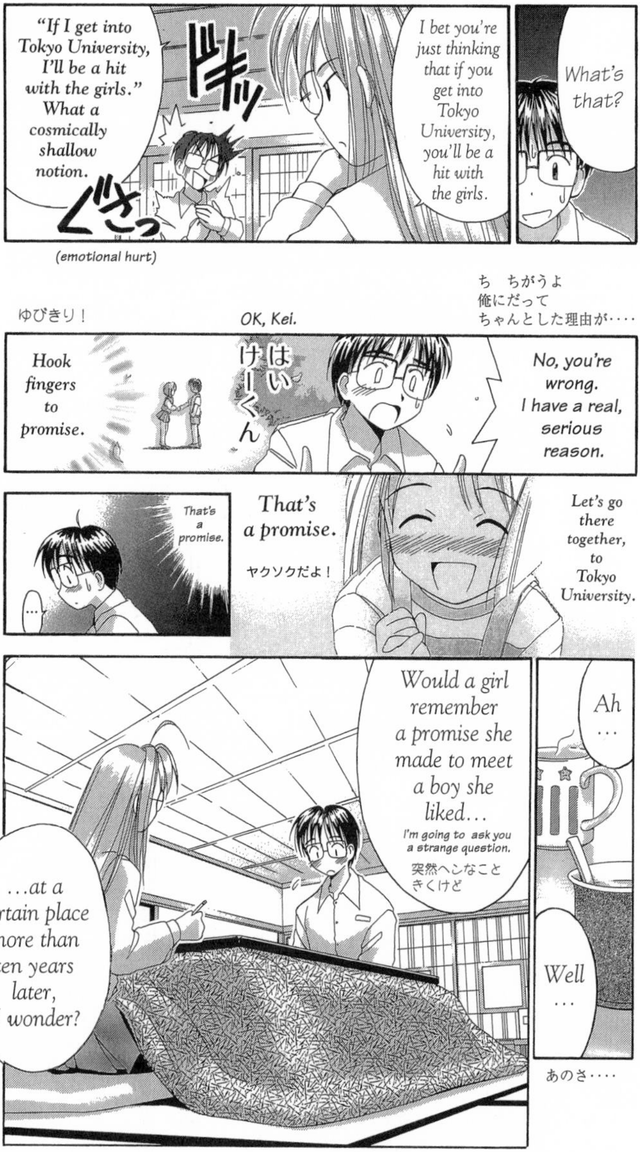

え・・・ な 何でって！
What's that?
どーせ東大に入って 女の子にモテよ —— とか思ったんでしょ
I bet you're just thinking that if you get into Tokyo University, you'll be a hit with the girls.
(shock)
大体 東大生なら女に モテるんじゃないかってゆー 発想自体が 宇宙的に浅はかよね
"If I get into Tokyo University, I'll be a hit with the girls." What a cosmically shallow notion.
(emotional hurt)
ち ちがうよ 俺にだって ちゃんとした理由が・・・・
No, you're wrong. I have a real, serious reason.
はい けーくん
OK, Kei.
ゆびきり！
Hook fingers to promise.
いっしょに行こーね トーダイ
Let's go there together, to Tokyo University.
ヤクソクだよ！
That's a promise.
ヤクソクだよ！
That's a promise.
...
・・・・あ
Ah ...
あのさ・・・・
Well ...
突然ヘンなこと きくけど
I'm going to ask you a strange question.
—— 女の子ってさ 子供の頃に 好きだった男の子と 「ある所で会おう」ってした約束を
Would a girl remember a promise she made to meet a boy she liked...
十何年たっても 覚えてるもんかなぁ・・・・
...at a certain place more than ten years later, I wonder?

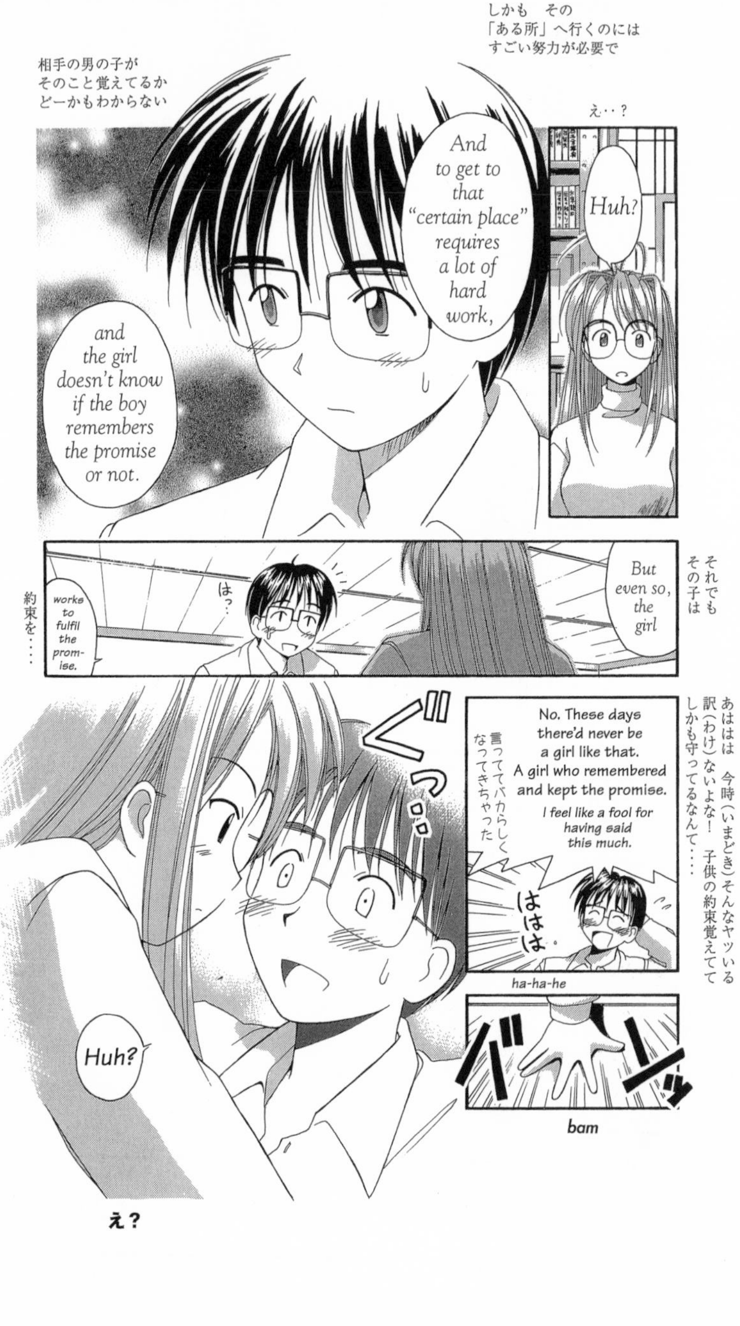

しかも　その
「ある所」へ行くのには
すごい努力が必要で
And to get to that "certain place" requires a lot of hard work,
え‥？
Huh?
相手の男の子が
そのこと覚えてるか
どーかもわからない
and the girl doesn't know if the boy remembers the promise or not.
それでも
その子は
But even so, the girl
はっ…
約束を‥‥
works to fulfil the prom-ise.
あははは　今時（いまどき）そんなヤツいる
訳（わけ）ないよな！　子供の約束覚えてて
しかも守ってるなんて‥‥
No. These days there'd never be a girl like that. A girl who remembered and kept the promise.
言っててバカらしく
なってきちゃった
I feel like a fool for having said this much.
ははは
ha-ha-he
バーン
bam
ぐっ
Huh?
え？

ぜったい

覚えてる！

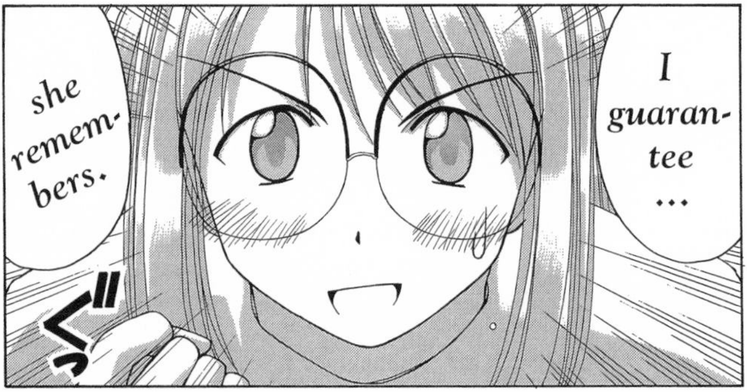

I guarantee…
she remembers.

え!?

taken aback

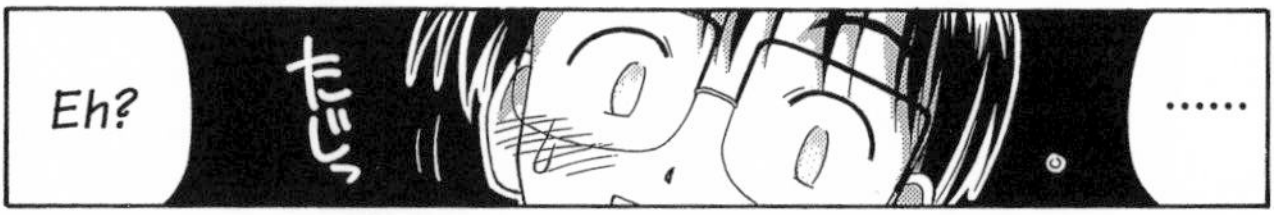

……
たじっ
Eh?

そ　そうかな…？

そうよ！　その子のこと
ホントに
好きだったなら

時間だって　何年たったって
関係ない　絶対
覚えてるはずよ !!

ホ　ホントに
そう思う？

うん

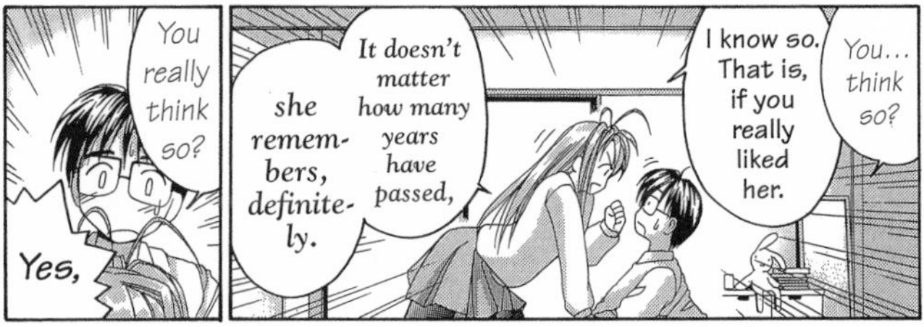

You… think so?
I know so. That is, if you really liked her.
It doesn't matter how many years have passed,
she remembers, definitely.
You really think so?
Yes,

たとえ　それがどんなに
大変で困難な目標だった
としても

きっと彼女は
がんばって

そのハードルを
越えて待ってると
思うわ

たとえば

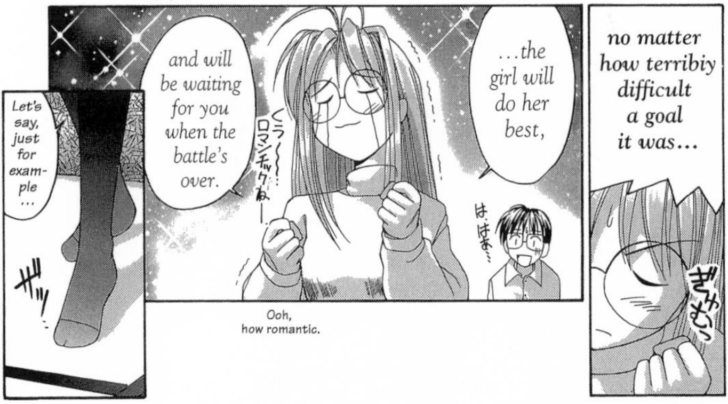

no matter how terribiy difficult a goal it was…
…the girl will do her best,
and will be waiting for you when the battle's over.
Let's say, just for example…

(clench)

Ooh,
how romantic.

(step)

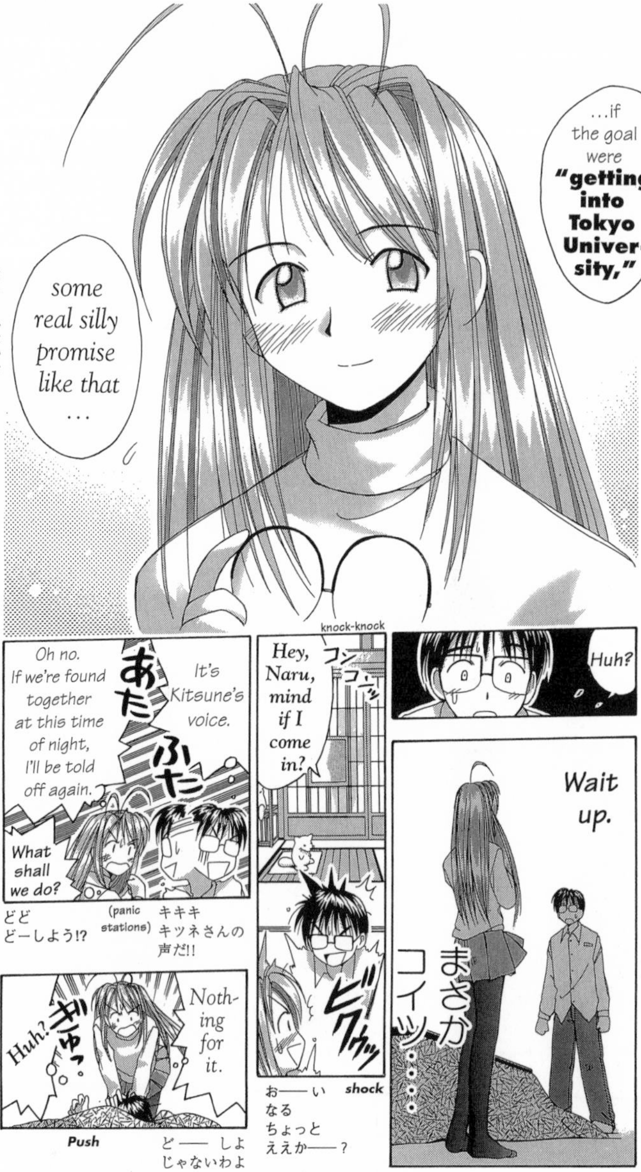

…if the goal were "getting into Tokyo University,"
それが「東大に入る」なんて
some real silly promise like that …
バッカみたいな約束だったとしてもね
Huh?
え？
Wait up.
ちょっとまてよ…
I don't believe it. You …?
まさかコイツ…
knock-knock
コンコンッ
Hey, Naru, mind if I come in?
ビクウッ
shock
お――い なる ちょっと ええか――？
It's Kitsune's voice.
キキキ キツネさんの 声だ!!
Oh no. If we're found together at this time of night, I'll be told off again.
ママママズいわ こんな時間に 二人きりでいるの見つかったら また なに言われるか
あたふた
(panic stations)
What shall we do?
どど どーしよう!?
Noth-ing for it.
ど―― しよ じゃないわよ
Huh?
ぎゅっ
Push
え――!?

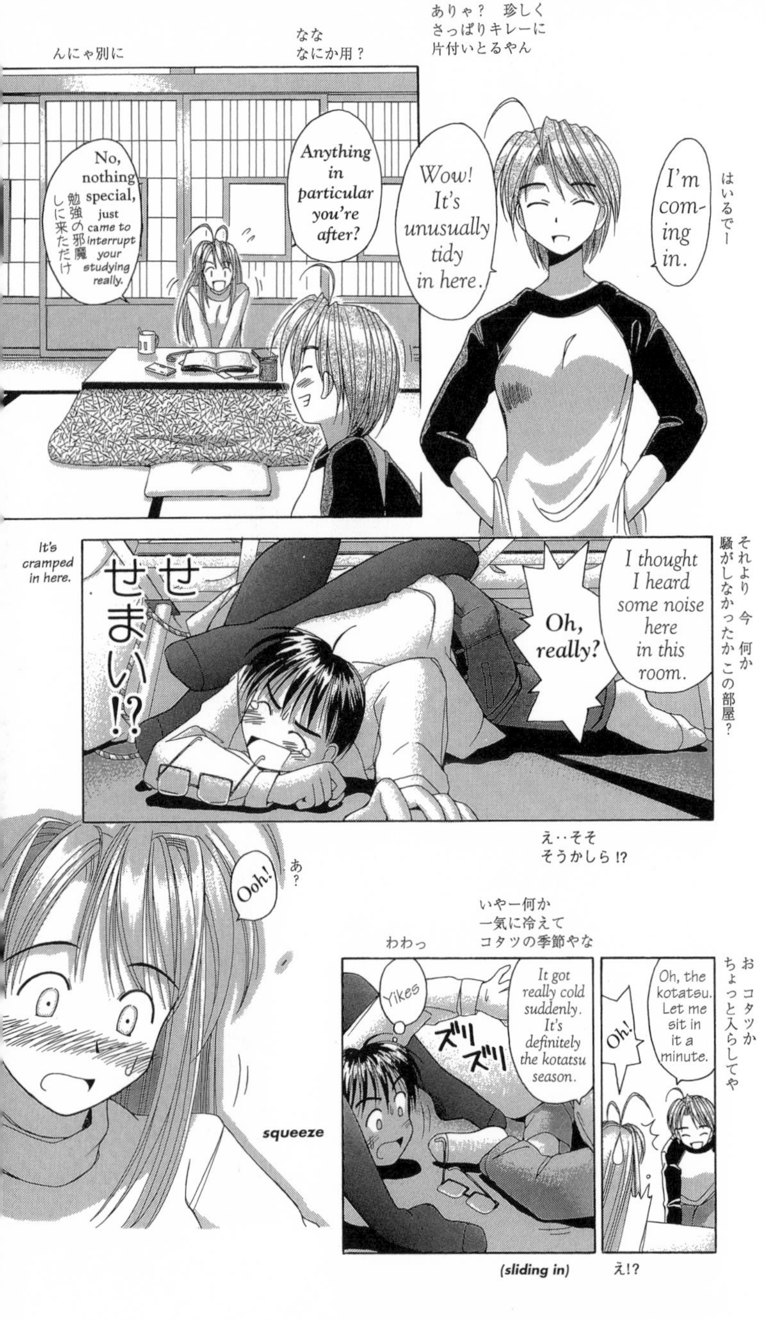

はいるでー
I'm com-ing in.
ありゃ？　珍しく さっぱりキレーに 片付いとるやん
Wow! It's unusually tidy in here.
なな なにか用？
Anything in particular you're after?
んにゃ別に
No, nothing special, 勉強の邪魔しに来ただけ just came to interrupt your studying really.
それより 今 何か 騒がしなかったかこの部屋？
I thought I heard some noise here in this room.
Oh, really?
せせまい!?
It's cramped in here.
え‥そそ そうかしら!?
あ？
Ooh!
squeeze
お コタツか ちょっと入らしてや
Oh, the kotatsu. Let me sit in it a minute.
Oh!
え!?
いやー何か 一気に冷えて コタツの季節やな
It got really cold suddenly. It's definitely the kotatsu season.
わわっ
Yikes
ズリズリ
(sliding in)

げげッ!?

ちょ
ちょっと

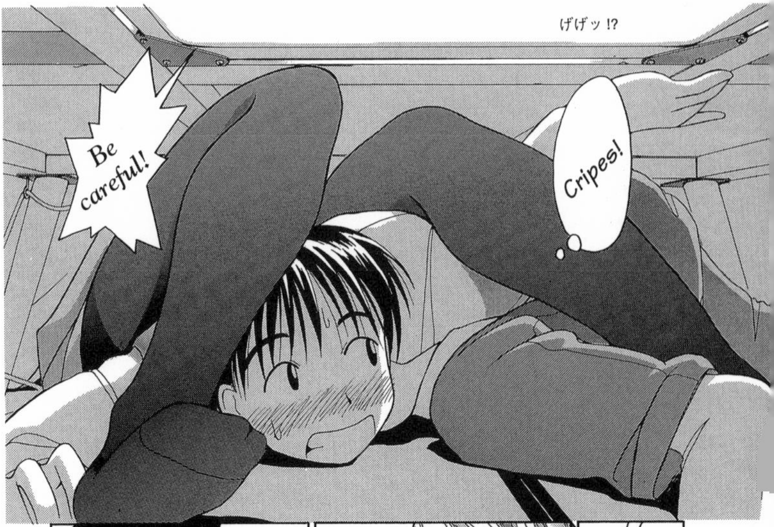
Cripes!
Be careful!

なんや　ヘンな
声だして？

いいえ
別にィ

あんまり
こっち来ないでよ——!!

そんなこと
言ったって〜〜〜

キツネさんがよってくんだもん仕方ないだろオ!!

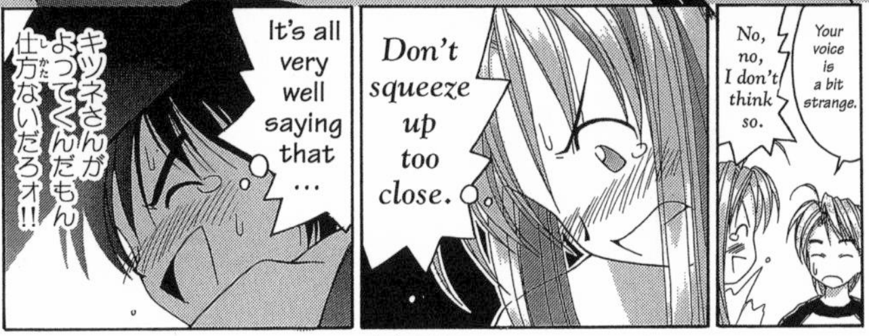
Your voice is a bit strange.
No, no, I don't think so.
Don't squeeze up too close.
It's all very well saying that …
キツネさんが
よってくんだもん
仕方ないだろオ!!

It can't be helped if Kitsune decides to move in close.

なる‥？

はいッ

なんか様子ヘン
ちゃうか？

そ
そうかしら？

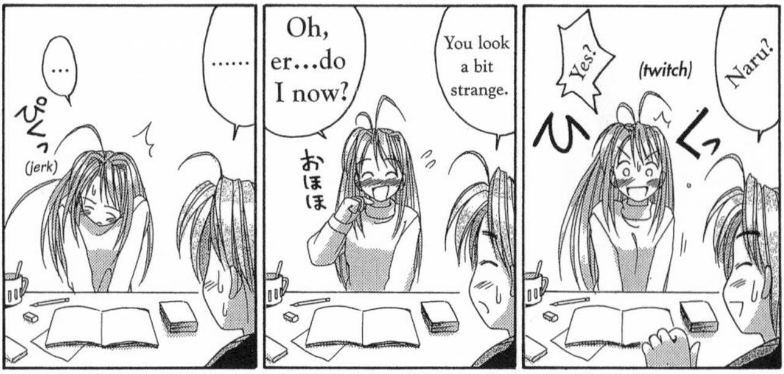
Naru?
(twitch)
Yes?
You look a bit strange.
Oh, er…do I now?
おほほ
……
…
ぴくっ
(jerk)

Ha-ha-ha

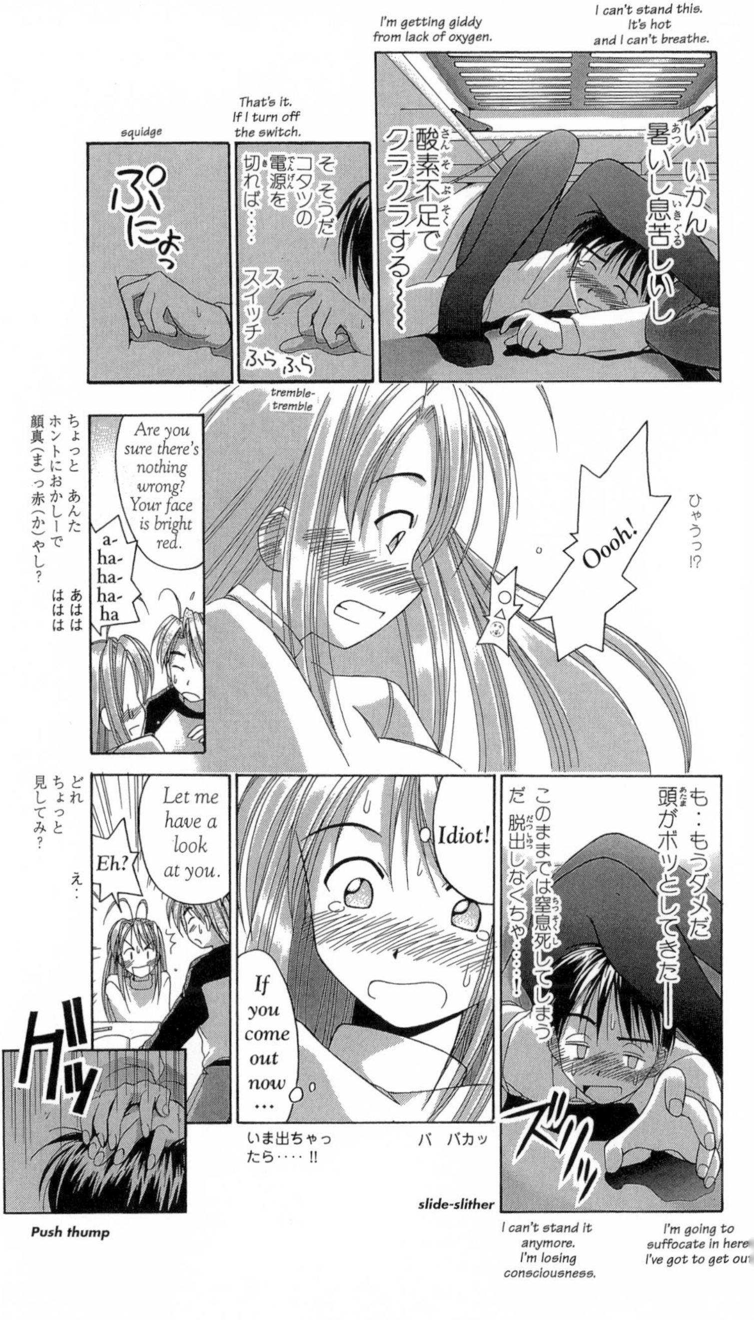

いいかん 暑いし息苦しいし
I can't stand this. It's hot and I can't breathe.
酸素不足でクラクラする～～
I'm getting giddy from lack of oxygen.
そそうだ コタツの電源を切れば‥‥
That's it. If I turn off the switch.
ススイッチ
ふらふら
tremble-tremble
ぷにょっ
squidge
ひゃうっ!?
Oooh!
ちょっと あんた ホントにおかしーで 顔真(ま)っ赤(か)やし?
Are you sure there's nothing wrong? Your face is bright red.
あははははは
a-ha-ha-ha-ha
も・・もうダメだ 頭がボッとしてきたー
このままでは窒息死してしまう だ 脱出しなくちゃ‥‥!
I can't stand it anymore. I'm losing consciousness.
I'm going to suffocate in here I've got to get out
ズルッ
slide-slither
バ バカッ
Idiot!
いま出ちゃったら‥‥!!
If you come out now…
どれ ちょっと 見してみ?
Let me have a look at you.
え・・
Eh?
グッ
Push thump

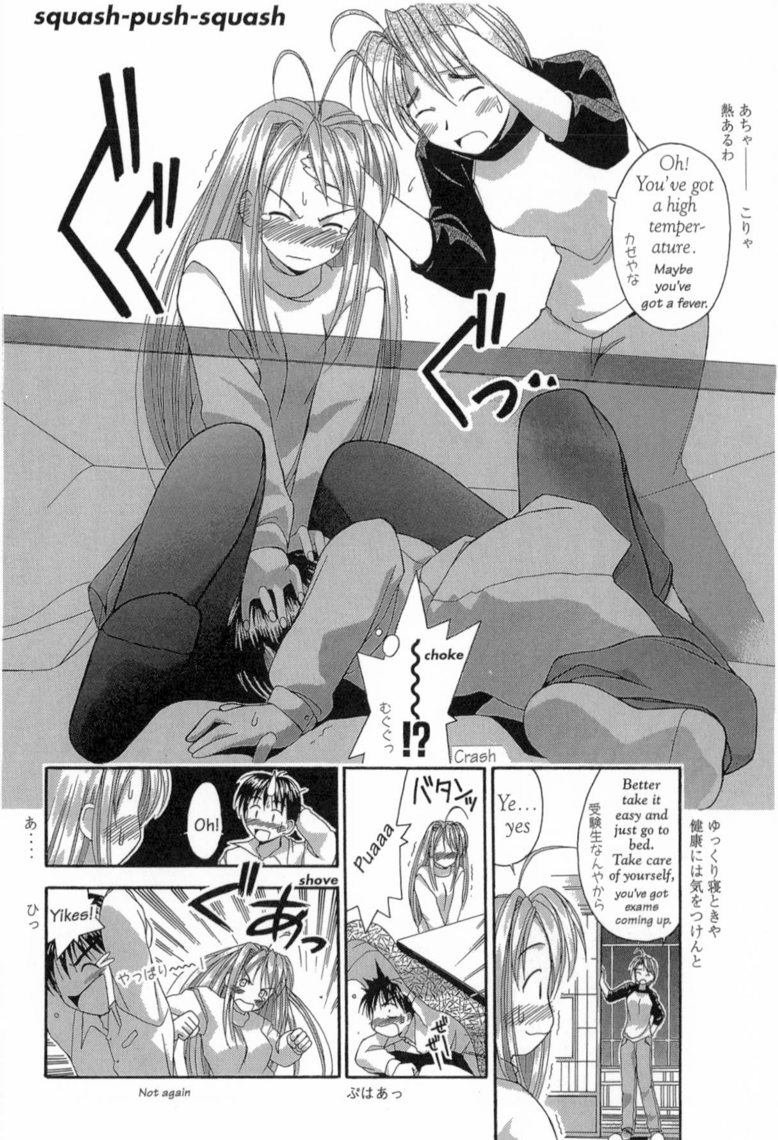
squash-push-squash
あちゃーーー こりゃ熱あるわ
Oh! You've got a high temperature.
カゼやな
Maybe you've got a fever.
choke
むぐぐっ
!?
Crash
ゆっくり寝ときや 健康には気をつけんと 受験生なんやから
Better take it easy and just go to bed. Take care of yourself, you've got exams coming up.
Ye... yes
う うん
バタンッ
Puaaa
ぷはあっ
あ……
Oh!
ひっ
Yikes!
shove
やっぱり〜〜!
Not again

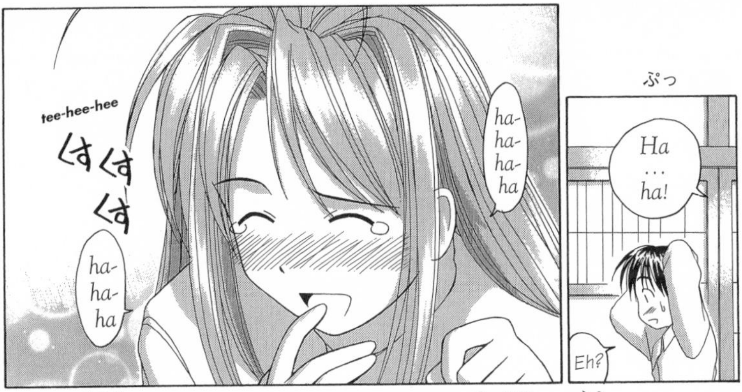

ぷっ
Ha … ha!
Eh?
ha-ha-ha-ha
tee-hee-hee
くすくすくす
ha-ha-ha

ははは は‥はは え？

な　何笑ってんだよ？

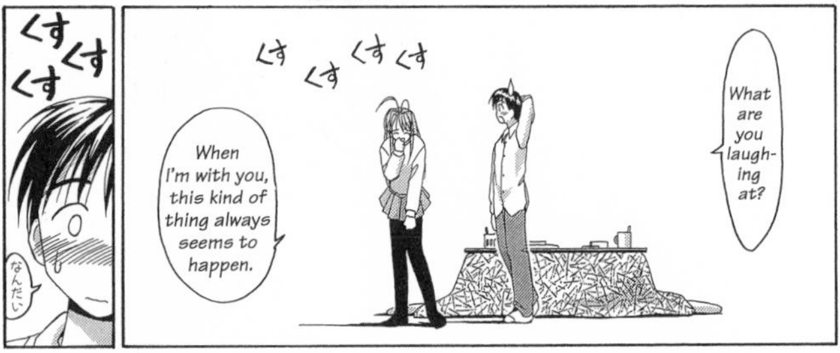

tee-hee-hee
What are you laughing at?
くすくすくすくす
When I'm with you, this kind of thing always seems to happen.
tee-hee-hee
くすくすくす
なんだい
What's this?

だって‥‥　あんたといると
いつも　こうなんだもん

なる——ちょ——ど
カゼに良ぉ効くクスリが
‥‥あ？

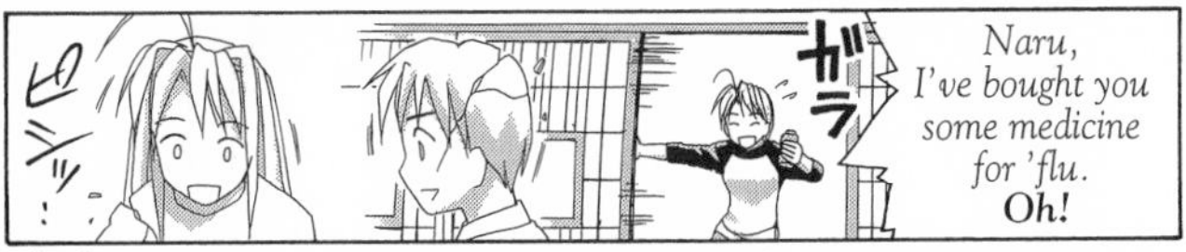

crash
ガラ
Naru, I've bought you some medicine for 'flu. Oh!
ピシッ
shock

そ——よ！
誤解よ——っ

ち　ちがう！
俺は勉強を!?

たいへんや——　景太郎がなるに
夜ばいかけとるで————!!

‥あんたら

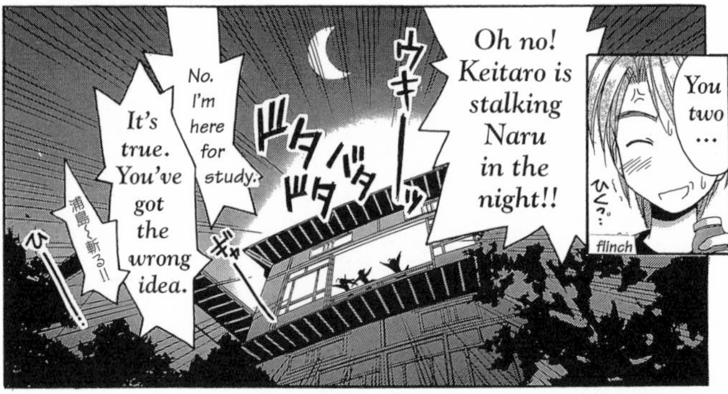

You two …
ひくっ…
flinch
Oh no! Keitaro is stalking Naru in the night!!
ウキーーッ
No. I'm here for study.
It's true. You've got the wrong idea.
ドタバタドタ
ギャー
浦島〜斬る!!
ひー
Urashima, I'm going to carve you up!
Yikes!
(commotion)
(scream)

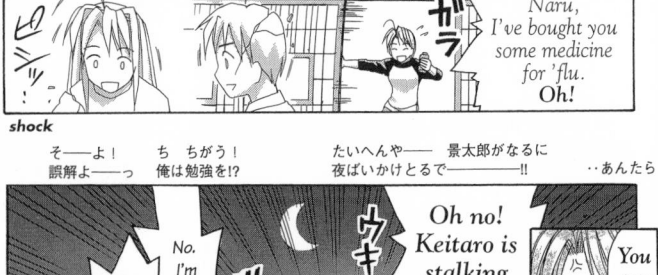

STAFF

Ken Akamatsu
Takashi Takemoto
Kenichi Nakamura
Takaaki Miyahara
Tomohiko Saito

EDITOR

Noboru Ohno
Tomoyuki Shiratsuchi

KC Editor

Mitsuei Ishii